# Developing Language and Literacy in English across the Secondary School Curriculum

Urszula Clark

# Developing Language and Literacy in English across the Secondary School Curriculum

## An Inclusive Approach

Urszula Clark
Department of English
Aston University
Birmingham, UK

ISBN 978-3-319-93238-5         ISBN 978-3-319-93239-2  (eBook)
https://doi.org/10.1007/978-3-319-93239-2

Library of Congress Control Number: 2018945058

© The Editor(s) (if applicable) and The Author(s) 2019
This work is subject to copyright. All rights are solely and exclusively licensed by the Publisher, whether the whole or part of the material is concerned, specifically the rights of translation, reprinting, reuse of illustrations, recitation, broadcasting, reproduction on microfilms or in any other physical way, and transmission or information storage and retrieval, electronic adaptation, computer software, or by similar or dissimilar methodology now known or hereafter developed.
The use of general descriptive names, registered names, trademarks, service marks, etc. in this publication does not imply, even in the absence of a specific statement, that such names are exempt from the relevant protective laws and regulations and therefore free for general use.
The publisher, the authors and the editors are safe to assume that the advice and information in this book are believed to be true and accurate at the date of publication. Neither the publisher nor the authors or the editors give a warranty, express or implied, with respect to the material contained herein or for any errors or omissions that may have been made. The publisher remains neutral with regard to jurisdictional claims in published maps and institutional affiliations.

Cover image: © voyata/Getty Images
Cover design by Tom Howey

Printed on acid-free paper

This Palgrave Macmillan imprint is published by the registered company Springer International Publishing AG part of Springer Nature
The registered company address is: Gewerbestrasse 11, 6330 Cham, Switzerland

# Acknowledgements

The research discussed in this volume was made possible through the commitment of the teachers who participated in it at the three schools involved. This book is dedicated to them and to all of the other inspiring teachers I have known.

# Contents

1. Introduction: Language and Literacy Across the Secondary School Curriculum — 1
2. Language, Literacy and Pedagogy — 37
3. Devising and Implementing Whole School Literacy across the Curriculum (LAC) strategies in the 11 to 19 Secondary School Curriculum — 89
4. Developing Literacy Across the Curriculum for Subject English — 127
5. Developing Literacy Across the Curriculum for the Humanities: RE, History and Geography — 159
6. Developing Literacy Across the Curriculum for Science and Maths — 195
7. Conclusion — 219

| | |
|---|---:|
| **Glossary** | 237 |
| **References** | 245 |
| **Index** | 263 |

# List of Figures

| | | |
|---|---|---|
| Fig. 2.1 | The mode/register continuum | 55 |
| Fig. 2.2 | Levels of language | 57 |
| Fig. 2.3 | Dimensions of register | 58 |
| Fig. 2.4 | Bernstein's theory of pedagogic discourse (Adapted from Bernstein 1991) | 70 |
| Fig. 2.5 | The learning and teaching cycle | 79 |

# List of Tables

| | | |
|---|---|---|
| Table 2.1 | Functions of language in schooling | 59 |
| Table 2.2 | Grammar overview | 60 |
| Table 2.3 | Functions within a clause | 62 |
| Table 2.4 | Constituent elements of the NC multi-clause sentence example | 64 |
| Table 3.1 | Overview of schools, subjects and year groups | 94 |
| Table 3.2 | Three-part answer structure for science | 111 |
| Table 3.3 | Assessment grid | 116 |
| Table 3.4 | Assessment Grid: revised | 123 |
| Table 4.1 | PETER support scaffold | 136 |
| Table 4.2 | Writing like Bryson: expanding phrases | 141 |
| Table 4.3 | Writers' checklist | 147 |
| Table 4.4 | Feedback sheet | 148 |
| Table 4.5 | Developing vocabulary through nominalisation | 149 |
| Table 5.1 | Planning writing in GCSE RE | 164 |
| Table 5.2 | Structuring writing in RE | 165 |
| Table 5.3 | IDEA in history | 171 |
| Table 5.4 | Interpreting sources in GCE history | 176 |
| Table 5.5 | Nominalisation in geography | 190 |

# List of Tables

Table 6.1  Structuring GCSE biology examination question answers  206
Table 6.2  Reflecting upon answer structure  207
Table 6.3  Three part answer structure  208

# 1

# Introduction: Language and Literacy Across the Secondary School Curriculum

## Overview

In this book, I draw upon research into teachers' practices in developing literacy across the curriculum initiatives in the 11–18 school curriculum undertaken in a UK context, that of England, informed theoretically by a *language based pedagogy* (LBP). Sometimes called *genre-based pedagogy* or *grammatics*, LBP draws upon a systemic functional approach to language and grammar (SFL/G). The main aim I seek to satisfy, is to provide an account of ways in which secondary schools in England can devise and implement coherent language and literacy across the curriculum policies and strategies that include explicit attention to grammar and associated metalanguage. Central to this endeavour is that implementing such policies and strategies is undertaken as an integral part of teachers' affordances and day to day curriculum practices in ways that are also theoretically credible.

This first chapter provides a context for the remainder of the book, by providing an overview of initiatives into developing language and literacy in English across the curriculum and associated teaching of grammar from the 1960s to the present day in Australia, the USA and

England. It discusses how developing language and literacy across the curriculum is nothing new, and has long been of concern in education in the UK and beyond. The realisation of the importance of language for learning characterised early work in the field by Barnes et al. (1971) and The Bullock Report of 1975. At that time, however, the theoretical underpinnings of what a pedagogic grammar (or as Halliday (1996) and latterly Macken-Horarick (2011) have called it, 'grammatics') could look like had yet to be developed, which it now has. I discuss the ideological clashes in relation to the teaching of grammar that characterised the introduction of the National Curriculum in the late 1980s in England through to the present day, and how various wholescale initiatives such as NLS in the 1990s and 2000s failed to impact upon teachers' imagination and pedagogic practices, particularly at secondary level (see, e.g., Goodwyn and Fuller 2011).

Such failure notwithstanding, in 2013 the government introduced Spelling, Punctuation and Grammar (SPaG) test, taken by all 10–11 year olds in England at the end of Key Stage 2. Consequently, pupils now enter secondary schools in England with an understanding of grammar. This was followed by national curriculum reforms that reintroduced explicit teaching of grammar, particularly at the primary school key stages 1 and 2 (4–7 and 8–11 year olds) and urge teachers at key stages 3 and 4 (11–14 and 14–16 year olds) to 'build upon' this knowledge. There is thus an opportunity to develop further pupils' and students' understanding of grammar and language. However, as Myhill (2018) says, this reintroduction has to be viewed in the context of the highly contested debates of recent decades that have been informed by polemic rather than informed debate, resulting in the incoherent nature of government policy documents regarding both what is meant by grammar and how it should be taught. Such documents and initiatives such as the SPaG test perpetuate the notion of grammar as the correction of error:

> **Quote**
>
> Our own cumulative set of research studies on the teaching of grammar in the L1 classroom in Anglophone settings has illustrated both the rich learning potential of grammar as a resource for supporting metalinguistic

> understanding about writing and improving writing outcomes, and some of the constraints, such as limitations in teachers' grammatical subject knowledge, and the pedagogical demands of managing high-quality talk about linguistic choices in writing, or using mentor texts in ways that support young writers' linguistic decision-making…grammar in Anglophone countries has had a contested past, and despite some recent resurgence in curricular emphasis on grammar, policy documents reveal the pedagogical incoherence of the positioning of grammar in the L1 classroom.
> (Myhill 2018: 18)

Myhill's research and that of others point to the ways in which the concept of grammar is moving away from error correction and towards developing an understanding of how the different genres or text types are constructed and the differing linguistic patternings therein. Thus, the teaching of grammar is currently being increasingly positioned within the context of developing young writers' writing, and especially in relation to the curriculum subject of English. Pupils' and students' understanding of English grammar is thus developed in the context of the texts they are required to read and to write, rather as decontextualized exercises centring upon error spotting. Developing pupils' and students' language and literacy across the secondary school curriculum and all subjects is also a central plank of recent curriculum reforms. In this context, the move away from grammar as error towards construing it in relation to the expression of subject knowledge related to textual organisation and language patternings within texts, provides the conditions whereby language and literacy can be developed incoherent and cross-curricular ways across secondary school subjects.

I show that paying explicit attention to the linguistic patterns and structures through which subject knowledge is realised—in other words, a pedagogic grammar—can be of benefit to all pupils and students regardless of their linguistic backgrounds in ways that are socially just and democratic. I also demonstrate how such an approach is not at odds with either pupils' own sociocultural as well as linguistic identities or teachers' subject identities, discussed in more detail below and in the next chapter. Indeed, the social justice aspect of learning grammar was first recognised in 1818 by the social reformer William Cobbett. Cobbett wrote a

*Grammar of the English Language* that ran to numerous editions throughout the nineteenth century until its final edition in 1901. Cobbett recognised the importance of grammar in relation to taking part in public life. He wrote the grammar as a series of letters, directly addressing a fictional nephew called James. It was not written as a school grammar, intended for the working man so he could learn the language of public discourse in order to take part in it. In the preface he writes:

> **Quote**
>
> The actions of men proceed from their thoughts. In order to obtain the co-operation, the concurrence, or the consent, of others, we must communicate our thoughts to them. The means of communication are words; and grammar teaches us how to make use of words. …to be able to choose the words which ought to be employed, and to place them where they ought to be placed, we must become acquainted with certain principles and rules; and these principles and rules constitute what is called Grammar.
> (Cobbett 1818: 10)

For Cobbett then, grammar was conceived in relation to textual organisation as well as sentence structure, and more in terms of rhetoric than the naming of parts.

> **Quote**
>
> The particular path of knowledge to be pursued by you, will be of your own choosing; but, as to knowledge connected with books, there is a step to be taken before you can enter upon any path. In the immense filed of this kind of knowledge, innumerable are the paths, and GRAMMAR is the gate of entrance to them all. And, if grammar is so useful in the attaining of knowledge, it is absolutely necessary in order to enable the possessor, to communicate, by writing, that knowledge to others, without which communication the possession must be comparatively useless to himself in many cases, and, in almost all cases, to the rest of mankind.
>    The actions of men proceed from their *thoughts.* In order to obtain the co-operation, the concurrence, or the consent, of others, we must communicate our thoughts to them. The means of communication are *words;* and grammar teaches us *how to make use of words* (p. 6).

> Grammar, as I observed to you before, teaches us *how to make use of words;*... as I used to teach you how to sow and plant the beds in the garden; for you could have throwed about seeds and stuck in plants of some sort or another without any teaching of mine; and so can any body, without rules or instructions, put mases of words onto paper; but to be able to choose the words which ought to be employed, and to place them where they ought to be placed, we must become acquainted with certain principles...called Grammar.
> (Cobbett 1818: 11)

Cobbett's sentiment is as true today as it was in 1818: namely, that grammar can be empowering, particularly when construed in relation to developing articulate and fluent expression of knowledge and thought. Chapter 2 explores this point further.

The challenge that faces educators today is (a) how grammar is construed and (b) how it should be taught. Research is telling us, including that undertaken for this book, it is most likely to have an impact upon language development if undertaken in the context of reading, analyzing and crafting texts, where attention is paid to function as well as form. Today, as Wyse (2017) so amply illustrates, we are more aware than ever of the inherently creative, diversity and richness of writing and its associated practices that move us ever increasingly away from the notion of writing as predicated upon an invariable set of rules.

Debates about teaching grammar today are also set against a changing demographic within England, where, in common with many urban areas of the UK, pupils and students have been born in England but have a home language other than English as their mother tongue. Throughout this book, I use the term *pupils* to refer to young people between the ages of 11 and 16 (key stages 3 and 4) and *students* to young people aged between 16 and 19 (Key Stage 5). A major education challenge facing schools and teachers is developing such pupils' and students' language and literacy across a curriculum designed for pupils and students for whom English is an L1. There is a growing body of research, particularly that undertaken in Australia (discussed further below) since the 1990s, that shows the ways in which explicit attention to language can accelerate pupils' and students' development of subject literacies as part of mainstream curricular practices, and of EAL pupils in particular. This research has been informed theoretically by SFL/G.

In mainstream schooling in England, pupils and students come from a wide variety of language backgrounds and those designated EAL are taught predominantly in mainstream classrooms, as illustrated by the three schools discussed from Chapter 3 onwards. The challenge teachers face in such situations, is how to adapt curricular and pedagogic practice so that pupils' and students' literacy develops through the key stages regardless of linguistic and social background. This is also in the face of the fact that pupils and students come to school with varying degrees of cultural capital that places many of them at a de facto disadvantage (Bourdieu 1973; Bourdieu and Passeron 1977). This point is picked up on and expanded in Chapter 2 in relation to the ways in which LBP draws upon Bernstein's (1991, 1996) theory of pedagogic discourse (see also Clark 2001, 2005). This chapter, together with Chapter 2, provides a background and context to the later chapters that draw upon research into teachers' own interpretations and practices in relation to LBP and identifying a pedagogic grammar in the context of their own curriculum and assessment goals.

The secondary schools in question are all too well aware of the fact that language and literacy lie at the heart of learning and academic achievement. However, like all others, they are struggling to find ways of developing language and literacy across the curriculum in ways that can be integrated into mainstream classroom teaching. In the words of one head teacher, whose own subject background is that of science:

> **Quote**
> ...the reason I've always been in favour of language work is because of the complexity of learning (.) you need the language to explain yourself in learning and if you don't have the language you can't explain yourself (.) so it's chicken and egg...

Developing language and literacy across the curriculum has long been recognised as an important aspect of pedagogic practice. It is only in recent years though that the notion of literacy has come to be accepted in the education context as extending beyond the teaching of initial literacy in the primary school to the development of subject literacies into the secondary curriculum (pupils and students aged 11–19). Such a move has not been without contestation, particularly on the part of those concerned with the secondary curriculum for English (Goodwyn and Fuller 2011). Nevertheless, recent assessment and curriculum changes introduced in the UK since 2013 that in England have included changes to GCSE and A Level examinations and new National Curriculum Framework documents that have revised the curriculum of all mainstream subjects (2014), all place language and literacy as a pillar or spine throughout all curriculum subjects. Whilst the introduction of this test has not gone uncontested, it does nevertheless mean that pupils enter secondary school aged 11 with some rudimentary metalinguistic terminology. At the same time, National Literacy Strategies (NLS) designed to support the teaching of literacy first introduced in the 1990s have been abandoned. Revisions to the latest iteration of the National Curriculum focus exclusively upon curriculum content and leave any associated pedagogic practice well alone.

Taken altogether, these changes make it increasingly incumbent upon secondary schools to develop language and literacy across the curriculum initiatives and strategies. Moreover, they are required to so do without any kind of government-endorsed national framework of support of the kind that has existed for the last thirty years or so through the NLS.

> **Quote**
>
> **6. Language and literacy**
>
> 6.1 Teachers should develop pupils' spoken language, reading, writing and vocabulary as integral aspects of the teaching of every subject. English is both a subject in its own right and the medium for teaching; for pupils, understanding the language provides access to the whole curriculum. Fluency in the English language is an essential foundation for success in all subjects.
>
> **Spoken language**
>
> 6.2 Pupils should be taught to speak clearly and convey ideas confidently using Standard English. They should learn to justify ideas with reasons; ask questions to check understanding; develop vocabulary and build knowledge; negotiate; evaluate and build on the ideas of others; and select the

> appropriate register for effective communication. They should be taught to give well-structured descriptions and explanations and develop their understanding through speculating, hypothesising and exploring ideas. This will enable them to clarify their thinking as well as organise their ideas for writing.
>
> **Reading and writing**
>
> 6.3 Teachers should develop pupils' reading and writing in all subjects to support their acquisition of knowledge. Pupils should be taught to read fluently, understand extended prose (both fiction and non-fiction) and be encouraged to read for pleasure. Schools should do everything to promote wider reading. They should provide library facilities and set ambitious expectations for reading at home. Pupils should develop the stamina and skills to write at length, with accurate spelling and punctuation. They should be taught the correct use of grammar. They should build on what they have been taught to expand the range of their writing and the variety of the grammar they use. The writing they do should include narratives, explanations, descriptions, comparisons, summaries and evaluations: such writing supports them in rehearsing, understanding and consolidating what they have heard or read.
>
> **Vocabulary development**
>
> 6.4 Pupils' acquisition and command of vocabulary are key to their learning and progress across the whole curriculum. Teachers should therefore develop vocabulary actively, building systematically on pupils' current knowledge. They should increase pupils' store of words in general; simultaneously, they should also make links between known and new vocabulary and discuss the shades of meaning in similar words. In this way, pupils expand the vocabulary choices that are available to them when they write. In addition, it is vital for pupils' comprehension that they understand the meanings of words they meet in their reading across all subjects, and older pupils should be taught the meaning of instruction verbs that they may meet in examination questions. It is particularly important to induct pupils into the language which defines each subject in its own right, such as accurate mathematical and scientific language.
>
> (The National Curriculum in England key stages 3 and 4 Framework Document, December 2014: 9–10)
> https://www.gov.uk/government/uploads/system/uploads/attachment_data/file/381754/SECONDARY_national_curriculum.pdf, accessed 31 August 2017.

Language and literacy as described above, relate most closely to the language and literacy practices encountered by pupils at school as academic or disciplinary literacies, rather than to the whole range of literary practices that include adult life, community, further education and work. Typically, this involves apprenticing them into the discourse practices associated with different subject disciplines, against which academic success is measured. In advocating an LBP approach I do not intend to deny the importance or place of other aspects of literacy work such as multimodality (Kendrick 2016; Maybin 2014), indexicality (Blommaert 2010), translanguaging (Garcia and Wei 2014; Blackledge and Creese 2014), or semiotic repertoires (Blommaert and Backus 2011), nor developments in the curriculum for English in relation to critical, new and multimodal literacies (e.g., Jewitt et al. 2016; Parry et al. 2016; Bragg et al. 2014; Gee 2012, 2014; Unsworth and Thomas 2014; Painter et al. 2013; Cope and Kalantziz 2012; Marsh et al. 2012; Pahl and Rowsell 2012; Knobel and Lankshear 2007; Kress 2003). Neither do I seek to deny the work that has been done in sociolinguistics which takes account of the increasingly global and superdiverse nature of today's world (Vertovec 2007; Blommaert 2010; Clark 2013), in which social media plays a significant part in young people's identity construction (Georgakopoulou 2014; Androutsopoulos and Georgakopoulou 2003). An LBP approach I argue, complements all the work being done in the areas summarised above in that it seeks to give all pupils a voice regardless of their economic, linguistic and sociocultural backgrounds. It is also consistent with the recent National Curriculum for key stages 3 and 4, since teachers are expected to build upon what their pupils have been taught at key stages 1 and 2, expanding the range of their writing and the variety of the grammar they use. No further guidance, however, is provided on how this should be done. Indeed, the approach taken, in line with de Silva Joyce and Feez (2016) and Coffin and Donohue (2014) and others, is that drawing upon SFL/G encompasses a social semiotic approach, in that it is multi-layered, taking into account language development. Multilayered, in that language is studied from three different but integrated perspectives, examining how linguistic patterns are: woven together to form texts at a textual level, structured into differing clause patterns and how words are expressed as sounds and the letters that correspond to sounds when written down.

> **Quote**
>
> This model reveals that semantic and phonological perspectives are complementary rather than incompatible views of language, and this suggests that possibilities for literacy pedagogy are diminished, if one perspective is favoured at the expense of another. Representing words in grammatical structures (lexicogrammar) as the intermediary between meaning and its expression in sounds (or letters) is a feature of this model that has proven to be particularly valuable for literacy researchers and practitioners.
> (De Silva Joyce and Feez 2016: 118–119)

In Australia and more recently in the USA, LBP has proved to be particularly effective in enriching disadvantaged pupils' curricular experiences, especially in the primary age phases and higher (see, e.g., Coffin and Donohue 2014; Nesi and Gardiner 2012). There is less research, however, into the secondary age phases than in relation to either primary or higher education, a gap which this book aims to fill. Humphrey's research (2016) undertaken in an Australian middle years context, for pupils aged between 9 and 14 years, has begun to address this in the context of the curriculum for English, as does that of Macken-Horararick et al. (2018). This book then, adds to a growing body of evidence by providing an account of how an LBP informed approach can be integrated into the secondary school curriculum for England in the context of developing literacy across the curriculum initiatives and strategies across the 11–19 age range.

My central argument is, that for any kind of literacy across the curriculum strategy to have any kind of purchase, it has to align with teachers' day to day affordances across all curriculum subjects. Not only that, it also has to take account of the local as well as the regional, national and global contexts within which they work, rather than as top-down, generic initiatives (such as those associated with the NLS) that are imposed upon them. A major challenge in recontextualising a 'grand theory' such as that of LPB into classroom practice then, is how to introduce it to teachers such that it can be drawn upon in ways that have affordance and purchase with their own pedagogic practices, knowledge about language and the wider cultural and policy contexts within which those practices are situated. As the next section demonstrates, it has often been assumed that such an introduction necessitates some kind of 'top-down' major curriculum initiative or professional development programme from which teachers are then expected to draw upon and incorporate into their own practices. Such programmes are by their nature very general, and provide little or no support in how to affect the translation or recontextualisation from abstract, generic principles into their own assessment and curriculum goals. Another way is a 'bottom-up' approach, through research initiatives where teachers' own goals are taken into account and worked with to introduce an LBP approach that is relevant to their own contexts.

It is certainly the case that research into the teaching of English grammar undertaken in the 1960s and particularly in England, did much to discredit the teaching of traditional grammar and its associated pedagogy that centred upon decontextualized grammar exercises (see, e.g., Clark 2001; Hudson and Walmsley 2005). The centrality and importance of learning and teaching language and literacy in relation to academic achievement is undisputed. However, since the late 1980s when national curricula began to be introduced in various parts of the world including Australia and England, the role of explicit teaching about grammar and language together with pedagogic practices has been the subject of much heated dispute in those countries, as well as in the USA and elsewhere (Clark 2005). In recent years, the debate has moved on to accept the teaching of grammar by the teaching profession, as Chapter 4 shows. The issue now is not so much *why* but *how* and of what kind.

LBP is informed by a language based theory of learning (Halliday 1993). It is also grounded in a social theory of meaning that recognises the central role language plays in the construction, mediation and realisation of academic/subject knowledge. An LBP approach integrates the explicit teaching of metalinguistic concepts and terminology as an integral part of—not apart from—subject content. Pupils are thus explicitly taught the linguistic structures through which subject knowledge is constructed, mediated and realised alongside knowledge itself as an integral part of reading and writing activities.

# A Review of Language and Literacy Curriculum Initiatives in Australia, the USA and England

In the last decade or so, there has been a growing move on the part of those concerned with the curriculum for secondary English, in particular, to reintroduce the teaching of grammar and knowledge about language into the curriculum in ways that are very different from those that existed before (e.g., Locke 2010; Myhill and Watson 2013a; Giovanelli and Clayton 2016). This has been coupled with a growing body of evidence over the past 30 years or so, particularly from Australia and more recently from the USA and England (e.g., Brisk 2015; Myhill and Watson 2014; Myhill 2018), which shows that explicitly teaching grammar and language in the context of and integrated into the teaching of subject knowledge across all curriculum subjects and all key stages of schooling, can have a positive effect upon pupils' and students' curriculum experience and educational attainment as discussed throughout this section. This research has spearheaded the move away from grammar's central concern being with error and more towards recognising language patterns (Gartland and Smolkin 2016). In the remaining sections of this chapter, I outline the extent to which LBP has influenced and informed curricular practices in the three contexts of Australia, the USA and the UK—particularly England—and takes each one in turn. Much of the research that has been undertaken, particularly in Australian and American contexts, has informed the growing development of LBP into what is now arguably a theoretically fully developed pedagogic approach.

## Australia

LBP has been developed more fully in Australia than anywhere else in the world. This is particularly in relation to the notion of school genres, discussed more fully in Chapter 2. Initially, genre-based literacy programs in Australia were developed during the 1980s out of a concern by teacher educators in the state of New South Wales, in relation to the quality of literacy education in the state's schools. This concern centred on the way in which since the 1960s, the teaching of writing had been dominated by way of process without hardly any—if at all—explicit teaching about language. Teacher educators began to observe the adverse effects of such an approach in relation to the range of writing tasks pupils and students undertook, particularly in schools with large numbers of working class, migrant or indigenous children, and the lack of explicit attention paid to their language development. They also noticed that pupils wrote in textual forms with which they were familiar from their oral culture such as narrative. However, pupils were not engaging as well with writing that was relevant in other subjects such as science, social science and the humanities, since these texts were not as familiar to them outside of school contexts.

As a response to this concern, academic staff from the University of Sydney, to help them to incorporate SFL/G into the teaching of language and literacy. Staff members from the University of Sydney's linguistics department began working with teachers and teacher educators to develop genre-based literacy programs to specifically address these challenges as part of the *New South Wales' Disadvantaged Schools' Program* and an associated project called *Write it Right*. These two projects produced a range of publications written in written in collaboration with teacher educators and linguists, including a series of genre-based books for students in the primary school with support books for teachers in under the general title of *Language as a Resource for Meaning* (Christie et al. 1990a, b, 1992); a book for teachers introducing genre theory (Derewianka 1990) and a number of resource books for teaching English, science, mathematics, history, art and geography (Rothery 1994; Coffin 1996 ; Humphrey 1996).

Since the late 1990s, various other initiatives have also taken place in other Australian states, centred upon developing LBP informed professional development materials for in-service teachers. The first of these was an accelerated literacy program designed to tackle low literacy levels in remote communities around Australia, particularly Indigenous communities in the Northern Territory (Rose et al. 1999). This initiative continues through a National Accelerated Literacy Network. Another initiative begun in 2001 has also focussed upon increasing literacy rates of all pupils, not only those of Australian Indigenous Aboriginal origin.

Called *Reading to Learn* (R2L), it shares some techniques with other literacy programs in Australia, such as the accelerated literacy program, but aims to provide teachers with far broader skills with which to integrate literacy with curriculum teaching in all year levels and subjects, including knowledge about language, texts across the curriculum, lesson planning and assessment. The R2L strategies also share some techniques with the New Zealand *Reading Recovery* programme, based upon Clay's (1991, 1993) research. R2L integrates the foundation's skills in reading similar to those in the *Reading Recovery* programme, and extends them into curriculum teaching at all year levels. R2L has also been introduced into European countries as part of a recently funded European Union initiative. More recently, some state departments, such as the South Australian Department for Education and Child Development (DECD) have published several LBP based CPD programmes to support that State's curriculum, some of which have international editions that are delivered worldwide.

In addition to programmes and resource development of the kind summarised above, research that took place during the 1980s as part of projects such as *Write it Right* began to be supplemented in the 1990s by that undertaken by individual researchers in both the primary and secondary sectors. The impetus for this research came largely as a way of rebutting criticism of LBP, and was undertaken in the main through researchers working directly with pupils themselves. From the late 1990s onwards, the work of researchers such as Williams showed how SFL/G could offer primary school children conceptual tools for reflection on language, and how an explicit focus on grammar could support critical thinking about a text (Williams 1998, 2000, 2004). He exemplified this through giving examples of 6 year olds using SFL metalanguage to talk about procedures and of 11 year olds including the use of cohesion to reflect on how they structured their texts. More recently, French (2012) has also provided evidence that SFL can help children develop more conscious control of their writing and more critical understanding of their reading.

Research by Quinn (2004) and O'Halloran (2005) into science and maths respectively show ways in which linguistic metalanguage drawn from SFL/G can be used in these subjects. Quinn highlighted the role of oral language in using linguistic metalanguage with students at 6th grade (12–13 year olds) to support their writing of explanations in science. Her research centred upon a case study of a student identified by her teacher as a 'poor writer', illustrating that using metalanguage enabled a less successful student to articulate more clearly what she had learnt than some of the more able students could. O'Halloran's research into secondary classroom discourse in mathematics shows how grammatical strategies in mathematics organise meaning in symbolic statements in ways that are different from those found in language. She shows how mathematical symbolism has developed in particular ways for the solution of mathematics problems and argues that mathematical symbolism reduces the amount of information on human feelings and ways of behaving. That is, that the components of a mathematical symbolic statement can be seen as embedded phrases that are concerned with operations. O'Halloran contends that this is a significant point in understanding how the grammar of mathematical symbolism is functionally organised to fulfil the goals of mathematics.

In relation to the humanities, Coffin (2006) developed research she had undertaken for the earlier *Write it Right* project. She researched the writing requirements of the history curriculum in the context of Australian secondary schools in Sydney, New South Wales, providing a linguistic analysis of student writing in secondary school history. This analysis was used to provide an empirical basis for creating teaching materials designed to develop pupils' writing skills whilst also expanding their historical knowledge and understanding. She found that partnership between educational linguists, literacy consultants and history teachers was pivotal to her research, in order to adapt the linguistic findings for classroom use and develop effective strategies for bringing to students' consciousness the way in which history writing is linguistically structured and shaped. Her study of 17 history teachers found that, although some teachers felt they needed more time to 'digest' the implications of the linguistic analysis and further support to implement it, the combined impact of the professional development sessions and in-class collaboration was enough to convince them of the value of the new approach. In particular, a significant shift in teacher use of language was observed, with a much higher level of explicitness in reference to the language system itself. In terms of changes in pupil attitudes and writing, outcomes were most evident in their control of text organisation.

Gibbons' (2006) 2-year qualitative study of 5th grade (11–12 year olds) science classrooms in an urban school of low socio-economic status with a high proportion of English Language Learners (ELLs), shows how pupils developed knowledge of language and science together over a period of time as their teachers engaged them in focused work on language in the context of learning about magnets. Teachers used SF/G metalanguage to talk about the forms language takes and explicitly taught pupils how to structure assigned oral and written tasks. Gibbons demonstrates how this metalanguage supported dialogic interaction with a simultaneous focus on science and language. Gibbons' study has been highly influential in adding the dimension of the Vygotskian concept of scaffolding into the LBP approach discussed in Chapter 2. As with other, later studies such as those undertaken by the authors in an edited volume by Hamond (2001) in the primary context, her work like much of the research undertaken, has focussed upon providing evidence of LBP as a curriculum intervention along with descriptions of key genres for learning. Polias and Dare (2006) also offer case studies of teachers using LBP to scaffold 7 year olds' writing of sequential explanations and 12 year olds' writing of narratives and arguments. They show how pupils designated EAL/ELLs gained increasing control of their writing through incorporating advanced language features typical of the genres they were required to write.

More recently, Martin (2013) has focused upon what knowledge looks like from the linguistic point of view in the secondary curriculum, and what it means to have an embedded, rather than a generic, literacy programme, where pupils read and write to learn and where what they are learning is the key factor that is addressed in shaping a curriculum subject and designing the pedagogy through which it is taught. Martin and his colleagues observed lessons in biology and history, and were struck by the ways in which teaching was characterised by skipping from one fragment of knowledge to another, rather than through any deliberate and explicit process of building knowledge. Pupils' knowledge thus remained fragmented, with lessons focusing on learning vocabulary associated with any given subject. He concluded that beyond their reading, if done at all, pupils are not presented with additional models, spoken or written, of the consolidated knowledge they need to produce for assessment purposes. Teachers' talk, but rarely ever model writing for their class: 'All this, in conjunction with the fact that reading and writing are not taught, results in a highly stratified set of outcomes, since only students from the right background are positioned to learn by osmosis what has to be learned but is never made explicit' (Martin 2013: 35).

In general, the biology and history units Martin and his colleagues observed start with the reading pupils are expected to have done (a textbook, screen text or photocopied handout) and end with writing for assessment purposes. Pupils have to learn more than can be covered in class and are assessed on their writing. Reading and writing are therefore 'high stakes tasks'. However, as Martin observes, reading and writing were not taught explicitly. Rather, it seemed to be assumed that students had acquired the necessary skills in primary school, which he observes is '…is an absurd assumption given the many unfamiliar genres packaging knowledge in secondary school and the unfamiliar power grammar students have not been expected to read or write before' (Martin 2013: 36).

What knowledge building did occur, happened through spoken interaction, with teachers explaining and unpacking unfamiliar technical and abstract vocabulary and then repacking it through spoken interaction and in notes on the board as consolidation and in preparation for writing. Such teaching, however, is rare, and leaves many pupils stranded in common sense, rather than abstract, knowledge.

Macken-Horarik et al. (2015), Herrington and Macken-Horarik (2015), Unsworth and Macken-Horarik (2015) and Macken-Horarick et al. (2018) have all shown the ways in which an LBP approach can underpin the teaching of English across the primary and secondary curriculum in all kinds of ways, from the teaching of spelling to interpreting visual images. One recent research project undertaken in in the context of the secondary curriculum for English and ELLs is that of Humphrey and Macnaught (2015) and Humphrey (2016) in an Australian urban, multicultural secondary school where 97.5% of pupils have language backgrounds other than English and with 42 cultural groups represented. Their research found that the students were able to interact fluently with both teachers and their peers in general class discussions. However, their writing was more often than not characterised by the use of informal language, and its resemblance to the spoken mode. The project thus centred upon introducing explicit instructional practices that included a shared metalanguage in order to make visible the patterns of language valued for discipline learning in relation to both developing pupils' writing and also in interpreting and understanding the success criteria of discipline-specific assessment tasks.

Research of the kind outlined above show the ways in which an LBP approach can be effected within the curriculum for English in ways that are focussed and targeted upon extending teachers' pedagogic practices, rather than replacing them with something completely new. Generic CPD programmes have a place and a part to play, but more and more research evidence, including that drawn upon in this book, shows that changing teachers' practices through the introduction of any kind of intervention such as LBP has more chance of success when it is embraced by all the staff in a school and any associated CPD is targeted and focussed upon teachers' own disciplines and the sociocultural contexts within which they work.

## USA

The American educational context is guided by learning standards, typically assessed by standardized tests. Until very recently, teachers were generally accountable to district and state standards that listed skills pupils and students need to develop, rather than to any national or state defined curriculum as in the case of the UK and Australia. However, in the spring of 2009, and unprecedented in the history of the US education, governors and state commissioners of education from across the United States formed the Common Core State Standards Initiative (CCSSI) that aims to develop a set of shared national standards, called Common Core State Standards (CCSS). Consequently, all states in America are currently engaged in writing their own State versions of the Common Core.

In the USA, the major influence upon the English Language Arts (ELA) curriculum has been in Rhetoric and Composition as well as Chomskyian formal linguistics. However, over the past decade or so, growing attention has been paid to the importance of writing for learning, including paying more attention to grammatical structure in the context of developing adolescents' literacy writing practices (Graham and Perin 2007). More recently, LBP has also begun to be theorised and applied to the American context and drawing from the Australian experience. Research into the impact of LBP has been undertaken by, for example, Schleppegrell et al. (2008), Achugar and Carpenter (2012) and Schleppegrell (2013). Schleppegrell's early research, like that of Greer and Taylor's, Achugar and Carpenter's (and Coffin's in Australia), centred upon academic/subject literacy in the secondary school curriculum for history. Schleppegrell's more recent research has taken place in primary schools where a majority of the population are bilingual students and many ELLs, focussing upon the upper primary curriculum. Her goal has been to use metalanguage drawn from SFL to develop approaches and materials that would assist teachers in engaging ELLs in talk about language in ways that would support their English language development.

Schleppegrell makes the point that the key challenge of applying the genre approach in American contexts as developed in Australia, is to develop genre descriptions that support the kinds of writing valued in American contexts. This involves taking into account local established expectations and pedagogies as well as teachers' own perspectives on language, grammar and genre. Schleppegrell contends that the American learning standards do not preclude a genre-based approach, and that the skills delineated in the standards need to be what she calls 'folded into' the genre approach and explicitly addressed. Schleppegrell and her team worked as instructional coaches with 26 teachers in six primary schools. Genre was a term used by teachers and pupils to 'name' different text types (e.g., Tall Tale, Legend, Memoir, Myth), during reading instruction. The writing genres in which pupils' engaged were in the main general and devoid of immediate social purpose (e.g., essay, report). The schools also used a commercial program for writing instruction that offered teachers generic scaffolds. Her research found that in order to focus teachers' and pupils' attention away from generic scaffolds to a focus on genre as choice in context for particular purposes, that disciplinary perspectives needed to be foregrounded and teachers helped to accomplish goals they already had for pupils' learning.

Identifying appropriate language features thus calls for developing a metalanguage within the classroom context in which it is used, so that it can serve as a means of talking about what texts are about, rather than as simply a labelling exercise. Schleppegrell found that a metalanguage drawn from SFG helped teachers and their students to talk about text, comprehend text and compose a written piece, in ways that contributed to a positive and motivating learning and teaching experience. Her research confirms that genres are ever-evolving and not static, and in work with teachers, genre descriptions may need to be adapted to local contexts so that they serve larger curricular purposes that are discipline-specific. She also found that the metalanguage associated with LBP cannot be brought into new contexts and taught as 'things'. Rather, it needed to be adapted by considering the kind of writing that teachers in a particular context want to support.

Most recently, Oliviera and Iddings (2014), in an edited volume devoted to language-based pedagogy in the USA, discuss LBP in the context of the CCSS for ELA, particularly with regard to applying the concept of genre as a way of scaffolding text types identified by the CCSS. The ELA standards demand that the responsibility for teaching reading, writing, speaking, listening and language is a responsibility shared by all teachers across all grade levels and content areas. The CCSS refers to three text types: argument, informative/explanatory and narrative. The CCSS includes illustrative examples by way of a compilation of student writing samples. Maune and Klassen (2014) analysed student writing samples taken from Grade 8 (13–14 year old) pupils using the two frameworks of CCSS and SFL to illustrate ways in which the two, far from being in conflict with one another, can work together very well. They show how both frameworks share the common goal of linking language, and view language as an activity that relates form to function. They point out that the text types identified by the CCSS overlap with Martin and Rose's definition of genre as 'stage-orientated, social processes' (2008: 6) and that text types share the common characteristic with genre of being goal oriented.

> **Quote**
> ...the stages that characterise genres and their corresponding social processes are unique to SFL and bring to our understanding of text discrete ways to teach students organisational strategies of text structures that accomplish some social purpose, thus helping them understand how specific language forms accomplish specific social functions.
>   (Oliviera and Iddings 2014: 122)

Oliviera and Iddings volume echoes and highlights Schleppegrell's research in drawing attention to the fact that since functional grammar theoretically situates language within a context of situation and culture, then it follows that developing an LBP approach in practice involves drawing from its theoretical base in ways that take account of the specific situation(s) and culture(s) within which it is realised.

# UK

In contrast with Australia and the USA, surprisingly little research has been undertaken in UK contexts into the application or integration of SFG/L or LBP with regards to the English and literacy curriculum. This is surprising, given that SFG/L has been drawn upon on four separate occasions since the 1960s in relation to materials written designed to support teachers in the teaching of grammar. The earliest research was that published in 1969/1971 by Barnes, Britton and Rosen and by Barnes in 1976/1992. All three individuals were highly influential at the time in relation to what has become known as the 'personal growth' model of English teaching and a process approach to the development of writing alluded to earlier in the Australian context. It is interesting to note that a key concept of SFG, that of *register*, is evident in their work.

In the volume, Barnes refers to 'the functions of subject-specific registers' and the importance of teachers' recognising the pedagogical implication of their own use of language. Barnes writes that: 'Teachers need a far more sophisticated insight into the implications of the language which they themselves use, especially the register which we have called the language of secondary education' (Barnes et al. 1971: 75). He also felt that teachers would benefit from a more sophisticated insight into their own use of language and also from recognising the important part that language plays in their pupils' learning.

SFG/L informed curriculum materials projects were also developed in the 1960s under the auspices of *The Schools Council Programme in Linguistics and Language Teaching*, led by Michael Halliday, before his departure to Australia. This project produced two sets of materials, which were the first ever set of SFG informed materials to have been developed. One set was written for primary school teachers called *Breakthrough to Literacy* and the second set written for secondary school teachers of English called *Language in Use* (Doughty et al. 1971). However, take up by teachers of English of the *Language in Use* materials was limited, and simultaneously failed to catch their attention and imagination for many and various reasons. Chief amongst these was that the status of the folder was unclear, since it did not appear to be a method book for teachers but neither was it a textbook for pupils. The materials tried to address both audiences at once with the result that it pleased neither. Its explanations were insufficient for the teacher who traditionally had studied English literature and its dull presentation did not make it attractive for use in the classroom. Added to this was the fact that the materials outlined sequences of lessons for the teacher without providing the supplementary materials that pupils and students would need to undertake them. Furthermore, the linguistic knowledge required by teachers to teach the materials was beyond the scope of many and the materials did not provide sufficient explanation of the linguistic theories on which the material was based. Anxious to avoid charges of prescriptivism, the materials' authors had described language neutrally, with the consequence that they failed to engage with the ways in which language is both a carrier *and* a conveyor of meaning and value.

Halliday (1991) later defended the authors of the *Language in Use* materials, pointing out how they had resisted the attempts made at the time to explain or describe the methods through which the materials would be translated into classroom practice, on the grounds that they did not wish to appear to be seen as prescribing or telling teachers how this was to be done. They had preferred instead to leave this particular issue to individual teachers. This strategy, however, meant that teachers were left to themselves to incorporate the materials into their own pedagogic practices with no support of any kind offered. Explicit teaching about language and linguistic terminology ceased being taught as part of the curriculum for English in primary and secondary schools from the early 1970s onwards and no longer formed part of formal examinations. It did continue however, as part of teaching Ancient and Modern Languages until well into the 1980s.

Interestingly, the *Language in use* materials were produced close to the time of the publication of The Bullock Report (1975), subtitled *A Language for Life*, a government report into the teaching of English that emphasised the importance of language across the curriculum. The importance of language for learning was well recognised by the authors of the Report, particularly Britton (1970). SFL/G was still, however, in its early stages of development and had yet to develop as a fully fledged theory of language. At the time, the teaching of traditional grammar, centred as it was upon sets of decontextualized exercises, had become increasingly discredited as a number of studies showed that such activity had little effect upon pupils' developing writing abilities. Consequently, the dominant paradigm for language across the curriculum that followed the Bullock Report emphasised the creative aspect of the English language in terms of pupils' developing abilities as writers. This was to be achieved mainly through engaging with the writing process itself rather than upon any explicit instruction into the formal and functional features of language use.

This paradigm dominated the teaching of English until the late 1980s, when the National Curriculum was introduced. Prior to introducing the one for English, a report was written that produced a model for the English Language, known as the Kingman Report (1988). This model went far beyond the teaching of grammar, and focussed instead on *knowledge about language* (KAL). The Kingman Model for KAL was broad and encompassing, and included a consideration of the differences and similarities between speech and writing, language variation and language change, alongside the form and structure of standard English, communication and comprehension and acquisition and development of literacy. However, whilst the model was incorporated into the original 1989 National Curriculum for English, it formed a separate strand, and, much like the *Language in Use* materials, the relationship between how language study in this strand related to the other areas of the English curriculum—speaking and listening, reading and writing—was not clear.

A national initiative called *Language in the National Curriculum* (LINC) was launched to support the Kingman Model of the English Language and the knowledge about language strand of the original National Curriculum for English. This national initiative ran from 1988 until 1991, with the aim of providing a set of CPD materials to support the Kingman Model upon which the *knowledge about language* (KAL) strand of the new National Curriculum for English was based. The LINC materials were informed by SFG, including by the then well-developed theories of *genre* and *register*. However, the materials' perceived failure on government policymakers' part to emphasise traditional teaching of English grammar meant that the initiative was abandoned before its work had been completed, and the training materials have never been published officially. They were, however, influential in supporting the growth of A Level English Language as a post-16 qualification, since topics at the heart of specifications since the early 1990s have been founded on the Kingman model. The knowledge about language strand of the first iteration of the National Curriculum was one of the most hotly debated issues at the time (e.g., Clark 1994). For teachers themselves, the research undertaken by the evaluation of the introduction of the National Curriculum found in its Report (Raban et al. 1994) that although teachers' collective understanding of the term 'Knowledge about Language' corresponded to the Kingman framework, there was a degree of uncertainty amongst individual teachers about the exact terms of reference and the precise area of English teaching to which it referred, particularly at key stages 1 and 2. This uncertainty lay in whether the term 'Knowledge about Language' included teaching about the organisation and use of language structured within texts and theoretical aspects of language, as well as teaching about the organisation and use of language related to words and sentences. English teachers at Key Stage 3 stated that it was the term 'Knowledge about Language' itself which was unfamiliar to them, rather than the area of English to which it referred, although many expressed a lack of confidence about teaching theoretical aspects of language, as they lacked the necessary expertise. Even so, secondary teachers of English found that stated that implementing the new curriculum had raised their awareness of the importance of teaching pupils' about sentence structure and punctuation, and increasingly structured their teaching and made their teaching of grammar more explicit. They did this largely in contextualised contexts as part of developing writing, such as explaining the use and structure of paragraphs followed by a practical activity. However, a change of government in 1992 led to the Report and its findings being ignored and the instantiation of a series of whole scale revisions to the National curriculum that have continued ever since.

A third initiative that began in 1994 and ended in 2013 centred upon *National Literacy Strategies* (NLS) and a *Framework for Teaching English* (FTE). Introduced first into primary schools, the NLS extended to secondary schools in 2001 for subject English, thereby extending the concept of literacy beyond primary education to secondary education. In a modern, post-industrial and technologised world, literacy has become ever more sophisticated, with the world of work demanding increasingly literate workers. Whilst various revisions of the NLS drew progressively upon elements of SFG and LBP, they lacked a coherent, explicit theoretical underpinning, and the degree of compromise between competing approaches to the teaching of literacy was evident within them. Its dissemination model was also far from effective with secondary teachers, who had no grounding in theoretical and applied linguistics, 'trained' by local authority advisors who knew very little themselves and then being asked to go back into schools to share their 'training' with colleagues. At the same time, Policy reviews into empirical studies into the teaching of grammar such as that undertaken by the Evidence for Policy and Practice Information and Co-ordinating Centre (EPPI) (Andrews et al.

2004a, b), continued to conclude that there was no evidence for any benefit of teaching grammar on writing quality. However, the studies upon which the reports were based were ones where grammar had been taught as a separate activity, and did not include any studies where it was taught in context. Research undertaken since then, such as that of Andrews (2005) and Andrews et al. (2006), has pointed to the benefits of an approach they called 'sentence combining', where pupils and students were taught to construct more complex and multi-clause sentences as part of contextualised learning, rather than as decontextualised exercises. Myhill et al. (2012) have also shown that where grammar is taught in context, then positive results can be achieved, in terms of improving the quality of pupils' and students' writing.

Both the NLS and the FTE were discontinued in 2013, after coming under much criticism from government's own reports (Ofsted 2009, 2012). This criticism centred upon the fact that although such initiatives had been designed to support the secondary curriculum for English, they had had a negative impact upon they its teaching. This led, unsurprisingly, to some schools using them in a fragmented way, and implementing them unthinkingly, 'often because they held no deeply held views about the nature of English as a subject and how it might be taught' (2009, paragraph 19). With regards to the teaching of grammar, such Reports also criticised government initiatives for overemphasising technical aspects such as punctuation or complex sentences, at the expense of helping pupils to develop and structure their ideas. Added to this, were the findings of international comparison tests such as those of the Programme for International Student Assessment (PISA), which showed that England was performing modestly at best against countries which did not have such prescriptive initiatives. As Ellis and Briggs (2011) say, the initiatives contained too much information with little guidance as to how to integrate its content into the curriculum as a whole, coupled with a very poor dissemination model. Other evidence, such as the research discussed in Denham and Lobeck (2010) also highlighted the failure of 'top-down' approaches to institutional change.

One of the major reasons for the failure of the NLS and the FTE in the UK is attributed to the micromanagement of teaching through policy with no corresponding pedagogic practice on how to integrate what was required into local contexts (Goodwyn and Fuller 2011). This lack of any 'hook' into day to day practices had the adverse effect of not only destabilising teachers' confidence but also their professionalism. At the same time, research undertaken as part of *Grammar for Writing* projects (Andrews et al. 2004a, b; Myhill et al. 2012; Myhill and Watson 2013b), argued against the decontextualising of grammar exercises as something 'outside' mainstream activity and for their integration into mainstream activities, especially those related to writing. They stressed the importance of pupils understanding the writing process in developing into more competent writers, rather than the simplistic and rigid interpretations of planning, drafting and revising evident in so many government produced documents. More recent research then, has begun to look at the benefits of teaching grammar that is contextualised and embedded within the teaching of writing and found significant benefit of a contextualised approach (Wyse et al. 2013; Myhill et al. 2012) that is characteristic of LBP.

A recent research project into an LBP approach has been that undertaken by McAlister and Ellis (2014) in Scotland has focused upon secondary geography in the upper primary and lower secondary curriculum. Their focus was to assess the impact of an LBP intervention upon pupils' attainment, and has shown that the intervention resulted in statistically significant impacts on pupil attainment in some contexts, but not all. Their research offers an analysis of the interplay between the affordances and the constraints of the classroom, school, subject and local authority policies which together form the contexts for teachers implementing literacy for learning across the curriculum. It also revealed the conflicting assumptions that are made about teachers' understandings of literacy teaching. Their study suggests that a more nuanced appreciation of the challenges posed by the call for 'literacy across or for learning' is called for if such initiatives are to be successful.

## Criticisms and Rebuttals

The adoption of an LBP approach in the various contexts summarised above has not been without criticism and fierce debate, particularly from theorists concerned with the teaching of English. Firstly, critical theorists have attacked genre-based approaches to teaching on the grounds that it accommodates learners to existing modes of practice and to the values and ideologies of the dominant culture that valued genres embody (e.g., Benesch 2001). Genre proponents, however, counter this argument on the grounds that such an argument can be levelled at almost any teaching approach. Learning about genres, rather than precluding critical analysis provides a necessary basis for critical engagement with cultural and textual practices. In this way genre-based literacy programmes informed by LBP have much in common with critical literacy as Hasan (1996), Rothery (1996), and Macken-Horarik (2008) have all argued. Secondly, proponents of process writing approaches claim that genre instruction inhibits writers' self-expression and straightjackets creativity through conformity and prescriptivism, such as Dixon (1991) and more recently Doecke and Breen (2013) and Rosen (2013). Clearly, the dangers of a static, decontextualized pedagogy are very real if teachers fail to acknowledge variation and apply what Freedman (1994: 46) called 'a recipe theory of genre'. But there is nothing inherently prescriptive in a genre approach, as the discussion in this chapter and the next makes clear. Rather, it has been the ways in which a genre approach has been interpreted as exemplars of practice that have led to such interpretation as being 'the' way, rather than 'a' way, as became apparent in the English NLS and FTE.

Teaching about genre implies instantiating the use of certain patterns not as a way of dictating what is written, but as a way of ensuring that appropriate patterns are selected in relation to the knowledge that is being expressed. It thus enables choices to be made and facilitates expression, particularly in relation to academic writing valued in upper secondary and higher education contexts. Even so-called process writing itself, in relation to writing certain texts common in the English syllabus such as writing imaginative newspaper articles, letters, emails or blog posts, has to pay attention to the language features of those genres (register) such as tense, use of first, second or third person, layout, headlines and so on if they are to be recognised as such. The difference between an LBP approach and a process one, is that the former explicitly makes language features visible through direct instruction, whilst the latter relies upon such features deriving 'naturally' and invisibly through practice. Finally, there is the claim that teaching grammatical terminology is in some way 'harmful' to pupils' and students' language development and that an LBP approach inhibits the development of writing if the main focus of assessment is on grammatical accuracy. However, this criticism seems to imply that the focus of LBP is (a) uncontextualised grammatical accuracy and (b) unrelated to the content and context of any individual writing task, when this is far from being the case.

## Conclusion

The sections in this chapter have summarised the ways in which initiatives into teaching about language have been undertaken over nearly half a century in different countries worldwide. The growing acknowledgement of the importance of the part language plays in learning has developed in tandem alongside modern grammars such as SFG. Within such a grammar, the unit of analysis has extended to include morphology (word structure) as well as syntax (clause structure) and textual organisation. Current debates thus centre not so much upon whether or not grammar should be taught, but *which* metalinguistic terminology should be used and *how* it should be taught. Part of the underlying tension with regards to teaching about language—including grammatical terminology and language structure—on the part of secondary school teachers of English, is that between the creativity and subversion evident in English teaching pedagogy are assumed to sit at odds with negative experiences of grammar pedagogy (Watson 2015). There is also the view that teaching about language is detrimental to the development of pupils' and students' creative expression. However, I would argue that whether or not such teaching is detrimental depends upon how teachers construe grammar, in relation to its purpose and its associated pedagogy.

The evidence base from around the world is steadily growing to show that an integrated approach to teaching grammar and about language that underpins LBP can be introduced to and practiced by teachers across secondary school curriculum in ways that transfer successfully into their curriculum aims, goals and practices. The assumption that teachers' metalinguistic knowledge awareness cannot be developed has proved to be unfounded, as has the assumption that explicitly teaching pupils and students metalinguistic terminology is either beyond their capabilities or somehow damaging to their language development. Indeed, much of the evidence points to the opposite: that explicit instruction and direct teaching of language structure in the context of its use improves, rather than inhibits, education outcomes particularly but not exclusively, for those pupils for whom English is an additional language and/or those from disadvantaged backgrounds.

# References

Achugar, M., & Carpenter, B. D. (2012). Developing disciplinary literacy in a multilingual history classroom. *Linguistics and Education, 23*(3), 262–276.

Andrews, R. (2005). Knowledge about the teaching of [sentence] grammar: The state of play. *English Teaching: Practice and Critique, 4*(3), 69–76.

Andrews R., Torgerson C., Beverton S., Locke T., Low G., Robinson A., & Zhu D. (2004a). *The effect of grammar teaching (syntax) in English on 5 to 16 year olds' accuracy and quality in written composition*. London: EPPI-Centre, Social Science Research Unit, Institute of Education. Retrieved December 12, 2005 from http://eppi.ioe.ac.uk/reel.

Andrews R., Torgerson C., Beverton S., Locke T., Low G., Robinson A., & Zhu D. (2004b). *The effect of grammar teaching (sentence-combining) in English on 5 to 16 year olds' accuracy and quality in written composition*. London: EPPI-Centre, Social Science Research Unit, Institute of Education. Retrieved December 12, 2005 from http://eppi.ioe.ac.uk/reel.

Andrews, R., Torgerson, C., Beverton, S., Freeman, A., Locke, T., Low, G., et al. (2006). The effect of grammar teaching on writing development. *British Educational Research Journal, 32*(1), 39–55.

Androutsopoulos, J., & Georgakopoulou, A. (2003). *Discourse constructions of youth identities*. Amsterdam: Benjamins.

Barnes, D. (1976/1992). *From communication to curriculum*. Portsmouth, NH: Boynton/Cook Heinemann.

Barnes, D., Britton, J., & Rosen, M. (1969/1971). *Language, the learner and the school*. London: Penguin Education.

Benesch, S. (2001). *Critical English for academic purposes*. Mahwah, NJ: Lawrence Erlbaum Associates Inc.

Bernstein, B. (1991). *The structuring of pedagogic discourse. Vol. 4. Class, codes and control*. London and New York: Routledge.

Bernstein, B. (1996). *Pedagogy, symbolic control and identity*. London: Taylor & Francis.

Blackledge, A., & Creese, A. (Eds.). (2014). *Heteroglossia as practice and pedagogy*. Dordrecht, Heidlelberg, New York and London: Springer.

Blommaert, J. (2010). *The sociolinguistics of globalisation*. Cambridge: Cambridge University Press.

Blommaert, J., & Backus, A. (2011). *Repertoires revisited: 'Knowing language' in superdiversity*. London: Kings College Working Papers in Language and Literacies.

Bourdieu, P. (1973). Cultural reproduction and social reproduction. In R. Brown (Ed.), *Knowledge, education and social change: Papers in the sociology of education*. Tavistock: Tavistock Publications.

Bourdieu, P., & Passeron, J. (1977). *Reproduction in education society and culture*. London: Sage.

Bragg, S., Kehily, M. J., & Buckingham, D. (Eds.). (2014). *Youth cultures in the age of global media*. Basingstoke: Palgrave Macmillan.

Brisk, M. (2015). *Engaging students in academic literacies: Genre based pedagogy for K-5 classrooms*. London and New York: Routledge.

Britton, J. (1970). *Language and learning*. London: Penguin.

Christie, F., Gray, P., Gray, B., Macken, M., Martin, J. R. & Rothery, J. (1990a, 1990b, 1992). *Language a resource for meaning: Procedures*. Books 1–4 and Teachers Manual; Reports Books 104 and Teachers' Manual; Explanations Books 1–4 and Teachers' Manual. Sydney: Harcourt Brace Jovanovich.

Clark, U. (1994). Bringing English to order. *English in Education, 28*(1), 33–38.

Clark, U. (2001). *War words: Language, history and the disciplining of English*. Oxford: Elsevier Science.

Clark, U. (2005). Bernstein's theory of pedagogic discourse: Linguistics, educational policy and practice in the UK English/literacy classroom. *English Teaching: Practice and Critique, 4*(3), 32–47.

Clark, U. (2013). *Language and identity in Englishes*. London: Routledge.
Clay, M. (1991). *Becoming literate: The construction of inner control*. London: Hienemann.
Clay, M. (1993). *An observation survey of early literacy development*. London: Heinemann.
Cobbett, W. (1818). *A grammar of the English language*. New York: Peter Eckler.
Coffin, C. (1996). *Exploring literacy in school history*. Sydney: Disadvantaged Schools Program.
Coffin, C. (2006). *Historical discourse: The language of time, cause and evaluation*. London: Continuum.
Coffin, C., & Donohue, J. (2014). *A language as a social-semiotic-based approach to teaching and learning in higher education*. Oxford: Wiley Blackwell.
Cope, B., & Kalantzis, M. (2012). *Literacies*. Cambridge: Cambridge University Press.
Denham, K., & Lobeck, A. (Eds.). (2010). *Linguistics at school: Language awareness in primary and secondary education*. Cambridge: Cambridge University Press.
Department of Education and Science (DES). (1975). *The Bullock Report. A Language for Life*. London: HMSO.
Department of Education and Science. (1988). *The Kingman Report. Report of the Committee of Inquiry into the Teaching of English Language*. London: HMSO.
Derewianka, B. (1990). *Exploring how texts work*. Rozelle, NSW: Primary English Association.
De Silva Joyce, H., & Feez, S. (2016). *Exploring literacies: Theory, research, practice*. Basingstoke: Palgrave Macmillan.
Dixon, J. (1991). *A schooling in English*. Milton Keynes: Open University Press.
Doecke, B., & Breen, L. (2013). Beginning again: A response to Rosen and Christie. *Changing English; Studies in Culture and Education, 20*(3), 292–305.
Doughty, P., Pearce, J., & Thornton, G. (1971). *Language in use*. London: Schools Council.
Ellis, V., & Briggs, J. (2011). Teacher education and applied linguistics: What needs to be understood about what, how and where beginning teachers learn. In S. Ellis & E. McCartney (Eds.), *Applied linguistics and primary school teaching* (pp. 276–289). Cambridge: Cambridge University Press.
Freedman, A. (1994). 'Do as I say': The relationship between teaching and learning new genres. In A. Freedman & P. Medway (Eds.), *Genre and the new rhetoric* (pp. 191–210). London: Taylor & Francis.

French, R. (2012). Learning the grammatics of quoted speech: Benefits for punctuation and expressive reading. *Australian Journal of Language and Literacy, 35*(2), 206–222.

Garcia, O., & Wei, L. (2014). *Translanguaging: Language, bilingualism and education.* Basingstoke: Palgrave Macmillan.

Gartland, L., & Smolkin, L. (2016). The histories and mysteries of grammar instruction. *The Reading Teacher, 69*(4), 391–399.

Gee, J. (2012). The old and the new in the new digital literacies. *Education Forum, 76*(4), 418–420.

Gee, J. (2014). Decontextualised language: A problem, not a solution. *International Multilingual Research, 8*(1), 9–23.

Georgakopoulou, A. (2014). 'Girlpower or girl (in) trouble?' Identities and discourses in the (new) media engagement of adolescents' school-based interaction. In J. Androutsopoulos (Ed.), *Mediatization and sociolinguistic change* (pp. 428–455). Berlin: Mouton de Gruyter.

Gibbons, P. (2006). *Bridging discourses in the ESL classroom: Students, teachers and researchers.* London: Continuum.

Giovanelli, M., & Clayton, D. (Eds.). (2016). *Knowing about language: Linguistics and the secondary English classroom.* London: Routledge.

Goodwyn, A., & Fuller, C. (2011). *The great literacy debate.* London: Routledge.

Graham, S., & Perin, D. (2007). *Writing next: Effective strategies to improve writing of adolescents in middle and high schools—A report to Carnegie corporation of New York.* Washington, DC: Alliance for Excellent Education.

Halliday, M. (1991). Linguistic perspectives on literacy: A systemic-functional approach. In F. Christie (Ed.), *Literacy in social processes: Papers from the Inaugural Australian Systemic Linguistics Conference.* Centre for Studies of Language in Education, Darwin.

Halliday, M. (1993). Towards a language-based theory of learning. *Linguistics and Education, 5*(2), 93–116.

Halliday, M. (1996). Literacy and linguistics: A functional perspective. In R. Hasan & G. Williams (Eds.), *Literacy in society* (pp. 339–376). London: Longman.

Hamond, J. (Ed.). (2001). *Scaffolding: Teaching and learning in language and literacy education.* Newtown: Primary English Teaching Association.

Herrington, M., & Macken-Horarik, M. (2015). Linguistically informed teaching of spelling: Toward a relational approach. *Australian Journal of Language and Literacy, 38*(2), 61–71.

Hudson, R., & Walmsley, J. (2005). The English patient: English grammar and teaching in the twentieth century. *Journal of Linguistics, 41*(3), 593–622.

Humphrey, S. (1996). *Exploring literacy in school geography.* Sydney: Metropolitan East Disadvantaged Schools Program.

Humphrey, S. (2016). *Academic literacies in the middle years: A framework for enhancing teacher knowledge and student achievement.* London and New York: Routledge.

Humphrey, S., & Macnaught, L. (2015). Functional language instruction and the writing growth of English language learners in the middle years. *TESOL Quarterly, 49*(4), 252–278.

Jewitt, C., Bezemer, J., & O Hallora, K. (2016). *Introducing multimodality.* London: Routledge.

Kendrick, M. (2016). *Literacy and multimodality across different global sites.* New York and London: Routledge.

Knobel, M., & Lankshear, C. (2007). *A New Literacies Sampler.* New York: Peter Lang.

Kress, G. (2003). *Literacy in the new media age.* London: Routledge Falmer.

Locke, T. (Ed.). (2010). *Beyond the grammar wars: A resource book for developing teachers and students language knowledge in the English/literacy classroom.* London and New York: Routledge.

Macken-Horarik, M. (2008). Multiliteracies and 'basic skills' accountability. In L. Unsworth (Ed.), *New literacies and the English curriculum: Multimodal perspectives* (pp. 283–308). London: Continuum.

Macken-Horarik, M. (2011). Why schools English needs a 'good enough' grammatics (and not more grammar). *Changing English: Studies in culture and education, 19*(2), 46–53.

Macken-Horarik, M., Love, K., & Horarik, S. (2018). Rethinking grammar in language arts: Insights from an Australian survey of teachers' subject knowledge. *Research in the Teaching of English, 52*(3), 288–316.

Macken-Horarik, M., Sandiford, C., Love, K., & Unsworth, L. (2015). New ways of working 'with grammar in mind' in school English: Insights from systemic functional grammatics. *Linguistics and Education, 31,* 145–158.

Marsh, J., Merchant, G., Gillen, J., & Davies, J. (2012). *Virtual literacies: Interactive spaces for children and young people.* New York: Routledge.

Martin, J. (2013). Embedded literacy: Knowledge as meaning. *Linguistics and Education, 24,* 23–37.

Martin, J., & Rose, D. (2008). *Genre relations: Mapping culture.* London: Equinox.

Maune, M., & Klassen, M. (2014). Filling in the gaps: Genre as a scaffold to the text types of the Common Core State Standards. In L. C. Oliveira & J. Iddings (Eds.), *Genre pedagogy across the curriculum: Theory and application in U.S. classrooms and contexts.* Sheffield and Bristol, CT: Equinox.

Maybin, J. (2014). Researching children's language and literacy practices in school. In C. McAlister & S. Ellis (Eds.), *Genre pedagogy and literacy across learning*. Paper presented at SERA Annual Conference 2014, Edinburgh, UK.
Myhill, D. (2018). Grammar as a meaning-making resource for improving writing. *L1. Educational Studies in Language and Literature, 18*, 1–21.
Myhill, D., & Watson, A. (2013a). Creating a language-rich classroom. In S. Capel, M. Leask, & T. Turner (Eds.), *Learning to teach in the secondary school: A companion to school experience* (pp. 403–413). London: Routledge.
Myhill, D., & Watson, A. (2013b). Grammar matters: How teachers' grammatical knowledge impacts on the teaching of writing. *Teaching and Teacher Education, 36*, 77–91.
Myhill, D., & Watson, A. (2014). The role of grammar in the writing curriculum: A review. *Journal of Child Language Teaching and Therapy, 30*(1), 41–62.
Myhill, D., Jones, S., Lines, H., & Watson, A. (2012). Re-thinking grammar: The impact of embedded grammar teaching on students' writing and students' metalinguistic understanding. *Research Papers Education, 27*(2), 139–166.
Nesi, H., & Gardener, S. (2012). *Genres across the disciplines: Students writing in higher education*. Cambridge: Cambridge University Press.
O'Halloran, K. L. (2005). *Mathematical discourse: Language, symbolism and visual images*. London and New York: Continuum.
Ofsted. (2009). *English at the crossroads: An evaluation of English in primary and secondary schools 2005/8*. London: HMSO.
Ofsted. (2012). *Moving English forward*. London: HMSO.
Oliveira, L. C., & Iddings, J. (2014). *Genre pedagogy across the curriculum: Theory and application in U.S. classrooms and contexts*. Sheffield and Bristol, CT: Equinox.
Pahl, K., & Roswell, J. (2012). *Literacy and education: The new literacy studies in the classroom* (2nd ed.). London: Sage.
Painter, C., Martin, J. R., & Unsworth, L. (2013). *Reading visual narratives: Image analysis of children's picture books*. London: Equinox.
Parry, B., Burnett, C., & Marchant, G. (Eds.). (2016). *Literacy, media, technology: Past, present and future*. London: Bloomsbury.
Polias, J., & Dare, B. (2006). Towards a pedagogic grammar. In R. Whittaker, M. O'Donnell, & A. McCabe (Eds.), *Language and literacy: Functional approaches*. London and New York: Continuum.
Quinn, M. (2004). Talking with Jess: Looking at how metalanguage assisted explanation writing in the middle years. *Australian Journal of Language and Literacy, 27*(3), 245–261.
Raban, B., Clark, U., & McIntyre, J. (1994). *Evaluation of the implementation of English in the national curriculum at key stages 1, 2 and 3 (1991–1993)*.

London: Schools Curriculum and Assessment Authority. http://www.educationengland.org.uk/documents/warwick/warwick1994.html.

Rose, D., Gray, B., & Cowey, W., (1999). Scaffolding reading and writing for indigenous children in school. In P. Wignell (Ed.), *Double power: English literacy in indigenous schooling* (pp. 23–60). Melbourne: NLLIA.

Rosen, M. (2013). How genre theory saved the world. *Changing English: Studies in Culture and Education, 20*(1), 3–10.

Rothery, J. (1994). *Exploring literacy in school English (write it right resources for literacy and learning)*. Sydney: Metropolitan East Disadvantaged Schools Program.

Rothery, J. (1996). Making changes: Developing an educational linguistics. In R. Hasan & G. Williams (Eds.), *Literacy in society* (pp. 86–123). London: Longman.

Schleppegrell, M. (2013). The role of metalanguage in supporting academic language development. *Language Learning, 63,* 153–170.

Schleppegrell, M., Greer, S., & Taylor, S. (2008). Literacy in history: Language and meaning. *Australian Journal of Language and Literacy, 31*(2), 174–187.

Unsworth, L., & Thomas, A. (Eds.). (2014). *English teaching and new literacies pedagogy: Interpreting and authoring digital multimedia narratives.* New York: Peter Lang.

Unsworth, L., & Macken-Horarik, M. (2015). Interpretive responses to images in picture books by primary and secondary school students: Exploring curriculum expectations of a 'visual grammatics'. *English in Education, 49*(1), 56–79.

Vertovec, S. (2007). Super-diversity and its implications. *Ethnic and Racial Studies, 30*(6), 1024–1054.

Watson, A. (2015). The problem of grammar teaching: A case study of the relationship between a teacher's beliefs and pedagogical practice. *Language and Education, 29*(4), 332–346.

Williams, G. (1998). Children entering literate worlds: Perspectives from the study of textual practice. In F. Christie & R. Misson (Eds.), *Literacy and schooling* (pp. 18–46). London and New York: Routledge.

Williams, G. (2000). Children's literature, children and uses of language description. In L. Unsworth (Ed.), *Researching language in schools and communities: A functional perspective* (pp. 111–129). London and New York: Continuum.

Williams, G. (2004). Ontogenesis and grammatics: Functions of metalanguage in pedagogic discourse. In G. Williams & A. Lukin (Eds.), *The development of language* (pp. 241–267). London and New York: Continuum.

Wyse, D. (2017). *How writing works: From the invention of the alphabet to the rise of social media.* Cambridge: Cambridge University Press.

Wyse, D., Jones, R., Bradford, H., & Anne, W. M. (2013). *Teaching English language and literacy* (3rd ed.). London and New York: Routledge.

# 2

# Language, Literacy and Pedagogy

In this chapter, I provide an overview of language based pedagogy (LBP) in terms of the various theoretical underpinnings upon which it draws. I discuss the importance of language for learning in general, particularly how teaching grammar and its metalanguage can help pupils and students to develop their apprenticeship into the discursive practices that characterise different subject disciplines. The key argument put forward in the chapter is that recontextualising grammar in the context of developing language and literacy across the secondary curriculum, relates to the expression of subject knowledge and associated discursive practices that characterise *all* school subjects, and not simply that of English. An approach such as LBP brings to the fore the importance of language for learning, and explicitly teaches metalanguage and the grammatical patterns of various registers that characterise different school subjects in ways that can aid adolescents' articulate expression in English. It is this particular aspect of LBP that makes it so suitable for adoption in contexts where a large majority of pupils and students are designated EAL in English L1 contexts. The approach also lends itself readily to adoption for all educational contexts in England and elsewhere, regardless of individual linguistic backgrounds, for reasons that will become clear.

Before providing this overview, in the section below I consider the relationship between the key concepts of *literacy, identity, standard English, dialect* and *register.* Often, these terms are perceived as being at odds with one another, when this does not have to be the case. Many of the controversies and tensions surrounding the teaching of grammar discussed briefly in Chapter 1, stem from the perception of grammar as an unvaried set of the conventions and norms associated with written standard English in particular, that are 'fixed' by grammars and dictionaries. Any deviation or alteration of such conventions is thus perceived as deficient, 'wrong' and illiterate. Such assumptions perpetuate the notion of grammar as 'error' and ignore advances in linguistic theory that have taken place over the last sixty years or so. Hudson (1992) reminds us that the history of grammar can be divided into two periods: The first period going back centuries to Ancient Greek and Roman times based upon prescriptive approaches to teaching grammar: that is language as it *ought* to be used. The second began in the twentieth century as modern linguistic theory shifted from prescriptive to descriptive approaches: how language *is actually* used. It was not until the 1950s that modern grammars of English began to appear that fundamentally shifted to descriptive approaches to grammar in fully fledged ways. In 1957 Chomsky published *Syntactic Structures* in the USA and in 1973 Halliday published *Explorations in the Functions of Language* in the UK. More recent developments include pattern grammar, a corpus-driven grammar of English (Hunston and Francis 2000) and cognitive grammar, where grammar is viewed as inherently meaningful (Langacker 1983). However, the development and teaching of these grammars has since the 1970s occurred within the university disciplines of English Language and Linguistics and not within the university discipline of English Literature, from which the majority of teachers of English are drawn.

The Kingman Report into the English Language that preceded the introduction of the National Curriculum in England (DES 1988) then, based its model of the English language upon contemporary descriptive linguistic theory rather than outdated, prescriptive theory that policymakers had expected. It was also heavily influenced by the sociolinguistic focus upon *dialects* rather than *language*. In linguistic terms, all dialects or varieties of a language such as English are rule governed, in the sense that phonological, lexical and morphosyntactic patterns can be identified that make them distinctive from one another. However, as Bourdieu (1973) has argued so convincingly, the cultural and social capital accorded to different languages and the dialects of which they are comprised differs. In a language such as English, the social dialect of standard English has greater cultural and social value above all others. It also serves a greater range of functions and purposes than any regional dialect. However, how we speak is an integral part of our individual, cultural and social identities. A challenge for the teaching of grammar then is how to do so in ways that do not denigrate or deny pupils' and students' sociocultural and linguistic origins. One way of so doing is to view grammar through the lens of 'register' rather than 'error'.

## Literacy, Identity, Standard English, Dialect and Register

Regional accents and dialects are varieties of language determined by 'who you are,' where 'who you are' means 'where do you come from' (Halliday et al. 1964). Social dialects, by contrast, are varieties of language where 'who you are' means 'to which social class you belong' (Hasan 1973). In sociolinguistic terms, any standard variety of a language is classed as a social dialect. Indeed, what counts as a language is socioculturally, not linguistically determined, a fact amply illustrated by the Ebonics debate in the USA (Clark 2001). Grammatical, lexical or phonological variation does not result in any meaning difference of the word in which it occurs, although it does say something about the region or social group with which the speaker identifies, either intentionally or unintentionally. Thus, for example, pronouncing a word such as *bath* or *grass* with a long /a/ sound or *car* as /kar/ or /ka/ does not alter the word's meaning, but indicates a regional and/or social affiliation. Equally, grammatical variation signifying negation such as *I haven't got no pencil* means the same thing as *I haven't got a pencil*. Linguistic features or variables in terms of *register* are the opposite, in that features of register perform a function linked to meaning, for example, the use of present tense in conversation.

Linguistic variables in dialect studies are almost always perceived as a choice between two variants, and concerned with identifying their formal properties. A variable score is then given in terms of their frequency and the relative preference of one over another. By contrast, linguistic variables in register are based upon identifying the rate of occurrence for any particular feature. The higher the rate, the greater need for the functions associated with the register. In this way, sociolinguistic 'styles' can be regarded as different registers.

Biber and Conrad (2009: 12) point out that it is possible to investigate the existence of functionally motivated linguistic variation across dialects. On the whole though, sociolinguists exclude this possibility based upon a theoretical/philosophical stance that all dialects are equivalent in their communicative potential. As a result, there has been much sociolinguistic research into variation in regional and social dialects, but not as much into register variation. Speech communities have been studied in relation to exclusive reference to variation across speakers, rather than across situations in which those speakers use language. Conversely, research in discourse analysis has focussed register variation without paying much attention paid to dialect variation. Although phonological variation has come increasingly to be widely accepted when speaking standard English, and a range of regional accents can now be heard in public broadcasting, there still remains a ladder of prejudice, with Received Pronunciation at the top, Northern accents in the middle and those of the West Midlands at the bottom (Coupland and Bishop 2007). There is no linguistic evidence for such prejudice, yet it remains deeply rooted and seated in the English psyche. When it comes to grammatical variation, public acceptance is not so tolerant. Whilst double negation of the kind exemplified above is a formal property of many regional dialects of English, it is perceived to be indicative of a low level of literacy in standard English (unless used self-consciously) and, by association, low intelligence.

With this in mind, it may be more helpful to reframe the dialect and grammar debate in ways that put the focus on register. Rather than thinking in terms of *dialect*, it is perhaps more useful to think in terms of *register*. Thus, whilst double negation is a register feature of regional dialects and used in face-to-face conversations, single negation is a register feature of standard English and widely used, particularly in formal written contexts. It is not so much that one is 'wrong' and the other 'right', but that the contexts and situations of their use is different. Register features thus relate to linguistic 'choice' realised as a set of linguistic features that are preferred in one register when compared to another. That is, speakers and writers choose from the entire inventory of phonological, lexico-grammatical characteristics of a language, selecting linguistic features that are best suited to their situations and common purposes.

The current **Grammar Glossary** for the programmes of study for English (2013) defines *register* as:

Classroom lessons, football commentaries and novels use different registers of the same language, recognised by differences of vocabulary and grammar. Registers are 'varieties' of a language which are each tied to a range of uses, in contrast with dialects, which are tied to groups of users. The examples given in the context of subject English, are:

- *I regret to inform you that Mr Joseph Smith has passed away* (formal letter);
- *Have you heard that Joe died?* (casual speech);
- *Joe falls down and dies, centre stage* (stage direction).

https://www.gov.uk/government/uploads/system/uploads/attachment_data/file/244216/English_Glossary.pdf

The examples given above are taken from different genres or text types characteristic of subject English, and clearly exemplify lexico-grammatical differences evident in each one. The examples also show how the concept of register also encompasses the full range of all spoken as well as written uses of language, regardless of their level of formality and in relation to their function. A focus upon register shifts the lens through which the English language is studied to the primacy of linguistic function in relation to determining linguistic form: that is, the context within which any speech or writing event occurs influences the linguistic choices we make for successful communication to occur. Our day-to-day linguistic interactions and the corresponding normative expectations shift as we move from one kind of activity to another in daily routines, and the opportunity for individual innovation is greater in some than in others. An understanding of register, then, is key in relation to language learning and the development of academic/subject literacy. This is because developing literacy within formal education contexts involves extending any individual's engagement with language—their linguistic repertoires—from the everyday, mainly context bound use to the academic language through which subject knowledge is expressed and academic success is measured—without denting their confidence.

## Language Learning, Learning Language

SFL/G, the linguistic theory upon which LBP is based is particularly suited to pedagogic contexts because it takes a developmental approach regarding linguistic usage. As Halliday (1993: 93) says: '…when children learn language, they are not simply engaging in one kind of learning among many; rather, they are learning the foundation of learning itself.'

Halliday goes on to say that when children learn to speak, they learn a semiotic system that has been evolving for centuries, thereby construing language as a social semiotic. Language mediates and organises our experiences and is an essential condition for expressing experience and knowledge, since it is the process through which our experiences become knowledge. Learning occurs through language and is an inherently semiotic process (Coffin and Donohue 2014; De Joyce and Feez 2016; Humphrey 2017). Knowledge, behaviours and language develop symbiotically. Painter (2005: 39) states that in SFL, the metaphor of *development* is more appropriate to language learning than *acquisition*. This is on the grounds that acquisition is suggestive of language as a commodity and the image thus conjured is language as unitary, monolithic or monoglossic and unchanging. Language is thus also perceived as something one either has, or has not. Painter argues that such a metaphor does not equate comfortably with the view that a living language such as English is a dynamic, infinite and variable resource for meaning that can develop indefinitely. One study which addresses this gap is that of Christie and Derewianka (2008). Their research has identified four key developmental phases in relation to school pupils' learning how to write that can be summarised as follows (2008: 218):

Phases of language development

- *Phase 1: early childhood*: 'Everyday' or simple 'commonsense' knowledge, expressed through congruent grammar (literal, one to one correspondence between word and meaning) with simple attitudinal expression.
- *Phase 2: late childhood to adolescence*: 'Commonsense' knowledge is elaborated as the grammar expands; attitudinal resources are extended.
- *Phase 3: mid-adolescence*: Knowledge becomes more 'uncommonsense', and is extended as grammatical resources are further amplified: attitudinal expression expands.
- *Phase 4: from late adolescence onwards*: 'Uncommonsense' knowledge is expressed through non-congruent grammar (words used in an increasingly metaphorical way and increased layers of abstraction), expressing abstraction, generalisation, value judgement and opinion.

As language development occurs most naturally through its use, then it would follow that the study of language itself should occur in a context of use. Such a pedagogy also does not automatically subscribe to the view that smaller units of language—or knowledge—need to be learnt before progressing to larger ones. Rather, development in both language and knowledge is viewed as both cumulative and recursive. Development in reading and writing does not follow a smooth, linear and unbroken progression, nor is it characterised by steady, incremental steps, but is more a matter of instability and 'regression' in some structures as others are learnt. Moreover, learning takes place across all three levels of word, sentence and text simultaneously. It is the degree to which any one is the focus of study that alters as pupils' progress from one stage of their education to another. It is also vital that teaching includes an interrogation and questioning of texts, of the kind advocated by proponents of critical literacy and critical language awareness. Language is created within a social context, and as such, pupils themselves are as much a part of that context as anyone else. The language system of a living language such as English is continually developing and changing because language is continually instantiated in the form of speech and writing. Developing our language abilities involves learning that we have choices when it comes to expressing ourselves, that some choices are more likely than others and that constraints surrounding choice of linguistic usage can be culturally, rather than inherently, determined.

A recent example of this is the emergence of a new variety of written English we now call *textspeak*. The initial restricted number of characters available for sending text messages on a mobile phone led to a series of abbreviations and alternative word spellings, which quickly transferred to informal online communication such as chat forums, blogs and social media. Examples of textspeak include *CU l8tr* for *see you later*, *lol* for *laugh out loud*, and *OMG* for *Oh My God*. The spelling of some words such as *was* have been changed to *wuz*, to represent an alternative pronunciation. Such abbreviations and spellings continue to be used in text messages and have crossed over into online communication, even though text messaging has not been character restricted for some time. Far from being a seemingly arbitrary and idiosyncratic mix of letters, numbers and symbols, Velghe and Blommaert (2014) have shown that textspeak has its own linguistic codes and rules of usage, so it is possible to get it 'wrong.' In 2015, textspeak was given a cultural stamp of approval in the UK in relation to the popular word game *Scrabble*, when *The Collins Scrabble Dictionary* included words such as *lol* and *wuz* for the first time. The point to be made is that *lol* and *wuz* are not 'wrong' linguistically in the context of textspeak and the game of *Scrabble*. However, such spellings have not (as yet), been adopted by more culturally authoritative dictionaries of English in general such as the Cambridge, Collins, or Oxford dictionaries. Nor are such features (as yet) acceptable in the more formal, academic contexts associated with the learning and teaching of literacy (except perhaps as part of creative or personal writing).

A common myth in relation to textspeak is that its use is impacting upon pupils' writing in school contexts. However, a recent corpus-based study undertaken by Cambridge Assessment (Elliot et al. 2016) and also Wood et al.'s research (2014), show that there is no evidence that pupils are using textspeak in their GCSE English examinations. This points to the fact that pupils and students have an implicit understanding of register and how language features in one context are not appropriate in another. Literacy is a key feature of modern, technological societies. Thus, language development refers to the development not only of speech but also of writing. Writing, however, is more than speech simply written down, and an appreciation of the differences as well as similarities between these two linguistic phenomena is fundamental to an LBP approach.

## Speech and Writing

A distinction can be made in relation to learning a language such as English between spoken and written forms of communication. There are ways in which both are similar, and ways in which they are very different, and there is still a great deal to be learnt about the process of children and adolescents embedding and disembedding spoken language structures in their writing. However, as Carter and McCarthy (2015: 2) say:

> We are still struggling under the burden of a grammatical metalanguage inherited from writing that does not seem always to work for speaking, and many teaching resources have yet to reflect what everyday speaking is really like. Meanwhile, technology forces us to re-think the conventional spoken/written distinction.

Learning one's first language (or more consecutively) typically begins from birth in familial contexts. Learning to read and to write any language, however, typically occurs in formal education contexts, and these linguistic skills are taught, rather than developed naturally as is the case with speech. Speech and writing, or oracy and literacy in a language such as English share many characteristic features but also have fundamentally different ones. Whilst both are the media of linguistic expression, the ways they are learnt are very different, as are the ways in which they operate in the world. Spoken and written language are different linguistic phenomena, with different purposes and distinct sets of characteristics. Halliday (1983: 93) also makes the point that speech and writing impose different grids upon experience, and create different realities, in that whilst talking creates a world of happenings, writing creates a world of things.

A second fundamental difference is that speech occurs predominantly in face-to-face or voice-to-voice conversation. By contrast, writing does not usually involve direct interaction (except for some kinds of online communication such as instant messaging). Speech involves activating organs of speech production and reception—our vocal organs and our ears—whilst writing involves activating organs of visual and spatial awareness—our eyes and our fingers and hands. Lillis (2013: 37) makes the point that linked to the visual dimension of writing is the spatial one, which includes considerations of, for example, the way writing occupies space, whether writing is written from left to right, or is organised on the page vertically or horizontally. She says that whilst speech occurs sequentially in time, writing is organised in units across time and space. 'Alphabet writing systems can be considered to 'border' speech and writing, in that whilst they are spatially displayed, they 'lean on' speech in being sequenced in time and 'mimicked' in writing by the spatial element of the line on which it is written'. Such a connection between speech and writing in a language such as English signals a greater proximity of writing to speech than in other languages that use characters or images for written representation such as Chinese, Japanese or Korean.

Olson (1994) points out that language users in non-literate societies do not have a conscious awareness of grammar and linguistic structure. People become interested in the nature of language—its phonology, morphology, grammar and lexis—once language is written down. The written mode of linguistic expression, in other words, induces a different kind of consciousness in people. Writing then, brings language into the material world and Olson takes as fundamental, the fact that in modern societies writing provides a model for speech. In the Western world and other parts of the globe, it is the literacy practices of the societies in which we live that provide a model for a national, standard sociolect of a language such as English. Thus, although in its primary form language occurs as speech and provides a model for a written equivalent, the written equivalent, in turn, has become a model for speech. Writing changes us from speakers to language users. Olson goes on to point out that in the course of learning to take part in a literate society, the concepts children appear to acquire 'naturally' are actually ones which have been worked out in particular historical and cultural contexts over two thousand years. Upward and Davidson (2011) also point out that writing, just like other systems in the modern world such as those of government, manufacturing and industry, arose in certain circumstances for certain purposes. In addition, the language of any society that depends upon the literacy of its members has its own conventions for converting speech to writing. Once these conventions have been applied and written texts created, then such texts become independent of speech.

A further difference between speech and writing is that the underlying grammatical structures of speech have often been thought to be less complex than writing. However, the invention of sound recording and the Internet has made it possible to turn speech into a material object through transcription and also the processing of large sets of data through corpus linguistic methods. Computers are able to store large numbers of texts, which can be compiled into a single corpus or several corpora, which can then be processed by using specialist software. Corpus-based linguistic analysis has allowed researchers to look in detail at recurring patterns of language use within spoken as well as written corpora and how they relate to the context in which they are used. Consequently, since the 1970s this has allowed much research into the structure of speech to be undertaken (e.g., Biber et al. 1999, Carter et al. 2011), and for corpora of spoken English to be created, such as the British Academic Spoken English (BASE) corpus, the Spoken British National Corpus and the Santa Barbara Corpus of

Spoken American English. Such research, and the corpora on which it has been based, shows that oral language is just as linguistically complex as written language, but that the complexity is of a different kind. The inevitable differences in the structures and use of speech and writing are also largely due to the fact that they are produced in very different communicative situations.

By and large and in general, informal English usage occurs more in spoken contexts and more formal ones in written contexts, although the exponential growth of technology and computer-mediated communication has given rise to written representations of speech as social interaction in new media such as text messaging, emails, Twitter and so on. Even so, public uses of English such as those demanded by education and the workplace still expect and require accuracy in the use of both spoken and written forms of standard English. Thus, as discussed above, whilst it may be acceptable to write *spk 2 u sn* (speak to you soon) in a text or email message to a friend, it is not usually acceptable to do so to a work colleague or teacher, or to use such abbreviated forms in formal writing contexts.

Sebba (2012: 43) makes the point that variation in the orthographic spelling of individual words is subject to linguistic limitations. He illustrates this with the word *dog*. The spelling <dog> has three letters which reflect its pronunciation. However, there are possible variations to this such as <dogg> which still conforms to the conventions of English, in surnames such as *Clegg* and *Rigg* and which the rapper Snoop Dogg also uses. One might inject humour into the spelling by calling a German Shepherd <dög>, with the use of the umlaut invoking 'foreignness', particularly German. At some point, however, variants of a word like <dog> become unintelligible. A spelling such as <Dd@gG> would appear to be losing the ability to represent the word *dog* in anything but a highly localised and ecologised context. Sebba uses the concept of the zone of social meaning to explain this phenomenon. As Sebba (2012: 6–7) says: 'The concept of the *zone of social meaning* refers to the fact that in order to be socially meaningful, an item must be different from some element of the repertoire in a specific way, but also be sufficiently similar that it can be *recognised* as a variant of, or alternative to, that thing.'

Sebba also points out that where the potential for variation exists, it is usually exploited and forms an increasingly integral part of the linguistic landscapes that surround us. If one subscribes to the belief that education is a key factor in social mobility and a key means to economic prosperity, and that in today's world a grasp of English is increasingly becoming a prerequisite for either, then ecologising literacy practices or designing curricula based upon the exclusion of any reference to culture beyond the immediate one of pupils' cultural-linguistic realities seems to promote, rather than mitigate against, social inequality. Literacy is as much a social as linguistic practice (Barton and Hamilton 2000) and as such, entails recognising multiple literacies that not only vary according to time and space but are also contested in relation to power, however, power is conceived. An LBP approach recognises the concept of multiple literacies and issues of power that surround language use. At the same time, it acknowledges the importance of normative functions and roles of standard varieties of English and the importance of learning and teaching the grammar and spelling of any standard variety of English for academic success.

Since the 1960s, sociolinguistic research has shown time and time again that linguistic difference does not automatically equate with intellectual deficit, yet such evidence does not appear as yet to have permeated and affected dominant discourses of linguistic hegemony. Lip service is paid to recognition of non-standard varieties of English as part of the curriculum for English in England for example, but only in so far as acknowledging that many pupils have linguistic repertoires comprising of more than one way of speaking English. Manifestations of linguistic variety other than that taught in schools are at best ignored, or at worst, continue to be the source of ritual humiliation in the classroom (Snell 2013). However, Carter (2004) illustrates clearly the inherent creativity manifested in everyday spoken language and how speakers adapt creatively to the conditions of use demanded by the situations in which we find ourselves. Thus, as adults, and paradoxically through becoming literate, many of us become increasingly aware of the range of linguistic resources upon which we can draw, including ways that mark identity, including identity linked to place (Clark 2013).

If one turns the focus away from dialect and standard English to that of register, then the 'constraints' of norms identified by researchers such as Snell fall away. Rather than the focus being upon standard English per se, the focus upon academic register aims to apprentice adolescents into talking and writing like historians, scientists, geographers and so on. Thus, it is possible for a pupil in a history lesson to ascribe the cause and consequence of World War One to the fact that 'some bloke got murdered by a shooter'. Acknowledging this statement and then asking the pupil to rephrase what they have said to 'sound like a historian' is a far more positive and validating experience than 'correcting' an informal register into a more formal one. Practices such as coaching pupils and students to rephrase their utterances and to reply to questions in complete sentences are two strategies that can work towards extending pupils' and students' range of language use.

The notion of *linguistic repertoire* is particularly salient here. Linguistic repertoire comprises sets of linguistic practices associated with specific speech communities, an interactional sociolinguistic concept attributed to Gumperz (1960) and developed since by poststructuralist researchers such as Busch (2012). Gumperz was particularly interested in the question of how linguistic choice relates or is tied to social categories and constraints.

> **Quote**
> Ultimately it is the individual who makes the decision, but his freedom to select is always subject both to grammatical and social constraints. ... The power of selection is [therefore] limited by commonly agreed upon conventions which serve to categorize speech forms as informal. Technical, vulgar, literary, humorous, etc...The social etiquette of language choice is leaned along with grammatical rules and once internalised it becomes a part of our linguistic equipment. Conversely, stylistic choice becomes a problem when we are away from our accustomed social surroundings.
> (Gumperz 1964: 138)

Alongside the notion of linguistic repertoire is that of *linguistic competence*. Chomsky (1965) introduced the notion of linguistic competence came into linguistics from Chomskyian transformational grammar, as the notion that the grammar of a language is an idealisation and that speakers know the rules of the 'correct' grammar of their language. However, such a notion has come under criticism from philosophers in particular.

> **Quote**
>
> One reason for philosophical abuse lies in some of the things Chomsky said about linguistic competence. In particular, he said that grammar is an idealization, and that the speaker knows – albeit tacitly – the rules of the grammar. It would seem that these remarks cannot both be true. If it is an idealization, then it does not characterize the actual speaker; in particular, it does not characterise his knowledge. But, in fact, they are both false.
>
> In pointing out the existence of a cognitive system which he called linguistic competence – and the existence of others like it – Chomsky made a significant contribution to the understanding of language and other complex psychological phenomena....But a theory of competence is not an idealization in any sense relevant to Chomsky's purpose. It is not necessary that speakers know or believe the rules of their language in order for the grammar to describe some real aspect of the speaker.
> (Tienson 1983: 101, 103)

Such criticisms notwithstanding, it has become well understood in linguistics that a speaker's linguistic or verbal repertoire defines her or his communicative competence in relation to both the grammatical construction of utterances/clauses and with respect to different social speech situations. Any speaker's competence is thus judged in relation to the ability to vary language use by applying different registers or styles. One of the major challenges for schools, particularly those located in socially disadvantaged areas, is how to extend the range of adolescents' linguistic repertoires and their corresponding communicative competence in ways that enable them to engage readily and positively with the discourses demanded by school-oriented speech communities that centre upon the classroom whilst at the same time also acknowledging and not denying their home and community ones. It is this challenge that LBP fundamentally addresses.

# An Overview of Language Based Pedagogy (LBP)

Theoretically, LBP draws from four disciplines: from linguistics it draws upon SFL/G as first developed by Halliday from the early 1960s onwards and subsequently by others such as Rothery (1989), Halliday in conjunction with Martin (1993), and Hasan (1976, 1985), Christie and Martin (2007), Martin and Rose (2007, 2008, 2012), Christie (2012) and Fontaine (2012). From cognitive and educational psychology it draws on theories of child language development as put forward by Bruner (1966, 1983, 1996), developing the work of Vygotsky (1962) and also Painter (2005). From education it draws upon the notion of the learning and teaching cycle or model as developed in Australia (Callaghan and Rothery 1988; Knapp and Watkins 1994; Rothery and Stenglin 1997; Gibbons 2002) in ways that are arguably similar to the American gradual release of responsibility (GRR) model (Pearson and Gallagher 1993; Fisher and Frey 2008). Finally, from sociology, it draws upon the work of Bernstein (1999, 1991, 1975), in relation to the ways in which education systems regulate, replicate and structure social inequality, developed more recently by Maton (2014.) The following sections take each of these four disciplines, in turn, discussing their specific contribution to LBP.

# Systemic Functional Linguistics and Grammar

Fundamental to SFG is the view that language is a semiotic system that creates, construes or realises experience, shaping, and also shaped by, sociocultural experience. A language such as English has evolved in human society to serve a range of broad functions, which are to do with negotiating and maintaining relationship, shaping experience and organising text to make coherent messages. A distinctive of SFG is its commitment to the notion of *system* in language and the associated notion of *choice* in learning and using language. It is thus not a *rule-driven* model of language, but a *choice-driven* one. In addition, in SFG the unit of study is the text, embracing both speech and writing. Finally, a distinctive feature of the theory is that learning language is fundamentally learning *how to mean*: that is, how to use language to construct and mediate our experiences in the world in ways that make sense to ourselves and to others.

> **Quote**
> Traditional grammar is often portrayed in opposition to functional grammar, as if traditional grammar represents everything that is bad about grammar while functional grammar represents its good side. Apart from being incorrect, such a position is completely unproductive. What is proposed here is that language is *formal* (it is put together in particular ways), *functional* (it performs particular social functions), and *figural* (it has the potential to communicate meanings beyond the literal/functional). One of the problems with traditional grammar was that it almost entirely emphasized the formal aspects of language. A similar problem exists with current approaches to functional grammar, where all the emphasis is placed on its functional aspects. The figural has traditionally been treated outside of grammar as 'figures of speech', although to separate this aspect of language outside of grammar is again unproductive. Not to take account of the interrelationships of all three aspects will result in less than satisfactory account of what language, and therefore grammar, can do. Unless teachers are themselves about how language works, there will be the potential for teaching students aspects of the English Language that are imprecise in places and confusing in others.
> (Knapp and Watkins 1994/2007: 32)

Drawing upon SFG in a pedagogic grammar does not necessarily involve transferring or superimposing all SFG categories into one that already exists. Rather, it is more of a case of recontextualising pedagogic grammar in ways that are influenced by SFG but not bound by it. Traditionally, pedagogic grammar has focused upon understanding word class/parts of speech and clause structure. One of the ways in which SFG has impacted upon pedagogic grammar is that the unit of analysis extends beyond the level of the sentence to that of the text, through the application of grammatical categories such as *cohesion*, *theme* and *rheme*. As such, the preferred unit of analysis is the *clause*, both in terms of how clauses are constructed and how they combine within and across sentences and utterances. *Genres* constitute different text types that have characteristic elements of structure, whilst the linguistic patternings characteristic of them are a function of *register*. It is a contention of SFG that text types emerge to meet the communicative needs of the communities they serve. Many of these have been developed over long periods of time (such as legal documents, religious documents, academic journal articles and so on) and others are more recent (newspaper articles, internet blogs, twitter posts). For example, a newspaper is a macro genre or text type that contains within it a range of subsets of identifiable text types such as news articles, horoscopes, letters to the editor, comic strips and so on. The linguistic patternings of the clauses that make up each of these text types can be, and often are, very different from one another and can be said to be characteristic of it. Register refers to the linguistic characteristics within the genre or text type, and connects them functionally to the situational context.

Studies into spoken English of the kind undertaken by Biber et al. (1998), Biber and Conrad (2009) and Carter and McCarthy (2004), amongst others, show that not only does speech have its own grammar which is distinct in many ways from that of writing, but that it, like writing, can also be described and ordered into grammatical categories where the concepts of *genre* and *register* are also key. Register thus refers to the set of linguistic features that are typically associated with a configuration of situational features across a range of genres and styles across the modes of speech and writing, on a continuum from informal to formal. An understanding of register is key to successful communication in both spoken and written contexts. The *mode or register continuum* (Halliday 1977; Halliday and Hasan 1985) is a continuum on which differing text types in speech and writing can be plotted, depending upon the levels of abstractness (Fig. 2.1).

As discussed earlier, understanding linguistic competence in terms of register and the differing nature of speech and writing shifts the focus of language learning from the concept of accuracy as singularly defined to one defined by matching language use to the context and purpose of a variety of different situations, spoken as well as written. As Christie (2007: 5) says: 'In SFG there is a 'hook up' between grammar and register. Some sets of choices relate primarily to activity, some primarily to

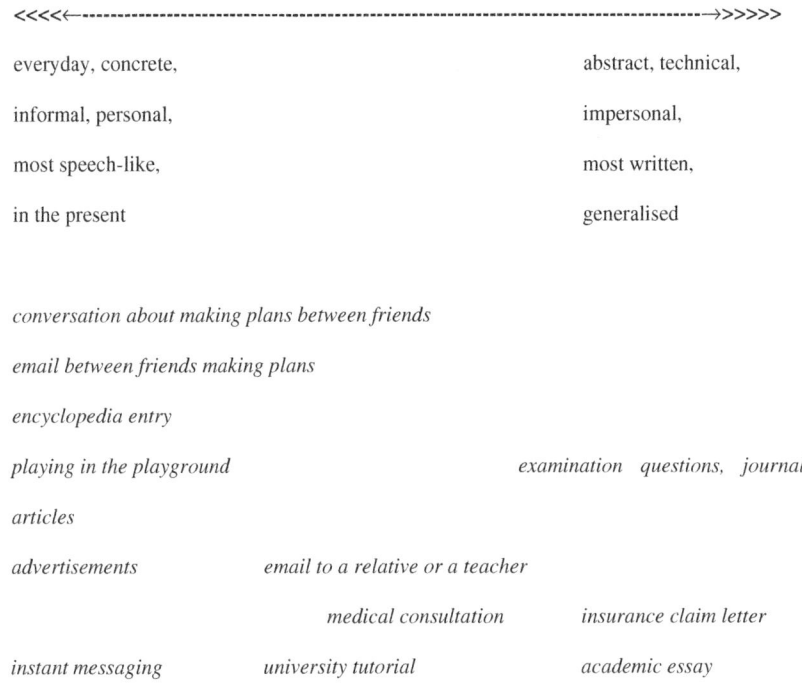

Fig. 2.1 The mode/register continuum

the nature of the relationship in construction, and others primarily to organization of the language as message'.

In terms of learning and teaching English and its grammar in education contexts then, the notion of register shifts the concept of accuracy from a singular notion to a more pluralistic one. That is, what may be appropriate and accurate linguistic use in one situation may not be appropriate and accurate in another. Another feature of SFG that makes it appropriate to be drawn upon in educational contexts is that the unit of analysis extends beyond the sentence to that of the text.

The National Curriculum, in *English—Appendix 2: Vocabulary, grammar and punctuation* https://www.gov.uk/government/uploads/system/uploads/attachment_data/file/335190/English_Appendix_2_-_Vocabulary_grammar_and_punctuation.pdf recognises the fact that when learning to write in primary school, pupils learn vocabulary, grammar and punctuation simultaneously in the contexts of words, how words combine into and are punctuated as sentences and how sentences combine into texts (see also Raban et al. 1994; Clark 2001). This begins at Key Stage 1 with writing to form short narratives based on everyday experience to writing to form a range of different text types associated with different school subjects by the end of Key Stage 2. One of the concerns of functional grammar is with the ways in which a culture has organised language use into different *genres* or *text types* for specific purposes and audiences. It is then concerned with identifying clusters of related linguistic features or language choices, that is, *register* as discussed above, that feature both within and across different genres or text types. Thus as Christie and Derewianka (2008) argue, in relation to language development, a functional model of language is concerned with the range of contexts within which learners are likely to participate. This involves learning the types of linguistic resources they need to develop if they are to communicate successfully. Consequently, it is central to SFG and LBP that such aspects of language learning are made explicit, as part of embedding language and literacy learning across content areas/disciplines, since every curriculum subject has its own specialised genres and registers and formal ways of presenting knowledge, developed over time.

Sets of linguistic features that are drawn upon in different registers are determined by three contextual variables as shown above in Fig. 2.2. Firstly, that of *field*, which answers the question: *what is going on?* Secondly, that of *tenor*, which answers the question: *who is involved?* Thirdly *mode*, which answers the question: *what role is language playing?* (Halliday 1977; Christie and Derewianka 2008) (Fig. 2.3).

Given a set of register variables then, the ways in which certain language choices are made from any language system can be predicted. For example, the ways in which two friends might discuss a novel they have both read when compared to writing a critical analysis of it for an English essay. The *field* may be the similar in that both refer to the novel, but the critical analysis would also include reference to other theoretical material. The *tenor* will be different, and characteristic of informal, context bound speech between friends in one case and written, non context specific, academic language on the other. The *mode* is also different, being speech in the first example and writing in the other.

```
                        Text

                     Paragraph

                      Sentence

                       Clause

Group                  Group                    Group

Word word word       word word word          word word word
```

**Text Level**                           **Sentence Level**

Visual layout, including                 Clauses (subject/verb/object)

Headings and diagrams                    Verbs: finites; modals;

Generic structure                        Tense: participles and auxilliaries

Thematic structure                       Nouns:

Paragraphing                             Noun groups; pronouns;

Cohesion                                 determiners and modifiers

Reference                                Prepositions

Conjunctions/connectives                 Modality

                                         Theme/rheme

**Word Level**

Graphological: spelling and punctuation

Morphological: singular/plural; tense; prefixes; suffixes; participles

**Fig. 2.2** Levels of language

All three aspects of *field, tenor* and *mode* have a part to play in constructing coherent and cohesive texts that will be understood by their receiver, be it in speech or writing. As they progress through their schooling, the texts pupils and students, in particular, write increasingly

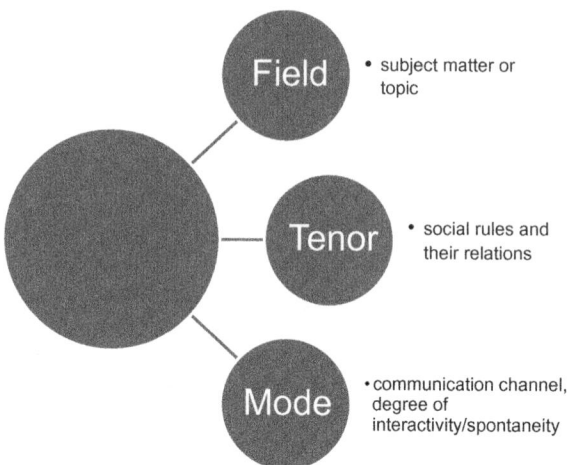

**Fig. 2.3** Dimensions of register

involve planning, revising and reworking to become more highly structured and readily recalled in examination conditions. Continuing to move from spoken to written modes that begins in primary education becomes ever increasingly more complex and sophisticated in the secondary school (Table 2.1).

In SFG, the central organising unit is the clause, which can be divided into three main 'bits' or 'chunks' of the noun group (including adjectivals), the verb group and adverbials. The following list of register variables provides an overview that is by no means exhaustive, but gives a 'flavour' of their different characteristics (Table 2.2).

The patterns of register that typify the written expression of different school subjects are drawn from the ways in which the different 'chunks' are realised and put together. So, for example, it may be common for an adverbial to begin—or front—a clause, such as: *happily, she skipped along the pavement* or to end it: *she skipped along the pavement happily*. Such patterns may appear in creative writing but, as Chapters 5 and 6 show, hardly ever if at all in geography, science or maths.

Table 2.1 Functions of language in schooling

| Function | Early childhood | Late adolescence |
|---|---|---|
| *Language for achieving different purposes* | Producing and interpreting small range of text types for specific purposes with basic structure | Producing and interpreting grater range of text types with a greater range of clause and textual structures |
| *Language for interacting with others* | Range of contexts informal, familiar and personal interaction; limited range of roles | Range of contexts extends to include formal contexts; expanded range of roles; critical awareness of how language can be used to position self and others |
| *Language representing experience* | Everyday, individualized, concrete, generalised, non-specialised subject matter | Dealing with more abstract, technical, subject specific matter |
| *Language for creating written and oral texts* | Face to face interaction; monologic; spontaneous, context-dependent | Distanced in time and space; crafted and planned contexts independent of immediate dialogues |

Adapted from Derewianka (1998: 6)

The basic unit of a sentence is a clause, which centres upon the verb group. Clauses such as *watch out! Help!* are comprised of a single verb group. More commonly though, a single clause comprises nominal or noun groups in addition to a verb group and often adverbials. Such components can also be categorised according to how they function within a clause, of which there are five main elements, though not every clause has all of them except for the verb group (Table 2.3).

Most commonly, sentences are made up of more than one clause known as a *clause complex*: a head or main clause together with other clauses that modify it in some way, such as elaborating upon it or adding verbal processes. The National Curriculum Glossary categorises clauses as *main, co-ordinate, subordinate* and *relative:*

Table 2.2 Grammar overview

| Those two cats from over the road | were caterwauling | late into the night |
|---|---|---|
| WHO? WHAT? | WHAT ARE THEY DOING? | WHERE? WHEN? HOW? WHY? |
| **Noun Group** | **Verb Group** | **Adverbials** |
| **Noun types** | **Verb types** | **Adverbs and adverbial phrases** |
| Living/non living (cat/rock) | material action (May *was prancing* down the street) | place: 'where' (away; to the shops) |
| Human/non-living (man/bed masculine/feminine/neuter | verbal (He *shouted* her name) | time: 'when' (today; at night) |
| General/particular (dog/Bramble) concrete/abstract (clock/time) | mental thinking, feeling, perceiving. (She *thought* he was right.) | manner: 'how?' quality: gladly; with glee. |
| Everyday/technical (flood tube/ Oesophagus) | (Kate *felt* unwell.) | means: by train; on a bike |
| Objective/subjective (girl/flirt) | (They *enjoyed* the meal.) | comparison: differently; like a bird |
| Countable/uncountable (trees/wood) common/proper (city, Coventry) | relational 'being' and 'having' | cause: 'why?' due to an accident; for her well-being |
| Collective (herd; class) singular/plural (man, men) | (Cats are fickle) | |
| Compound (handbag; suitcase) | (They *have* sharp claws) | accompaniment: 'with Whom? (together; with Kim) |

(continued)

Table 2.2 (continued)

| Noun Group<br>WHO? WHAT? | Verb Group<br>WHAT ARE THEY DOING? | Adverbials<br>WHERE? WHEN? HOW? WHY? |
|---|---|---|
| Those two cats from over the road | were caterwauling | late into the night |
| **Noun types** | **Verb types** | **Adverbs and adverbial phrases** |

| Adjectivals | Tense | Other types of adverbials |
|---|---|---|
| Articles a/an, the, this, those | Present (Cows *chew* grass.) (Lucy *is chewing* gum.) | point of view, comment pointing words: (in my view; fortunately) |
| Possessives: her's, John's | Past (She *ate* slowly) (They *were eating* together) (They *have eaten* it all) | degree (more loudly; most quantity loudly; too sweet) |
| adjectives: few, 1 | | modal adverbs: perhaps, factual focus- |
| Opinion adjectives: happy; sad | | sing and |
| adjectives: green; circle | Future (aspect) (I *will* eat later) | emphasising: even; only |
| Comparing adjectives: Big, bigger, biggest; more | (He *will be eating* later) | |
| classifying adjectives: aircraft carrier; war plane | Regular/irregular verbs | |
| adjectival phrases (including prepositions) | Active/passive forms | |
| The car on the road | Modals (might; could; must) | |
| Girls with long hair | Negative forms (did; didn't) | |
| Adjectival clauses | | |
| (The car *that I drive*) | | |
| (The girls *lying up the back*) | | |
| **Pronouns** | Multiword/phrasal verbs *began to laugh; had a laugh* | |
| Personal: I, he, she, her, us | | |
| Possessive: hers, his, mine | | |
| Relative pronouns: which, that | | |
| Question pronouns: who? What? | | |

Adapted from Derewianka (1998: 9)

Table 2.3 Functions within a clause

| | |
|---|---|
| S = subject<br>Noun group | A noun group which is the topic of the clause.<br>Normally appears first in the clause |
| P = predicator<br>Verb group | A verb group which expresses the process involved;<br>material action; mental; verbal and relational |
| O = object<br>Noun group | A noun group which refers to the subject in verbs<br>that are *transitive:* one that needs to transfer its<br>action onto someone or something |
| C = complement<br>Noun group or adjectival | A noun group or adjectival which comes after<br>the predicator and adds information about the<br>SUBJECT and sometimes the OBJECT |
| A = Adverbial | When, where or how some action happened |

## Quote

### Main clause

A sentence contains at least one clause which is not a subordinate clause; such a clause is a main clause. A main clause may contain any number of subordinate clauses.

*It was raining but the sun was shining.* [two main clauses]

*The man* who wrote it *told me* that it was true. [one main clause containing two subordinate clauses.]

*She said, "It rained all day."* [one main clause containing another.]

### co-ordinate, co-ordination

Words or phrases are co-ordinated if they are linked as an equal pair by a co-ordinating conjunction (i.e. *and, but, or*).

In the examples on the right, the co- ordinated elements are shown in bold, and the conjunction is underlined. The difference between co-ordination and subordination is that, in subordination, the two linked elements are not equal.

**Susan** and **Amra** met in a cafe. [links the words *Susan* and *Amra* as an equal pair]

**They talked** and **drank tea** for an hour. [links two clauses as an equal pair]

**Susan got a bus** but **Amra walked**. [links two clauses as an equal pair]

Not co-ordination: *They ate before they met.* [*before* introduces a subordinate clause]

### Relative clause

A relative clause is a special type of subordinate clause that modifies a noun. It often does this by using a relative pronoun such as *who* or *that* to

refer back to that noun, though the relative pronoun *that* is often omitted. *That's the **boy** who lives near school.* [*who* refers back to *boy*]
  *The **prize** that I won was a book.* [*that* refers back to *prize*]
  *The **prize** I won was a book.* [the pronoun *that* is omitted]
  ***Tom broke the game**, which annoyed Ali.* [*which* refers back to the whole clause]

**Subordinate clause**
A clause which is subordinate to some other part of the same sentence is a subordinate clause; for example, in *The apple that I ate was sour*, the clause *that I ate* is subordinate to *apple* (which it modifies). Subordinate clauses contrast with co-ordinate clauses as in *It was sour but looked very tasty*. (Contrast: main clause) However, clauses that are directly quoted as direct speech are not subordinate clauses.

A relative clause may also be attached to a clause. In that case, the pronoun refers back to the whole clause, rather than referring back to a noun.

In the examples, the relative clauses are underlined, and both the pronouns and the words they refer back to are in bold.

*That's the street where Ben lives.* [relative clause; modifies *street*]
*He watched her as she disappeared.* [adverbial; modifies *watched*]
*What you said was very nice.* [acts as subject of *was*]
*She noticed an hour had passed.* [acts as object of *noticed*]
Not subordinate: *He shouted, "Look out!"*
(Adapted from *Glossary for the Programmes of Study for English*) https://www.gov.uk/government/uploads/system/uploads/attachment_data/file/244216/English_Glossary.pdf

Having defined clauses as above, the definition for 'sentence' in The Glossary talks in terms of single- and multi-clause sentences: It states:

**Quote**

**Sentence**
The form of a sentence's main clause shows whether it is being used as a statement, a question, a command or an exclamation.

A sentence may consist of a single clause or it may contain several clauses held together by subordination or co-ordination. Classifying sentences as 'simple', 'complex' or 'compound' can be confusing, because a 'simple' sentence may be complicated, and a 'complex' one may be

> straightforward. The terms **'single- clause sentence'** and **'multi-clause sentence'** may be more helpful.
> *You are my friend.* [statement]
> *Are you my friend?* [question]
> *Be my friend!* [command]
> *What a good friend you are!* [exclamation]
> *Ali went home on his bike to his goldfish and his current library book about pets.* [single-clause sentence]
> *She went shopping but took back everything she had bought because she didn't like any of it.* [multi-clause sentence]
> (Glossary for the Programmes of Study for English) https://www.gov.uk/government/uploads/system/uploads/attachment_data/file/244216/English_Glossary.pdf

The Glossary uses the term *multi-clause sentence* to describe a combination of a main clause and any number of co-ordinating, subordinate or relative clauses, which SFG calls a *clause complex*. The example given above of a clause complex though, does not identify its constituent parts (Table 2.4).

She went shopping (*first coordinating clause*) but (*coordinating conjunction*) took back everything she had bought (*second coordinating clause, including a defining relative clause 'she had bought' modifying 'everything'—relative pronoun 'she' ellipsed*) because (*subordinating conjunction*) she didn't like any of it (*subordinate clause, dependent on the second coordinating clause*).

Sentences can also be crafted as taking either an *active* or *passive* voice. The NC Glossary defines these as follows:

**Table 2.4** Constituent elements of the NC multi-clause sentence example

| She **went** shopping | but **took back** everything [[she **had bought**]] | because she **didn't like** any of it |
|---|---|---|
| Clause 1: main/head clause | Clause 2a: co-ordinating [with an embedded relative clause] | Clause 2b: subordinate clause |

**Quote**

| Term | Guidance | Example |
|---|---|---|
| Active voice | An active verb has its usual pattern of subject and object (in contrast with the passive) | Active: The school arranged a visit. Passive: A visit was arranged by the school |
| Passive | The sentence *It was eaten by our dog* is the passive of *Our dog ate it*. A passive is recognisable from:<br>• the past participle form eaten the normal object (it) turned into the subject<br>• the normal subject (our dog) turned into an optional preposition phrase with by as its head<br>• the verb be (was), or some other verb such as get. Contrast active<br>A verb is not 'passive' just because it has a passive meaning: it must be the passive version of an active verb | A visit was <u>arranged</u> by the school. Our cat got <u>run</u> over by a bus. Active versions:<br>• The school arranged a visit<br>• A bus ran over our cat<br>Not passive:<br>• He received a warning. [past tense, active *received*]<br>• We had an accident. [past tense, active *had*] |

The fundamental difference between the two voices is that in the active voice, the person, animal or thing performing the action is the subject of the sentence. In the passive voice, the subject of the sentence becomes the entity upon which the action of the verb is performed. For example:

*The police shot dead ten people* becomes *ten people were shot (by the police).*

Passive constructions such as the one above are typically used to hide agency. In science, where the emphasis is upon what has happened rather than who is performing any action, then the passive voice is used more commonly than the active.

The outlines given above intend to provide an overview and are by no means exhaustive, but serve to illustrate the main grammatical patterns associated with groups/phrases and clauses that form sentences which in turn combine together to form texts. It is also evident from the discussion in Chapters 3–6 that clause patterning differs in the writing of different school subjects. In science, for example, the most common clause structure is main/single, co-ordinating and subordinate, with complexity lying in the formation of expanded three or four word noun groups rather than clause structure. The subjects of sentences also tend to be physical properties of some kind, rather than people, places or things. For example, in an AS and A Level specification for physical chemistry atomic structure is described as follows:

> The chemical properties of elements **depend** on their atomic structure and in particular on the arrangement of electrons around the nucleus (1). The arrangement of electrons in orbitals **is linked** to **the way in which** elements **are organised** in the Periodic Table (2). Chemists **can measure** the mass of atoms and molecules to a high degree of accuracy in a mass spectrometer (3). The principles of operation of a modern mass spectrometer **are studied** (4).
>
> http://filestore.aqa.org.uk/resources/chemistry/specifications/AQA-7404-7405-SP-2015.PDF

There are six clauses in the text above: the first sentence is a single clause; the second is a clause complex and the last two are single clause sentences. They also consist entirely of noun and verb groups with no pronouns, one comparing adjective (high), and no adverbials. The second sentence: *The arrangement of electrons in orbitals* ***is linked*** *to* **the way in which** *elements* ***are organised*** *in the Periodic Table* is a single main clause which includes within it a defining relative (or embedded) clause ('in which…Table') that in turn modifies the noun group 'the way'. The relative pronoun is 'which'. This is in stark contrast to patterns of register found in other subjects such as English, history and RE, where it is more common to find clause-complex sentences.

Why bother? As Chapter 1 has discussed, understanding the grammatical patterns of the register through which subject knowledge is expressed in the context of subject-specific learning and teaching, can provide adolescents with the linguistic tools with which to articulate their thought and in turn, increase their own confidence in their educational abilities. Giving them access to the genres and registers through which subject knowledge is realised is what empowers them to succeed academically in ways that a sole reliance on process writing or recounting of personal experiences can ever do. LBP explicitly teaches adolescents how to write the different academic literacies of different school subjects explicitly. It also teaches them to read with critical understanding and to conceptualise texts as partners in the exchange of knowledge and meaning. To do otherwise risks locking them into the limits of their linguistic ability and perpetuating a cycle of social as well as linguistic inequality.

## LBP and the Linguistic Structuring of Inequality

Language makes possible individual speech. However, discursive practices and their patterns of language use are also regulated- and in educational contexts particularly—through a complex network of systems amongst and between education policymakers, education practitioners, teachers, schools, learners, families and communities. These networks, in turn, are regulated by wider sociocultural structures and systems. Bernstein's (1991, 1996) concept of *pedagogic discourse* provides a way of accounting for the ways in which such networks function. Better known for his work on codes, Bernstein's theory of pedagogic discourse is one of cultural reproduction, which attempts to explain the structures through which pedagogic discourse is realised and thus to uncover the processes of symbolic control. As such, it follows on from the work of cultural theorists such as Foucault (1972) and Bourdieu and Passeron (1977), who, in analysing the relationship between education and the reproduction of class relations, reject the notion of schools as independent of external forces. Instead, schools are viewed as playing an important part in legitimating, reproducing and reflecting hierarchically arranged bodies of knowledge which serve to reinforce the interests of the dominant social class. However, Bernstein argues that such theorists take for granted the discourse which is subject to their analysis and view pedagogic discourse as a medium for other social voices or discourses such as class, gender and race. Although they acknowledge the distinction between the message—what is relayed—and its carrier or relay, Bernstein takes them to task for failing to distinguish sufficiently between them.

Bernstein defines pedagogic discourse as 'a principle for appropriating other discourses and bringing them into special relation with each other for the purposes of their selective transmission and acquisition' (Bernstein 1991: 181). Consequently, pedagogic discourse is distinct from many others in that it is totally dependent upon others drawn from outside itself in forming its own. Furthermore, Bernstein is concerned with the structuring of pedagogic discourse rather than its realisation as a specific discourse. His theory, therefore, makes it possible to take account not only of how groups resist and oppose pedagogic communication, but are also positioned by it. In Bernsteinian terms then, pedagogic discourse is not physics, chemistry or any other subject but a principle for the circulation and re-ordering of discourses into a pedagogic subject. It de-locates, re-locates and re-focuses a discourse from its original site and moves it to a pedagogic one. It creates a gap or space in which ideology can play. Furthermore, as the pedagogic device mediates discourse from its primary site it is also transformed into a virtual or imaginary discourse. The reproduction of knowledge in formal education contexts, Bernstein argued, is thus governed by socially constructed and not intrinsically logical facts. In Bernsteinian terms then, pedagogic discourse is not physics, chemistry or any other subject, but a principle for the circulation and re-ordering of discourses into a pedagogic subject. It de-locates, re-locates and re-focuses a discourse from its original site and moves it to a pedagogic one. In so doing, it creates a gap or space in which ideology can play.

Bernstein maintains that no discourse moves without bringing ideology into play and as it moves it is ideologically transformed. Furthermore, as the pedagogic device mediates discourse from its primary site it is also transformed into a virtual or imaginary discourse. Consequently, pedagogic discourse selectively creates imaginary subjects. He illustrates his theory further with the curriculum subject of physics in secondary schools, arguing that the principal site for physics is in universities, from which it is recontextualised as a pedagogic subject. In another example within school, time spent in a room with wooden benches, saws, hammers and chisels was 'woodwork', but which outside pedagogy was the practice of carpentry. Since Bernstein's time of course, 'woodwork' has been recontextualised and subsumed under school 'Art and Design' or 'Design and Technology'.

The merit of Bernstein's theory is that its framework provides an explanation of the wider political, social and cultural contexts which influence how any pedagogic subject is configured at any given moment in time. What most theories of cultural reproduction lack, Bernstein argues, is an analysis of the internal logic of pedagogic relay and its relation to what is relayed. If a theory is weak on 'relations within', then, according to Bernstein, it is not possible to realise rules for the description of the agencies or processes with which it is concerned. If transmission is to be understood, then the relation between 'relation to' and 'relation within', both macro and micro levels of operation and their internal logic, have to be taken into account. Bernstein proposes something he calls the 'pedagogic device', akin to the Chomskyan notion of a language device, to account for this logic. For example, the introduction of a national curriculum for English in the early 1990s was very weak on 'relations within' the subject, with the macro level of government policy being entirely at odds with the micro level of what went on in classrooms, especially in relation to teaching language structures and their uses (Clark 2001, 2005, 2010).

Bernstein's pedagogic device has three hierarchically-interrelated rules, each with a different function, which are rules of distribution; recontextualisation and evaluation. These rules stand in hierarchical relation to one another, and are thus also concerned with power in that recontextualising rules are derived from the distributive rules and the evaluative rules from the recontextualising. The distributive rules regulate 'the fundamental relationship between power, social groups, forms of consciousness and practice, and their reproductions and productions' (Bernstein 1991: 180). In a nutshell, Rules of Distribution are regulated by the State and any servant of the State, such as the Department for Education and associated satellites, and the now defunct National Curriuculum Council and Qualifications and Curriculum Authority. Rules of Recontextualisation, in turn, regulate the constitution of specific pedagogic discourse and the texts privileged within it. Rules of Recontextualisation are based upon how government departments such as the Department for Education recontextualise previous versions of a curriculum and theorists writing or editing books and journals. Rules of Evaluation constitute pedagogic practice. That is, the practices in which teachers engage when they interpret method and policy into their own teaching in the classroom on a day to day basis. Figure 2.4 shows this theory in tabular form.

In attempting to answer the question of how differently valorised and rewarded forms of knowledge are distributed differently in society, Bernstein makes a distinction between two types of pedagogic discourse, namely *horizontal* and *vertical* discourse (Bernstein 1999).

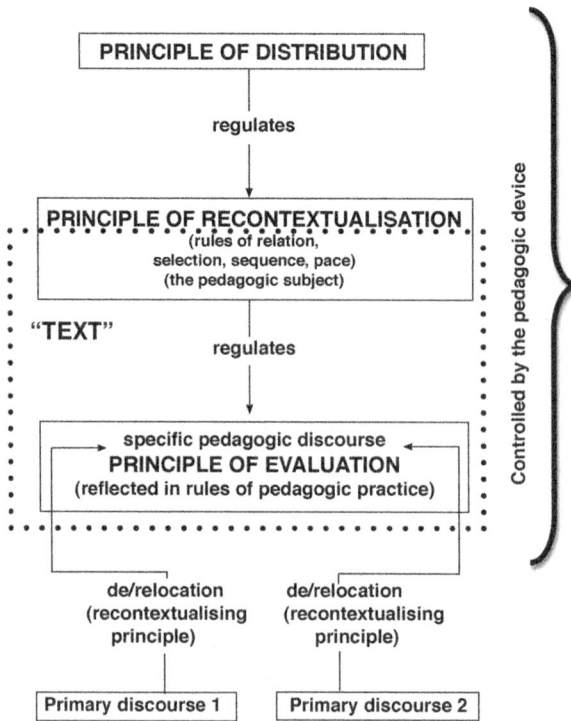

Fig. 2.4 Bernstein's theory of pedagogic discourse (Adapted from Bernstein 1991)

*Horizontal* discourse is typically 'common sense knowledge' in the sense that we all have potential access to it and it is concerned mainly with common problems associated with living and dying. It is thus most usually oral, local and context-dependent with all the features of everyday language use. The crucial aspect of horizontal discourse for Bernstein is that it is segmentally organised. By segmental, Bernstein means the site within which the discourse is realised. 'The realization of this discourse varies with the way the culture segments and specializes activities and practices' (Bernstein 1999: 159). This is not to say that all segments have equal importance, since some will be more important than others. *Vertical discourse*, by contrast, is acquired in formal institutional settings such as schools and universities, comprising specialised forms of knowledge abstracted from actual contexts of situation.

> **Quote**
>
> In brief, a vertical discourse takes the form of a coherent, explicit, and systematically principled structure, hierarchically organized, as in the sciences, or it takes the form of a series of specialized languages with specialised modes of interrogation and specialised criteria for the production and circulation of texts, as in the social sciences and humanities.
> (Bernstein 1999: 159)

Normally, vertical discourse circulates through Bernstein's three principles of pedagogic discourse, in explicit forms of recontextualisation and evaluation, motivated by strong distributive features. Vertical discourse also has two different "modalities": *hierarchical knowledge structure* and *horizontal knowledge structure*. Bernstein defines *hierarchical knowledge structure* as 'a coherent, explicit and systematically principled structure, hierarchically organised' that 'attempts to create very general propositions and theories, and which integrate knowledge at lower levels, and in this way shows underlying uniformities across an expanding range of different phenomena' (Bernstein 1999: 161–162). This form of knowledge, exemplified by the natural sciences, is represented visually as a triangle, motivated towards building an apex of greater integrating propositions. In contrast, *horizontal knowledge structure* is defined as 'a series of specialized languages with specialized modes of interrogation and criteria for the construction and circulation of texts' (Bernstein: 162). As Maton and Muller (2007: 24) point out, a key difference between the two knowledge structures lies in how they have been developed. The hierarchical knowledge structure typical of the natural sciences widens the base and sharpens to the tip of a triangle. Intellectual progress is made by defining, integrating and subsuming existing ideas within more general and overarching propositions. Bernstein quotes the Nobel Prize winning physicist Richard Feymann to illustrate this point: 'Physics has a history of synthesizing many phenomena into a few theories' (1999: 163).

In contrast, horizontal knowledge structures develop through the addition of new languages or discourses, typically in the humanities and social sciences. For example, in sociology they refer to its wide array of competing theoretical approaches. The different knowledge structures thus specialise consciousness differently. They also, as Maton and Muller point out, 'shape social practices and forms of pedagogy, and differently specialize consciousness within their intellectual fields (2007: 24). The questions then arise, as to who has access to what form of knowledge, and whether or not they also constitute curriculum or pedagogic structure? A school curriculum does not, as Maton and Muller point out, equate with either horizontal or hierarchical knowledge structure. Rather, the question is more one of the issues highlighted by these concepts, such as the degree to which knowledge structures develop through integrating and subsuming past ideas, particularly in the humanities. For example, Christie and Macken-Horarik (2007) highlight how pupils experience a trajectory of schooling in subject English in ways that go against the integration of already learnt knowledge. Rather than building upon pupils' past learning, the invisible pedagogy of the English curriculum renders educational knowledge structures less visible. This, in turn, has the effect of pupils often experiencing segmental rather than integrative acquisition of educational knowledge.

From an SFL perspective, pedagogic discourse is realised through two sets of language choices: firstly, those of a first order or regulative register, that are to do with the goals, purposes, and directions of classroom activities and secondly, those of a second order or instructional register, that have to do with the 'content' that is taught and learnt (Christie 2002). Instructional register—that is, the talk that actually goes on in classrooms—is determined or governed by the regulative register. Together, the two registers create pedagogic discourse. The ways in which they interact determines the ways in which curriculum subjects are constructed and how pupils and students develop an understanding of the 'common knowledge' (Mercer and Edwards 1987) of a culture. Such 'common knowledge' is different from Bernstein's concept of the common culture of horizontal discourse, in that it is learnt, regulated and reproduced in education and thus through vertical discourse.

It is clear that developing and learning language during the upper primary and secondary school years goes hand in hand with developing and learning the knowledge of the various academic disciplines and subjects that are taught. However, as Humphrey (2015) points out, developing control of academic English and its associated literacies is by no means automatic. She points out that there is a wealth of evidence to show that sociocultural, economic, pedagogic and political constraints and opportunities have a significant impact on the development of academic language, as demonstrated in curriculum learning and performance on standardised measures of literacy. As Humphrey also goes on to point out, from the perspective of pupils and students for whom standard English is an additional language or dialect, there is a danger of assuming academic language competence from evidence of fluency in everyday language, which may be learned quite rapidly in conversational contexts. Martin (2009: 16) also makes the point that '…in classrooms where knowledge of the language in which genres are composed cannot be assumed, discussing the relation of lexis, grammar and discourse structure to genre is inescapable – since the lower level resources have to be brought to consciousness and taught'.

A further aspect that has to be taken into consideration is the nature of knowledge itself. In a constructivist tradition, knowledge is conceived of as an object.

> **Quote**
> Educational research has ... typically backgrounded knowledge as an object. Key issues for research are exploring processes of learning and revealing whose knowledge is being learned. What is being learned and how it shapes these processes of learning and power relations among knowers have been largely obscured. Such knowledge-blindness thus proceeds as if the nature of what is taught and learned has little relevance. Accordingly, debates over teaching have oscillated between 'traditional' and 'constructivist' pedagogies that are generalized across the curriculum, and knowledge-building has been typically understood generically, as accumulation of content or ill-defined skills such as 'critical thinking'. How the forms taken by educational knowledge may enable or constrain cumulative teaching and learning remains relatively under-researched.
> (Maton 2013: 9)

Following Bernstein (1991), Maton distinguishes between two *legitimation codes* in order to differentiate between the nature of specialisation involved: the *knowledge code* and the *knower code*. Areas of study such as those associated with the sciences 'legitimate' their work by referencing an object of study and evoke a knowledge code. Where the object of study involves personal attitudes and/or characteristics of a subject such as those that make up the arts and humanities, then a knower code is evoked. An important aspect of both codes is that acquisition of knowledge is cumulative. In addition, they have drawn attention to the ways in which language functions in relation to building cumulative knowledge through the concept of *semantic waves*. Maton conceptualises knowledge-building as cumulative in nature in terms of features of the knowledge itself, and the significance of what he calls semantic waves for cumulative teaching. Martin (2013) has also explored the ways in which linguistic resources are drawn upon to achieve semantic waves in teaching, identifying a trio of complexes he terms 'power words', 'power grammar' and 'power composition'. Using the metaphor of surfing a wave, the wave is 'caught' in classroom discourse through teachers and students engaging with subject-specific concepts, which are packed in (typically written) text as decontextualised condensed meanings. When riding 'down the wave', the concepts are unpacked to relatively simplified contextualised meanings in classroom discussion through explanation and examples. Crucial to cumulative knowledge building, though, is the move back 'up the wave' to support students to repack meanings into the condensed forms which will allow relationships to be made with broader subject-based concepts.

The semantic wave is characterised by the twin concepts of *semantic density* and *semantic gravity*. *Semantic density* refers to the degree of condensation of meaning in sociocultural contexts, whereas semantic gravity refers to the degree to which meaning relates to context. Part of the process of accumulating subject knowledge is learning the degree to which discipline-specific concepts are firstly, defined in dense and metaphorical ways and secondly, the discourses that surround explanation and realisation of the concepts themselves. For example, Martin (2013) shows how the term *cilia* is situated by the academic discourse of biology within the compositional structures that describe the physical constituents of *cilia* and of what constitutes *cilia*. Taxonomic structures are evoked or used that involve different ways of classifying parts of the body and a range of biological processes and causal explanations in which cilia play a role. In terms of the semantic structure of the intellectual field of Biology, *cilia* possesses a semantic density of considerable strength. This strength, Martin and Maton both argue, is not essential or intrinsic to the term itself, and the semantic density characterising 'cilia' in research publications is likely to be stronger than that characterising the term's use within school textbooks, which in turn may be stronger than its use in classroom discourse or student work products. Indeed, when I mentioned Martin and Maton's observations to Denise, the biology teacher referred to in Chapter 3, she concurred immediately and enthusiastically. Chapter 3 and those that follow, illustrate ways in which knowledge is built up across a range of secondary curriculum subjects through applying the concepts of semantic waves, semantic density and gravity to the analysis of classroom activity.

## Language Learning and Pedagogy

Bernstein's theory has influenced another recent development in pedagogy particularly in the UK and Australia known as *dialogic teaching*, as developed by Wells (1999), Mercer (2000), Alexander (2008) and Martin and Rose (2012). For the purposes of this chapter, the term dialogic teaching encompasses all such approaches. The concept of dialogic teaching also draws upon Bakhtinian theory and Vygotsky's notion of the zone of proximal development discussed in the next section. Alexander's research into UK primary classrooms showed that teachers do not make as much use of talk for learning as they might, nor do they give routinely corrective verbal feedback. According to Alexander, dialogic teaching:

> **Quote**
> ...harnesses the power of talk to stimulate and extend students' thinking and advance their learning and understanding. It helps the teacher more precisely to diagnose students' needs, frame their learning tasks and assess their progress. It empowers the student for lifelong learning and active citizenship. Dialogic teaching is not just any talk. It is as distinct from the question-answer and listen-tell routines of traditional teaching as it is from the casual conversation of informal discussion.
> http://www.robinalexander.org.uk/dialogic-teaching/ accessed 16th June 2017

Dialogic teaching then, encourages patterns of interaction such as exploratory talk, argumentation and dialogue between teachers and learners and amongst learners in order to promote high-level thinking and intellectual development. This is achieved through teachers and their pupils working together in partnership as they participate in joint acts of knowledge construction. At the same time, the practice of making such an approach visible needs not to be lost, as the section above has pointed out.

The pedagogic practices upon which LBP draws also include what Vygotsky (1972) called the Zone of Proximal Development (ZPD), a notion he developed from his observations of children playing. Play, he contended, is a condensed form of all developmental tendencies and itself a major source of development, since it creates a ZPD. The idea here is that the best kind of play to foster development is with older peers or adults who 'scaffold' the learning process of the younger child and through interaction, provide the mediational tools to promote development.

Vygotsky, in common with other psychologists concerned with first language acquisition and development, also noticed that children acquire language in progressive stages, moving from the concrete to the abstract. His studies led him to conclude that the study of grammar was of paramount importance for the mental development of the child, particularly in understanding the nature of the linguistic sign as symbolic of thought. Formal instruction is thus crucial in developing pupils' and students' abilities to a higher level of speech development, since it brings to consciousness that which is unconscious. Although children unconsciously learn the pronunciation, morphological and grammatical structures and patternings of their language long before they begin school, Vygotsky argued that instruction in grammar and writing enables the child to use language in a more conscious and controlled way.

A fundamental premise of the notion of ZPD, and the instructional cycles and models outlined above is that language development is as much a sociocultural as a psychological activity. Developmental processes take place through participating in cultural, historic and linguistically informed settings such as family life and peer group interaction and institutionally through the contexts of schooling, the workplace and organised sports activities (Lantolf and Thorne 2007: 198). Language mediates our experience, and transmission of meaning between one language and another occurs not through any kind of transparent process of input and output but rather, through the use of "psychological tools" such as language, symbols, behaviour and so on, through which we construct meaning between ourselves. Lantolf and Thorne (2007) use the analogy of a shovel to explain the concept of mediation. We can imitate an animal digging by using our hands. Digging though, can be enhanced and increased greatly through the use of a shovel, which is a human created artifact. Our language is used in much the same way as a tool such as a shovel. It is through use that language exerts its power to mediate our experience, and as a tool, it is only as useful in so far as it is able to make meaning.

An LBP approach also draws upon pedagogic approaches to language learning that have developed the notion of the ZPD. For example, in Australia Callaghan and Rothery (1988) building upon Martin and Rothery (1986) in relation primarily to the teaching of writing, developed the notion of the *learning and teaching cycle* (LTC) or what Knapp and Watkins (1994/2007) call the Learning/Teaching Model (LTM).

The LTC, although developed in the context of pupils' needs from socio-economically disadvantaged backgrounds, has also been widely recognised as a means of scaffolding learning for mainstream students, EAL/ESL learners (Gibbons 2002) and adult ESL learners (Burns and Joyce 1991). It is based upon two important premises: firstly, that writing is learnt through the practice of writing, and writing tasks that pupils and students are set should be commensurate with their stage of language development and their linguistic ability. Secondly, that grammar is taught and learnt in the context of pupils' own writing.

The LTC comprises of three interlinked stages.

- **Phase One**. Building a strong connection between the language of experience and the language of writing. As pupils and students are introduced to content knowledge (the field) explicit connections are made between the language and cognitive processes used to deal with it. Connections can be made at this stage between subject knowledge and language not only through describing and explaining, providing reading models and note-taking activities but also through defining key concepts and associated vocabulary.
- **Phase Two**. Providing an explicit framework to construct texts through which the content/knowledge of stage 1 is expressed. The framework is provided by scaffolding research activities to exemplify the structure of the texts to be written. As part of this, teachers may choose or write a mentor or model text, which is pulled apart or deconstructed to draw attention to the textual organisation that pupils and students will be expected to draw upon in their own written texts. They may also engage in activities where writing is produced jointly between a teacher and groups of pupils and students.
- **Phase Three**. Developing well-defined editing skills based on the generic purpose, structure and grammar of texts. Grammar is taught through writing and as part of drafting and editing their writing. Pupils and students learn the grammar of writing through

understanding the ways that their own writing works, including giving grammatical names and functions of the language they are using.
- **Phase Four.** Independent writing for summative assessment purposes.

The phases outlined above can also be represented as Fig. 2.5.

The LTC also develops Alexander's principle of *cumulation* in relation to dialogic talk. Although the focus of the LTC is upon teaching pupils and students how to write in ways that are appropriate to the subject being taught, much of the teaching occurs through talk, in ways that are dialogic, between the teacher and the whole class, between pupils in small groups and pupils or students reporting back to the teacher. Dialogic talk and the LTC both serve to make classrooms more democratic in terms of their approach to linguistic use. Thus, rather than focusing upon 'inaccurate' or 'accurate' use of speaking English, interaction between teacher and pupils and students focuses upon learning

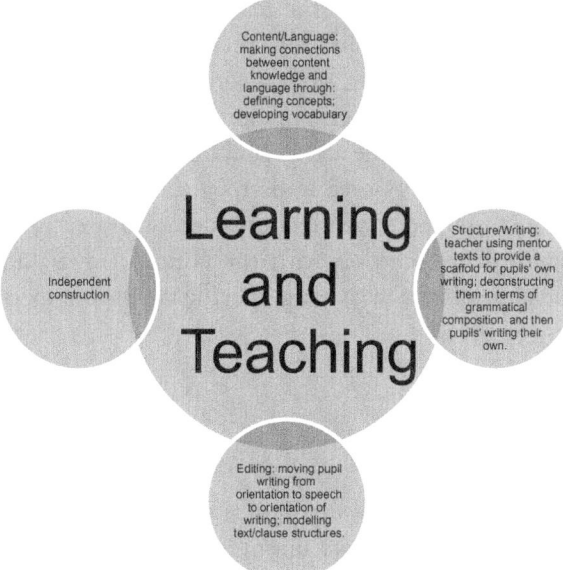

Fig. 2.5 The learning and teaching cycle

to use different registers of language use according to audience, context and purpose. Chapter 4 provides further exemplification of the model in classroom practice.

Martin and Rose (2012) show how the LTC can also be applied to the teaching of reading as well as writing. They point out that implicit with each phase of writing pedagogy is supported practice in reading. Learning to read, they point out, includes not only extracting subject matter from texts but also learning, importantly, the language patterns, including various discourse and grammatical features related to genre and register through which subject matter is constructed. They also point out that whilst writing may play a part in reinforcing knowledge, its primary function is for the assessment of knowledge learnt. They propose a three move cycle in relation to the teaching of reading in the secondary curriculum, comprised of: *prepare, task* and *elaborate*, in a way that mirrors parent–child interaction in reading and ties into the LTC for writing. The first phase of *prepare* is designed not only to elicit a response but also includes scaffolding activities in preparation for a response; *task* includes not only the teacher giving feedback comments on pupil or student responses but also includes drawing attention to the textual features of the reading undertaken and in the *elaborate* phase, where interpretation of reading is made, feedback is always affirmatory and positive. In this way, the cycle enables all pupils and students to always respond successfully and leads to greater participation on their part, as subsequent chapters of this book demonstrate. Such a structure shares a great deal in common with the concept of dialogic talk, but with the crucial addition of paying specific attention to the language features of any text read.

## Conclusion

This chapter has discussed the theoretical principles that underpin LBP, and the ways in which it draws upon research in education, psychology and sociology as well as linguistics in its formulation. In Bernstein's sociological theory of pedagogic discourse, *recontextualisation* is the concept that underpins curriculum reform, mediated through government policy (*distribution*) and teacher's own practices (*evaluation*). Account is also taken of the discursive structures through which knowledge is realised and learnt, as well as the pacing and sequencing of classroom activity. The grammatical aspect of LBP recontextualises aspects of SFG from its primary university research context into a pedagogic one in so far as it links with both government policy and teachers' evaluative practices. The aspects of SFG that are arguably the most beneficial in terms of developing a pedagogic grammar are (a) extending the unit of analysis above the clause to the text and below it to the word, (b) teaching grammar in the context of adolescents' own reading and writing practices, and (c) developing the notion of register and the linguistic repertoire. SFG also moves the concept of grammar away from one centred upon 'error' to one centred upon grammar as patterns of choice in language.

Account also has to be taken of the fact that the time given to delivering curriculum objectives and preparing adolescents for assessment, is finite. As too are school's financial resources. It thus follows, that incorporating LBP into initial teacher education programmes or professional development courses for in-service teachers has a greater chance of success if it is focused and targeted in the context of subject-specific literacy development. The pacing and sequencing of activities centred around the notion of apprenticeship and scaffolding that underpin the LTC also imply a change in teachers' pedagogic practices. For such change to warrant the time commitment needed, then it has to link into teachers' everyday affordances in ways that make sense to them. It follows too that LBP can be drawn upon in any educational context, whatever the language of instruction may be. However, since in LBP context is everything, it also follows that LBP informed curricula will differ in their realisations and relate to specific sociocultural contexts in which they occur.

LBP is an approach that is essentially dialogic in nature between teachers and their pupils and students. It does not seek to dictate or prescribe the pace or sequence of learning and teaching activities. Rather, pacing and sequencing is left to the teacher to determine, governed by the educational needs of the pupils and students they teach and the communities within which they are situated. In this respect, an LBP approach is teacher, rather than method, driven. It is also appropriate as a pedagogy for children and adolescents for whom English is an L1 as it is for those for whom English is an additional language. This is because explicit attention is paid to the development of language, alongside knowledge, in symbiotic relationship.

An LBP approach also integrates the writing required for assessment as part of the curriculum learning experience, rather than as something separate from it. In this respect, an LBP approach is also consistent with a growing trend towards assessment for learning (Black and Wiliam 1998; Gardiner 2006; Stiggins 2007). LBP draws upon SFL/G and recontextualises it into a pedagogic grammar of English that in turn, links into the framework of the curriculum not only for English but also that of other school subjects. Grammar is not a religion, and the key here is the recontextualisation of as many key concepts drawn from SFG as are necessary for a pedagogic context. Such a recontextualisation as discussed throughout this book selects and draws upon SFG in so far as it adds, extends and reconfigures existing traditions and practices in ways that also take account of and build upon teachers' knowledge base and in turn, those of their pupils and students.

## References

Alexander, R. (2008). *Towards dialogic teaching: Rethinking classroom talk*. York: Dialogos.

Barton, D., & Hamilton, M. (2000). Literacy practices. In D. Barton, S. Hamilton, & R. Ivanic (Eds.), *Situated literacies* (pp. 7–15). London and New York: Routledge.

Bernstein, B. (1975). *Class and pedagogies: Visible and invisible*. Paris: Centre for Educational Research and Innovation (CERI).

Bernstein, B. (1991). *The structuring of pedagogic discourse. Vol. 4. Class, codes and control*. London and New York: Routledge.

Bernstein, B. (1996). *Pedagogy, symbolic control and identity*. London: Taylor & Francis.

Bernstein, B. (1999). Horizontal and vertical discourse: An essay. *British Journal of the Sociology of Education, 20*(2), 157–173.

Biber, D., & Conrad, S. (2009). *Register, genre and style*. Cambridge: Cambridge University Press.

Biber, D., Conrad, S., & Randi, R. (1998). *Corpus linguistics: Investigating language structure and use.* Cambridge: Cambridge University Press.

Biber, D., Johansson, S., Leech, G., Conrad, S., & Finnegan, E. (1999). *The Longman Grammar of spoken and written English.* London: Longman.

Black, P., & William, D. (1998). Assessment and classroom learning. *Assessment in Education: Policy & Practice, 5*(1), 7–74.

Bourdieu, P. (1973). Cultural Reproduction and Social Reproduction. In R. Brown (Ed.), *Knowledge, education and social change: Papers in the sociology of education.* Tavistock: Tavistock Publications.

Bourdieu, P., & Passeron, J. (1977). *Reproduction in education, society and culture.* London: Sage.

Bruner, J. S. (1966). *Towards a theory of instruction.* Cambridge, MA: Belkapp Press.

Bruner, J. S. (1983). *Child's talk: Learning to use language.* New York: W.W. Norton.

Bruner, J. S. (1996). *The culture of education.* Cambridge, MA: Harvard University Press.

Burns, A., & Joyce, H. (1991). The teaching-learning cycle. In J. Hamond, A. Burns, & H. Joyce (Eds.), *English for social purposes.* Sydney: National Centre for English Language Teaching and Research.

Busch, B. (2012). The linguistic repertoire revisited. *Applied Linguistics, 33*(5), 1–22.

Callaghan, M., & Rothery, J. (1988). *Teaching factual writing: A genre based approach.* Erskeneville, NSW: Metropolitan East Disadvantaged Schools' Program.

Carter, R. A. (2004). *Language and creativity: The art of common talk.* London: Routledge.

Carter, R. A., & McCarthy, M. J. (2015). Spoken grammar: Where are we and where are we going? *Applied Linguistics, 38*(1), 1–20.

Carter, R. A., & McCarthy, M. J. (2004). Talking, creating: Interactional language, creativity and context. *Applied Linguistics, 25*(1), 62–88.

Carter, R. A., McCarthy, M. J., Mark, G., & O'Keefe, A. (2011). *English grammar today: An A-Z of spoken and written grammar.* Cambridge: Cambridge University Press.

Chomsky, N. (1965). *Aspects of the theory of syntax.* Cambridge: MIT Press.

Christie, F. (2002). The development of abstraction in adolescence in subject English. In M. Schleppegrell & M. Colombi (Eds.), *Developing advanced literacy in first and second languages* (pp. 45–66). Mahwah, NJ and London: Erlbaum.

Christie, F. (2007). Ongoing dialogue: Functional language and Bernsteinian sociological perspectives in education. In F. Christie & J. Martin (Eds.),

*Language, knowledge and pedagogy: Functional linguistic and sociological perspectives* (pp. 3–13). London and New York: Continuum.

Christie, F. (2012) *Language education throughout the school years: A functional perspective*. Chichester, West Sussex and Malden, MA: Wiley-Blackwell.

Christie, F., & Derewianka, B. (2008). *School discourse: Learning to write across the years of schooling*. London and New York: Continuum.

Christie, F., & Macken-Horarik, M. (2007). Building vertically in subject English. In F. Christie & J. R. Martin (Eds.), *Language, knowledge and pedagogy: Functional linguistics and sociological perspectives* (pp. 14–36). London and New York: Continuum.

Christie, F., & Martin, J. R. (Eds.). (2007). *Language, knowledge and pedagogy: Functional linguistic and sociological perspectives*. London and New York: Continuum.

Clark, U. (2001). *War words: Language, history and the disciplining of English*. Oxford: Elsevier Science.

Clark, U. (2005). Bernstein's theory of pedagogic discourse: Linguistics, educational policy and practice in the UK English/literacy classroom. *English Teaching: Practice and Critique, 4*(3), 32–47.

Clark, U. (2010). The problematics of prescribing grammatical knowledge: The case in England. In T. Locke (Ed.), *Beyond the grammar wars: A resource for teachers and students on developing language knowledge in the English/literacy classroom* (pp. 120–136). London: Routledge.

Clark, U. (2013). *Language and identity in Englishes*. London: Routledge.

Coffin, C., & Donohue, J. (2014). *A language as a social-semiotic-based approach to teaching and learning in higher education*. Oxford: Wiley-Blackwell.

Coupland, N., & Bishop, H. (2007). The ideologised values for British accents. *Journal of Sociolinguistics, 11*(1), 74–93.

Department of Education and Science. (1988). *The Kingman report. Report of the committee of inquiry into the teaching of English language*. London: HMSO.

Derewianka, B. (1998). *A grammar companion for primary teachers*. Sydney: Primary English Teaching Association.

De Silva Joyce, H., & Feez, S. (2016). *Exploring literacies: Theory, research, practice*. Basingstoke: Palgrave.

Elliot, G., Green, S., Constantinou, F., Vitello, S., Chambers, L., Rushton, N., et al. (2016). Variations in aspects of writing in 16+ examinations between 1980 and 2014. *Research matters: A Cambridge assessment publication,*

*Special Issue 4*. http://cambridgeassessment.org.uk/Images/340982-research-matters-special-issue-4-aspects-of-writing-1980-2014.pdf.

Fisher, D., & Frey, N. (2008). *Better learning through structured teaching: A framework for the gradual release of responsibility*. Alexandria, VA: Association for Supervision and Curriculum Development.

Fontaine, L. (2012). *Analysing English grammar*. Cambridge: Cambridge University Press.

Foucault, M. (1972). *The archeology of knowledge*. New York: Pantheon Books.

Gardiner, J. (2006). *Assessment and Learning*. London: Sage.

Gibbons, P. (2002). *Bridging discourses in the ESL classroom: Students, teachers and researchers*. London: Continuum.

Gumperz, J. (1960). Formal and informal standards in the Hindi regional language area (with C. M. Naim). In C. Ferguson & J. Gumperz (Eds.), *Linguistic diversity in South Asia*. Bloomington: Indiana University Research Center.

Gumperz, J. (1964). On the ethnology of linguistic change. In *Proceedings of the UCLA Sociolinguistics Conference*. Los Angeles, CA: Mouton & Company.

Halliday, M. (1977). Text as semantic choice in social context. In T. van Dijk & J. Petofi (Eds.), *Grammars and descriptions* (pp. 176–225). Berlin: Mouton de Gruyter.

Halliday, M. (1983). *Spoken and written language*. Geelong, VIC: Deakin University Press (Republished by OUP 1989).

Halliday, M. (1993). Towards a language-based theory of learning. *Linguistics and Education, 5*(2), 93–116.

Halliday, M., & Hasan, R. (1976). *Cohesion in English*. London: Longman.

Halliday, M., & Hasan, R. (1985). *Language, context and text: Aspects of language in a social semiotic perspective*. Oxford: Oxford University Press.

Halliday, M., & Martin, J. (1993). *Writing science: Literacy and discursive power*. London: Routledge.

Halliday, M., McIntosh, A., & Stevens, P. (2007 [1964]). The users and uses of language. In J. J. Webster (Ed.), *Language and society. Volume 10 in the Collected works of M. A. K. Halliday* (pp. 5–37). London and New York: Continuum.

Hasan, R. (1973). Code, register and social dialect. In B. Bernstein (Ed.), *Class, codes and control, Vol. 11: Applied studies towards a sociology of language* (pp. 253–292). London: Routledge and Kegan Paul.

Hudson, R. (1992). *Teaching grammar: A guide for the national curriculum*. Oxford: Blackwell.

Hudson, S., & Francis, G. (2000). *Pattern grammar: A corpus-driven approach to the lexical grammar of English.* Amsterdam: John Benjamins.

Humphrey, S. (2015). A 4×4 literacy toolkit for employment: English language learners for academic literacies. In M. B. Schaefer (Ed.), *Research on teaching and learning with the literacies of young adolescents* (pp. 49–72). Charlotte, NC: Information Age Publishing.

Humphrey, S. (2016). *Academic literacies in the middle years: A framework for enhancing teacher knowledge and student achievement.* New York: Routledge.

Knapp, P., & Watkins, M. (1994). *Context-text-grammar: Teaching the genres and grammar of school writing in infant and primary schools.* Broadway, NSW: Text productions.

Langacker, R. W. (1983). *Foundations of cognitive grammar.* Indiana: Indiana University Press.

Lantolf, J., & Thorne, S. L. (2007). Sociocultural theory and Second language learning. In B. van Patten & J. Williams (Eds). *Theories in second language acquisition.* Mahwah, NJ: Lawrence Erlbaum Associates.

Lillis, T. (2013). *The sociolinguistics of writing.* Edinburgh: Edinburgh University Press.

Martin, J. (2009). Genre and language learning: A social semiotic perspective. *Linguistics and Education, 20,* 10–21.

Martin, J. (2013). Embedded literacy: Knowledge as meaning. *Linguistics and Education, 24,* 23–37.

Martin, J., & Rose, D. (2007). *Working with discourse* (2nd ed.). London: Continuum.

Martin, J., & Rose, D. (2008). *Genre relations: Mapping culture.* London: Equinox.

Martin, J., & Rose, D. (2012). *Learning to write: Reading to learn: Genre, knowledge and pedagogy in the Sydney school.* London: Equinox Publishing.

Martin, J., & Rothery, J. (1986). Writing Project: Report. *Working Papers in Linguistics 4.* Sydney: Department of Linguistics, University of Sydney.

Maton, K. (2013). Making semantic waves: A key to cumulative knowledge-building. *Linguistics and Education, 24*(1), 8–22.

Maton, K. (2014). *Knowledge-building: Educational studies in Legitimation Code Theory.* London and NY: Routledge.

Maton, K., & Muller, J. (2007). A sociology for the transmission of knowledges. In F. Christie & J. Martin (Eds.), *Language, knowledge and pedagogy: Functional linguistic and sociological perspectives* (pp. 14–33). London: Continuum.

Mercer, N. (2000). *Words and minds: How we learn to think together*. London: Routledge.

Mercer, N., & Edwards, D. (1987). *Common knowledge: The development of understanding in the classroom*. London: Methuen and Routledge.

Olson, D. (1994). *The world on paper: The conceptual and cognitive implications of writing and reading*. Cambridge: Cambridge University Press.

→Painter, C. (2005). *Learning through language in early childhood*. London: Continuum.

Pearson, P., & Gallagher, M. (1993). The instruction of reading comprehension. *Contemporary Educational Psychology, 8*, 317–344.

Raban, B, Clark, U., & McIntyre, J. (1994). *Evaluation of the implementation of English in the national Curriculum at key stages 1, 2 and 3 (1991–1993)*. London: Schools Curriculum and Assessment Authority. http://www.educationengland.org.uk/documents/warwick/warwick1994.html.

Rothery, J. (1989). Learning about language. In R. Hasan & J. Martin (Eds.), *Language development: Learning language, learning culture* (pp. 152–198). Norwood, NJ: Ablex Publishing.

Rothery, J., & Stenglin, M. (Eds.). (1997). Exploring experience through story. In F. Christie & J. Martin (Eds.), *Genres and institutions: Social processes in the workplace and school* (pp. 231–263). London: Pinter.

Sebba, M. (2012). Orthography as social action: Scripts, spelling, power and identity. In A. Jaffe, J. Androutsopoulos, M. Sebba, & S. Johnson (Eds.), *Orthography as social action: Scripts, spelling, power and identity* (pp. 1–20). Berlin: Mouton de Gruyter.

Snell, J. (2013). Dialect, interaction and class positioning at school: From deficit to difference to repertoire. *Language and Education, 27*(2), 110–128.

→Stiggins, R. (2007). Assessment through the student's eye. *Educational Leadership, 64*(8), 22–26.

Tienson, J. (1983). Linguistic competence. *Transactions of the Nebraska Academy of Sciences and Affiliated Societies*. Paper 259. http://digitalcommons.unl.edu/tnas/259.

→Upward, C., & Davidson, G. (2011). *The history of English spelling*. Oxford: Wiley-Blackwell.

Velghe, F., & Blommaert, J. (2014). Emergent new literacies and the mobile phone: Informal languages learning, voice and identity in a South African township. In B. Geraghty & J. Conacher (Eds.), *Intercultural contact, language learning and migration* (pp. 89–111). London: Bloomsbury.

Vygotsky, L. (1962). *Thought and language*. Cambridge: MIT.

Wells, G. (1999). *Dialogic inquiry: Towards a sociocultural practice and theory of education.* Cambridge: Cambridge University Press.

Wood, C., Kemp, N., & Plester, B. (2014). *Text messaging and its impact on literacy skills: The evidence.* London: Routledge.

# 3

# Devising and Implementing Whole School Literacy across the Curriculum (LAC) strategies in the 11 to 19 Secondary School Curriculum

## Introduction

Two often cited and perceived barriers to an LBP approach to developing language and literacy in education contexts are first, the ostensible gap in many teachers' knowledge about language, which in turn is due to their own education history touched upon in Chapter 1. Second, that teachers do not have time within lessons and in an already overcrowded curriculum to add anything they perceive to be 'extra' into their existing pedagogic practices. A key challenge in relation to introducing an intervention such as LBP then, is how to overcome such barriers. Like Schleppergrell's and Humphrey's research discussed in Chapter 1, the approach I took was to locate and situate developing teachers' knowledge about language in the context of their pedagogic goals, objectives and practices.

For the last 10 years or so many urban areas of England, as elsewhere in the UK and other English L1 contexts, have experienced an unprecedented upsurge in immigration, particularly, from parts of Asia and Eastern Europe. As a result, some English regions have seen a sharp rise in the number of EAL pupils and students. Any pupil or student

© The Author(s) 2019
U. Clark, *Developing Language and Literacy in English across the Secondary School Curriculum*, https://doi.org/10.1007/978-3-319-93239-2_3

who speaks a language other than English at home falls into the EAL category. It therefore includes all those who were born in England and speak a language different from English at home as well as the newly arrived who speak no English at all. In 2013–2014, just over one million children fell into the EAL category, accounting for 16.2% of all pupils, a proportion which has more than doubled since 1997 (7.6%) and is forecast to continue to rise. It is likely, therefore, that EAL will be a key characteristic of student bodies in many schools for the foreseeable future (Strand 2015; Murphy 2015). In some schools, particularly in densely populated urban areas, EAL pupils and students thus defined can make up virtually 100% of the school population. Often, a significant number of children born in England and having attended primary school begin secondary school at age 11 with the literacy levels of seven year olds, as measured against Key Stage 1 standardised assessment tests (SATs). The sheer volume of numbers however, means that it is impractical to either withdraw pupils for small group intensive teaching or, given the diverse range of language backgrounds, implement any kind of bilingual or translanguaging programme. Consequently, ways need to be found of integrating EAL pupils' English language development as part and parcel of mainstream learning and teaching activities for all but the most newly arrived who speaks little or no English at all.

Recontextualising language and literacy for learning across the secondary curriculum under such circumstances is thus a challenge many schools in the UK are currently facing. The collapse of the NLS and FTE initiatives in 2013 also coincided with phased revisions to the National Curriculum for all subjects across all key stages and new syllabi introduced for GCSE and A Level examinations with corresponding changes to assessment. These changes included reduced assessment by coursework from 40 to 20%; introduced more assessment by examination and increased subject knowledge content. A number of appendices were also included to the curriculum for English at key stages 1 and 2, namely a *Vocabulary, grammar and punctuation* appendix, a grammar glossary and a phonics chart. Alongside curriculum and assessment reform then at key stages 4 and 5, policy documents urge secondary school teachers to use or 'build upon' the appendices, and the grammar glossary in particular, in their own teaching throughout key stages 3,

4 and 5. Such a recommendation is challenging for secondary school, teachers to effect, particularly for the large majority of them where the formal teaching of grammar did not form part of their own schooling, even for teachers of English.

In this chapter, I thus also discuss how teachers' own metalinguistic awareness is bound up with their own teacher autobiographies and experiences of their own schooling. Despite the fact that many teachers reported they could not recall having been taught any grammar and did not know the differences between different parts of speech/word classes never mind clause structures, I took as fundamental the notion that secondary school teachers are expert in the discursive practices that characterise their subject disciplines. I show ways in which teachers' implicit knowledge about language can be brought to the surface remarkably quickly when CPD activity is focused and targeted upon both in relation to their own subject programme specifications and the local context in which they teach. I also illustrate ways in which teachers from different curriculum areas/departments can be brought to work together to develop literacy across the curriculum initiatives, something which, given their nature, is far more of a challenge in secondary schools than in primary ones.

## Literacy Intervention Research Design

In order to undertake research in schools in England today, they have to be approached individually. I was able to gain access to three schools via personal contact by offering my services to the Head teachers as a CPD consultant, to develop their embryonic literacy across the curriculum initiatives. In return, I collected data from teachers for subsequent analysis, in the form of the pupil and student writing samples and individual teacher interviews in addition to the CPD sessions themselves. The writing samples comprised of pre-, during- and post-intervention texts. I faced two major challenges in introducing an LBP approach to language and literacy across the curriculum initiatives in these schools. First, there is a widespread assumption that such initiatives are the responsibility of the English department. Second, given the absence of explicit grammar teaching in the curriculum for the last 50 years or so—despite Kingman, LINC, various iterations of the national curriculum, NLS and FTE—teachers' own knowledge about language—including that of teachers of English—was either non-existent or acquired as part of learning other languages such as Latin, French or German.

Research into teacher beliefs has shown that they play an important part in influencing pedagogy, particularly in relation to contested areas of the curriculum such as that of grammar teaching. Watson (2015) shows how negative attitudes towards grammar that have been observed repeatedly in the profession relate to a general lack of confidence in linguistic subject knowledge. Her study reveals a more complex picture in relation to a perceived dichotomy between grammar and creativity. She argues that attempts to advance any kind of rhetorical and contextual approach to grammar, such as the LBP one advocated in this book, and as evident in parts of the English National Curriculum, must take into account the impact of teachers' beliefs about grammar. Giovanelli (2015), in the context of teachers teaching A Level English Language for the first time, has also researched how having to teach 'language' affected teachers' personal and professional identities. He found that despite initial feelings of anxiety and low self-confidence, they ended up with a more positive outlook.

Teachers are expert in the linguistic patterns—or register features—that characterise discursive practice—or communicative competence—of their own subjects/disciplines, by the very fact of the qualifications they have needed to acquire to become teachers. An underlying aim of my research then was how to make teachers' largely invisible discursive practices become more visible, in line with the theoretical principles of LBP outlined in Chapter 2. I identified two further major challenges in respect of reaching this goal. First, how to work with teachers in ways that would support them to explicitly engage their pupils and students with the discursive practices associated with any curriculum subject, when such practices may be very different from the everyday language they are used to using at home and in the community. Second, how to do so in ways that recognised yet did not denigrate or disparage adolescents' home and linguistic backgrounds—in other words, without compromising pupil, student and teacher identities.

Following Humphrey (2016) and Schleppegrell (2015) my research design was based upon a combination of semi-ethnographic participant observation via my role as a provider of CPD set within the paradigm of Design-Based Research (DBR). DBR is a method derived from science-based research, especially psychology (Sandoval and Bell 2004), that has been developed in the education context. DBR has evolved in recent years through the work of researchers such as Anderson and Shattuck (2012) in response to the challenge of developing a methodology of experimenting with intervention designs in situ to develop theories of learning (and teaching) that accounted for the multiple interactions of people acting in a complex social setting.

Schleppegrell (2015) has summarised the principles of a DBR in education contexts as comprising of:

- An analysis of a school's or group of schools' needs.
- Developing a theory of change that addresses the needs identified.
- The inclusion of principles of evaluation in the research design.

Like Schleppegrell and Humphrey, I sought to address the issue of how a 'grand theory' such as LBP outlined in Chapter 2 can be recontextualised into pedagogic practice in ways that tangibly support adolescents' language development in the context of subject learning through the inclusion of explicit, contextualised grammatical instruction. I thus followed the DBR iterative cycle of design, implementation and evaluation, with each cycle exploring and reflecting upon the one previously undertaken. The theory of change with which I engaged was an inductive one, based upon grounded theory (Glazer and Strauss 1967; Charmaz 2014), with discovery and interaction between myself and the participating teachers, in a spirit of open inquiry and dialogue. My position was that of linguistics expert; the teachers that of subject expert. Change was thus teacher-led, informed but not determined by, LBP method.

Three schools located in two different English cities took part in my study between 2014 and 2017, all 11–19 schools, with varying proportions of EAL pupils and students. School A, Makepeace School, was an all girls' comprehensive school in a socially deprived area where the majority of adolescents were EAL took part in an initial pilot in 2015/2016. School B, Greenford School, a mixed comprehensive in a more socially mixed area with 55% EAL and School C, Farming School, a selective all boys' school with negligible adolescents designated EAL took part in addition to School A in the larger scale project 2016/2017 (Table 3.1).

In addition to the teachers teaching the subjects listed above, in School A, Makepeace, the school librarian also wished to take part in the project, and supported the teachers of English and history through library displays and activities designed to advance reading and comprehension. In School B, Greenford, in place of teaching assistants, the school employed literacy coaches to support pupils and students in small groups of two or three, and one of these also took part in the project. The remainder of this chapter discusses the pilot phases of the project which took place in Makepeace School in 2015/2016. Chapters 4–6 includes discussion of the project at all three schools.

In terms of analysing any school's needs, account had to be taken of its demographic context. School A, Makepeace School, is situated in a densely populated area within which live people predominantly of

Table 3.1 Overview of schools, subjects and year groups

| Subject | School A, Makepeace, 11–18 girls' comprehensive | School B, Greenford, 11–18 mixed comprehensive | School C, 11–18 boys' selective |
|---|---|---|---|
| Art |  | Year 11 |  |
| Business studies |  | Year 12 |  |
| Drama |  | Year 10 |  |
| English |  |  | Years 8 and 9 |
| English literature | Year 12 | Year 10 | Years 10 and 11 |
| Geography | Year 9 |  | Years 8 and 9 |
| History | Year 12 |  |  |
| Law |  | Year 12 |  |
| Maths | Year 12 |  |  |
| MFL (French and Urdu) | Year 10 |  |  |
| RE | Year 11 |  |  |
| Science (Biology) | Year 10 |  |  |
| Sociology |  | Year 13 |  |

a Pakistani and Muslim heritage. Over 90% of the girls at the school are of Pakistani and Muslim heritage, all of whom are designated EAL. Nearly half of them are eligible for free school meals, one of the major UK indicators of social disadvantage and thus eligible for Pupil Premium, an additional sum that is added to school's budgets to support such adolescents. Consequently, whilst the community from which the school draws is located in an English city, its sense of place and belonging is constructed as much by parents' homelands as by the host city and the host country of England. This is signified by the way people dress, the food that they eat, the shops and cafes that serve the community and the linguistic exchanges between parents and administrative staff particularly at the school, many of whom are drawn from the local community and thus speak the community language. Nevertheless, despite significant socio-economic and linguistic disadvantages, in 2014 the school was rated by OFSTED as 'outstanding', mainly on the basis of its GCSE results. Despite the fact that many girls at the school start out with below average attainment, the proportion gaining five or more A* to C grades (now 9 to 5) at GCSE is above the national average.

Teachers at the school prided themselves on the work they already did in language, but it remained largely compartmentalised in different curriculum areas and thus lacked any sense of coherence and integration. For example, teachers in the humanities department, comprising history, geography and RE, had some years previously introduced a 'pause for literacy' session in all lessons, but what this 'pause' consisted of, how often it happened and how it was monitored was left to individual teachers to determine. In addition, teachers of these subjects, albeit to a greater or lesser extent, already incorporated a textual organisation tool that had formed part of the defunct NLS around the notion of IDEA (Identify, describe, evidence, analyse), sometimes manifested as PEE/L (point, evidence, explanation, link) or PEA/L (point, explanation, analysis/link). However, it became clear through discussion with the teachers that focusing upon the register features of each constituent part of textual organisation was not given explicit attention.

I began the pilot project at the school with a 90-minute CPD session held over an extended lunchtime. In this session, I outlined key LBP concepts of *register* and *genre*, accompanied by exemplars of some ways in which attention these concepts could be integrated into their teaching. I then moved on to clause-level analysis, and at this point, when I was explaining different parts of speech/word class to the group, Bruno, the teacher of English charged with leading the LBP initiative, said: 'what, so you mean we should actually use the terms nouns, adjectives, verbs/processes and so on when we're teaching?' This generated a discussion amongst the group about their own anxieties about using grammatical terms that ranged from one teacher (the biology teacher discussed further below) saying she did this all the time to others, notably the geography and RE teachers, saying they could not recall ever having been taught any grammar and would find it hard to so do. I also introduced the LTC to them as discussed in Chapter 2, which brought to the surface the concern over the change to the pacing and sequencing of lessons this would necessitate as discussed in Chapter 2. A number of the teachers voiced this concern in relation to their feeling that designing LBP informed activities would impact negatively upon pacing and sequencing, by taking time away from delivering subject content. The profile of the vast majority of the girls in the school was such that their level of subject knowledge was generally lower than average, and required a great deal of teacher input. For them to 'add onto' their existing practices was could only be undertaken if it linked directly to their existing pedagogic practices and could guarantee a positive return, measured in terms of an increase in pupil and student attainment.

Such reservations notwithstanding, the group agreed that they would attempt to incorporate activities informed by LBP as far as they were so able to do with one of the classes they currently taught. Their motivation for participation lay in the significant changes to public examinations at GCSE and A Level that had (a) shifted assessment away from coursework to examination and (b) in many cases doubled the marks and thus the length pupils and students were required to write. The session then moved on to a discussion of the ways in which teachers could incorporate any aspect of what I had introduced to them into their teaching. Changes to assessment at GCSE and A Level at 16+ and 18+ as outlined above meant that the teachers were in the process of revising their lesson plans/schemes of work to take account of them. In the main these changes around assessment by examination rather than coursework in A Level English Literature and, in subjects more routinely assessed by examination such as GCSE science ones, more marks being awarded per question which meant writing at greater length. The participating teachers thus chose to incorporate LBP strategies introduced to them mainly with the classes they taught in the 14–18 age range, rather than with the younger, Key Stage 3 pupils aged 11–14. I also offered to provide individual email support as needed, taken up by the teachers of English and geography.

All of them agreed that they would trial activities that focused upon pupils' and students' writing in relation to its textual organisation, as this was something they all agreed was something with which their students and pupils struggled. I then explained the principles of evaluation associated with the project, which were, that over the course of a half term in 2016, as follows:

**Project Design**

- Teachers identified one class from any key stage with whom an LBP-based activity would be trialled and if possible, identified a parallel control class;
- The class (or classes) undertook a written task individually in advance of the LBP activity to act as a control measure, either as an end summative piece of the sequence of lessons preceding the LBP intervention or at the start as a formative one;
- Lessons and associated resources were planned to introduce explicit attention to literacy in the context of specific subject teaching, including the use of mentor texts, group work, and paying attention to the phases of the LTC described in Chapter 2;
- Teachers undertook a sequence of lessons in which LBP was introduced;
- A second individually written task was undertaken at the end of the sequence of lessons;
- I as researcher analysed the pupils' and students' written tasks in order to identify subject specific patterns of register and genre/text type.
- I as researcher interviewed the teachers involved about their experiences.

I held a second one-hour CPD session some two months after the first, where those who had taught their classes as outlined above shared their experiences with me and the rest of the group for the first time. Those who had already begun to incorporate aspects of LBP into their teaching reported very positive experiences, with the history teacher, who had trialled the intervention with her A level Year 12 class, reporting that her class had made significant improvement between their first written task and the second, with one student gaining a grade A where previously she had obtained a grade E. Focussing upon deconstructing assessment questions and unpicking the structure of source material with her students had made the teacher that the student had not grasped how to integrate source material into her written essay on her first attempt. Once, this had been explicitly worked upon, she reported that all her students' marks had improved overall. Chapter 5 discusses this case study in more detail. A final one-hour session was then held to preliminarily evaluate the project as a whole, where all agreed that the project had been a success, particularly in relation to affecting changes to their pedagogic practice as discussed in the remainder of this chapter and the three that follow. Between the second- and third-group CPD sessions, I also held interviews with each teacher individually to obtain a sense of their biographies and subject identities as teachers; their experience of integrating aspects of LBP into their pedagogic practice and how that practice had changed subsequently. The LBP pilot project was also disseminated to the staff as a whole through two whole school CPD days, held in March and July of 2016. At the second of these, teachers taking part in the project demonstrated an LBP approach in action.

In 2016/2017, both Makepeace and Greenford schools took part in the project in the context of Joint Practice Development (JPD). Unless an organised conduit of dissemination exists, cross-curricular initiatives such as LBP under a standard CPD model impact upon individual teachers across departments but do not extend to all other subject area/departmental/faculty colleagues. One such conduit is reconfiguring CPD in schools to that of JPD. The idea of JPD is similar to that of action research, and centres upon teachers as researchers, working together on research lessons as part of a network. Teachers in any one network are drawn from a number of schools, with the aim of developing lessons that innovate new practices in order to raise standards of learning, teaching and assessment. Fielding et al. (2005) define JPD as '…learning new ways of working through mutual engagement that opens up and shares practices with others'.

Traditional approaches to CPD are largely based on the transferring knowledge or 'best practices' from an expert presenter to his or her audience, which research has shown to be rarely effective. By contrast, JPD is a process by which individuals, schools or other organisations learn from one another. It has three key characteristics. It

- involves interaction and mutual development related to practice
- recognises that each partner in the interaction has something to offer and, as such, is based on the assumption of mutually beneficial learning
- is research-informed, often involving collaborative enquiry.

Powerful professional learning: a school leader's guide to joint practice development www.gov.uk/government/uploads/system/uploads/attachment_data/file/329717/powerful-professional-learning-a-school-leaders-guide-to-joint-practice-development.pdf, accessed 28th February 2018.

Although originally intended for networks across schools, JPD has evolved to create networks within schools. Schools A and B had, since 2016/2017, recontextualised their CPD activities as JPD, and the LBP initiative was thus subsumed as part of a whole school JPD initiative. JPD involves teachers from different curriculum areas/subjects working together on a particular theme divided into groups of three, including the teachers observing one another teach. Developing LBP informed LLAC in the secondary context then, can be undertaken in contexts where teachers work together in cross-curricular groups as with a focus upon improving pupils' and students' learning and as part of whole-school JPD initiatives.

The remainder of this chapter provides vignettes of teachers integrating LBP informed language and literacy activities into their classroom practice. Specifically, at each of the key stages 3, 4 and 5 in geography, biology and English, respectively, as a precursory overview to the subject centred discussion in Chapters 4–6.

## Key Stage 3 Geography

Mary, the geography teacher at Makepeace School, chose to take part in the project since she reported that she is always keen to explore new ways of developing and refreshing her teaching. She enjoyed taking part in CPD activities she could then go on to introduce with her class. She had been a teacher for 10 years, the last five of which had been at the school and she was second in the department of Humanities to which geography belonged. She had attended a comprehensive school and could not recall ever having been taught grammar. She said that the pupils at Makepeace were characterised by below average literacy levels in general, coupled with very little general knowledge of the world at large. She had taken part in the first CPD session that had introduced an LBP approach because of the change in assessment requirements that meant pupils at Key Stage 4 had to undertake pieces of extended writing, where previously the requirement had centred upon short answer questions. She was thus conscious of the fact that she needed to pay more attention to developing her pupils' control over their written expression in response to such changes.

She reported that she had never been taught the literacy aspects of her subject as part of her teacher education, was not particularly confident of her own knowledge of grammar and linguistic terminology given that she could not recall ever having been taught grammar. Nevertheless, she was attracted to an LBP approach because she believed it could develop her abilities to teach her pupils how to develop control over their written expression, particularly in relation to EAL pupils who were developing language and literacy in English alongside curriculum knowledge. As preparation for Key Stage 4, she decided to incorporate elements of LBP with a Year 9 (13- to 14-year old, end of Key Stage 3) middle to low ability class of 28 pupils on the topic of *Uneven world development: for richer, for poorer.* The reading age of this group was lower than average and ranged from between eight years seven months to 16 years 10 months, with the majority falling between 10 and 11 years. All pupils were designated EAL, from predominantly Pakistani backgrounds (22) with four Somalians and two Bangladeshi. 16 of the

28 pupils (45%) came from low socioeconomic backgrounds. In terms of genre, she decided to focus upon that of an informative magazine article, since this is what pupils are currently required to write for assessment. In terms of register, she chose to focus upon the use of conjunctions and nominalisation. This was because her experience had shown her that linking ideas across a text and using more abstract language of the kind expressed through nominalisation were key weaknesses in her pupils' writing.

The Humanities department had focused their development of the genre in relation to IDEA as described above. As identified by Humphrey (1996), the *tenor* (see Chapter 2) of written texts in geography (the relationship established between the writer and the reader) is generally impersonal, and the technicality of the *field* itself is also expressed in ways that create an impersonal, objective relationship. Textbooks and course materials are written in an authoritative, 'expert' to learner way, whilst texts written by pupils and students are generally written for teachers or examiners, as a learner to 'expert'. In both cases, the relationship is unequal, and there is no reason to establish a personal relationship with the reader unlike say, in writing a diary entry or a story. However, writing tasks in humanities subjects such as geography and history make use of genres through which to write explanations such as a magazine article, as in the activity described below.

An important aspect of *tenor* is the way writers can use language to persuade or 'position' their readers in particular ways. For example, readers can be positioned to see an environmental issue from a particular point of view, as in the topic under discussion here. In relation to *mode*, whilst geography makes great use of direct observations such as visual images and oral explanations to accompany writing, learning to handle the written mode becomes increasingly important for pupils as they progress through secondary school. Mary was thus aware that she needed to be much more explicit in relation to teaching her pupils aspects of *tenor* and *mode*.

Mary taught the topic content in her usual way over eight 50-minute lessons. She then introduced the assessment and gave out the task sheet:

*Year 9 Assessment: For Richer, For Poorer*

*Your task is to produce a **magazine article** about **uneven world development**. Below shows what you must include in your article, which will then be assessed according to the criteria on the back of the sheet.*

*Remember, each paragraph of your article must use the IDEA structure that your teacher will show you.*

*You must use graphs, tables, diagrams and/or maps to support your points. You will also need to use the subheadings below that are in bold in your article.*

*A reminder that 'copy and paste' will get zero marks as this is plagiarism.*

In addition, and as a departure from her usual practice, she devised a mark sheet to accompany the task sheet, which also provided a structure for writing an article:

**Title of the article: For Richer, For Poorer.**
**Assessment**
**Introduction:**
Define the key terms that are important in the article. Start by defining 'uneven development'. You may want to define words such as *poverty, development gap* and *aid*. Use your keyword sheet to help you to identify the most important items.

**What is uneven development?**
In this paragraph, you must explain what uneven development is by using evidence. For example, you might have a map which shows where some of the world's poorest and richest places are. You then write your IDEA paragraph using this evidence.

**Why does uneven development exist today?**
You need to explain the reasons why some countries are in poverty. You can use particular countries to focus on (in the lesson we looked at Haiti, Ethiopia, Zimbabwe and Afghanistan for example). Consider factors such as civil war.

**What needs to be done to reduce the development gap?**
You need to explain the different types of aid and what effective ad is. You could include an example of effective aid and explain why you think it works.

**Conclusion:**
Here, you need to identify what the main points of your article are and explain how you think you are connected to this issue of uneven development. Yu may also want to consider what you think should be done about the development gap and how it may change in future.

Mary also reminded the pupils that the assessment criteria for the task were written in relation to IDEA:

- IDENTIFIED what development and uneven development means. You have identified some ideas why uneven development exists and you identify what can be done about it.
- DESCRIBED using evidence to show what development and undevelopment means. You describe where is undeveloped and the reasons why. You describe what can be done to reduce poverty.
- EXPLAINED and given reasons why places are undeveloped. You explain causes and effects. You explain the solutions using specific evidence.
- ANALYSED which factors are more significant in causing unequal development. You explain the solutions and evaluate strengths and weaknesses.

At Key Stage 3, learning in geography is characterised by developing specialised understandings or ways of classifying and categorising the world. Places are classified according to their biophysical and built environments, as this example topic illustrates. Variations and human modifications to places and the causes and effects of those modifications are typical categories of investigation. Thus, in subjects like geography, pupils are moving from concrete to abstract understandings and from specific to generalised understandings where abstract and generalised phenomena contrast with the concrete and specific physical phenomena that can be observed. Whilst particular places are always of interest to a geographer, by Key Stage 3 pupils are no longer concerned with simply describing specific features, but are also required to explain generalised principles and hypotheses about the future using specific events and other phenomena as evidence or examples. Pupils must, therefore, be able to move backwards and forwards between specific and general knowledge and between different kinds of knowledge. Thus, in the assessment task given to the pupils, the first task they are asked to undertake is to explain the abstract phenomena expressed through nominalisation of *uneven development*. Secondly, they are then required to move between different parts of the world to evidence the identified phenomenon as examples. Third, they are asked to explain contemporary manifestations of the phenomenon based upon the examples given, including any other factors to be taken into consideration such as in this case, civil war, as to why the phenomenon currently exists. Finally, they are asked to generate a hypothesis about the future.

In preparation for her pupils' writing task, Mary went through the different stages of IDEA and wrote phrases on the board that might help the pupils in their written expression. They then began the assessment in class individually and completed it at home, handed in two weeks later, after a one week half term holiday. Mary marked the first paragraph of each individual piece of work in detail in relation to both content and literacy, something she had never done before. She gave back the pupils' their marked work, and took time to go round and to supplement the individual written feedback with individual oral feedback.

At the introductory LBP session, I had introduced the teachers to the concept of *PEEL: Point, evidence, elaboration, linking back* as a possible organisational principle for extended pieces of writing. Mary remembered using a PEE structure as part of her own GCSE geography fifteen years previously, and decided to replace IDEA with PEEL, as it seemed to her to better reflect the ways in which geographic knowledge is expressed. She then talked the pupils through the feedback she gave them of their first attempt at writing the article. She identified aspects she wished them to include in their second draft of the assessment, only this time, the writing took the form of an explanation as written for assessment purposes, not a magazine article. This change of genre meant that the tenor of the writing in which pupils wrote was altered to become more academic. To help prepare her pupils for this change in tenor, she asked her class:

- To identify how we can *structure* our answers in a more formal way using *nominalisation*.
- To identify 3 *explaining conjunctions* to use in our own assessment.
- To practice using the PEEL structure by working in pairs to produce a model answer.

The Humanities department had developed a chart listing different categories of conjunctions, comprising single words and phrases that pupils would find useful. Mary asked the pupils to identify three that they would use when they explained each point they made at the front of their exercise books, and to ensure they included them in all future work. She then went on to give an explanation of nominalisation, illustrated through an example:

**Every day language**
*Uneven development is unfairer between people and places but not just about how much money you have and if you are in poverty and if a country is develop. It's about if someone educates you and employs you.*

**Academic language**
*Development can be measured in various ways—including economic and human developments. Being developed is about how things change and how their lives change. I am going to explain this in my article which is an assessment.*

First, she asked her pupils to give alternatives to complete the sentence: *Uneven development is…* such as *Uneven development refers to the ways in which resources and wealth are distributed across different parts of the world.*

She also drew their attention to a register feature common to geography, which is the use of nominalisations as the noun group with which sentences often begin: **Uneven development** *is…,* **Development** *can be measured in various ways……* She advised them not to use the pronoun *I* and the active voice when writing for the purposes of assessment in geography. Finally, she explained PEEL as follows:

- Point—your topic sentence
- Examples— use statistics, place names, maps etc.

- Explain—use your explaining connectives
- Link—go back to the question/topic sentence.

The pupils then wrote their assessment piece for a second time. In marking these, Mary realised that she had pitched her explanation of nominalisation at a level that was too advanced for her pupils to grasp and had not scaffolded the explanations sufficiently. She identified that she had not provided enough exemplary activities to consolidate her pupils' learning of this concept. Even so, she felt that taking the time to draft written responses and providing mentor paragraphs had a positive impact upon her pupils' written expression overall, and were aspects of the LBP that she would incorporate into her classroom practice from now on. These included giving more time in class to explaining register features of the writing she asked her pupils to do, particularly in relation to concepts such as nominalisation. She was also encouraged to so because in terms of pupil progress between the first and second attempts, the majority improved their mark overall.

For Mary, marking two versions of the same assessment had been a useful exercise for her. She planned to make more use of joint construction in class and the setting of shorter writing tasks for formative purposes that led up to writing a final piece for assessment. Despite the set back she had experienced, Mary was sufficiently convinced of the central importance of nominalisation as a key aspect of developing her pupils' written expression in geography and has gone on to plan giving more time to explanation of nominalisation as part of the next topic the pupils were to study on the geography of disease, discussed further in Chapter 5. Grasping the concept of nominalisation also led Mary to understand the related linguistic concepts of noun and verb.

## Key Stage 4 Biology

Denise, the biology teacher, chose to take part in the project because of changes to examinations at GCSE that required pupils to write extended responses. She had observed that although pupils learnt key vocabulary, they did not have the writing skills needed to incorporate it into coherent written responses to questions. The class with whom she chose to pilot an LBP approach was comprised of 27 girls, 16 of whom were by ethnicity Pakistani, seven Somalian, one Arab, one Afro Caribbean, one other Asian and one not known. They were the second from top class in Year 10, following a newly revised GCSE syllabus.

Coincidentally, a week before the first LBP CPD session, she told me that she had asked her class to find a scientific way of explaining using oxygen. One student replied: to *respirate*. Denise responded by telling the pupil that the term needed was *respire*. The pupil's insistence on understanding the difference between the two terms led Denise to a discussion of nominalisation processes, although she was unaware at the time that this was what she was doing. She wrote up on the board a list of verbs and their corresponding nominalisations, such as *move/ movement; respire/respiration* and *ventilate/ventilation*. Denise had been educated in the private sector and had studied Latin as part of her own schooling and thus she was very familiar with traditional grammatical categories and morphological aspects such as *prefix, suffix* and the fact that much vocabulary in biology is derived from Latin. In explaining the term *intravascular*, for example, she was able to point out to her class that the word was a compound of *intra* meaning *inside* and *vascular* meaning a *vessel*, which in biology, is the vein. She also routinely explained other vocabulary differences that came from Latin such as singular and plural terms, for example, *stomatum* and *stoma*, with the aim of providing the pupils with strategies to decode unfamiliar words. Consequently, her classes were well used to language interventions as part of lesson content.

In the half term before the Christmas break, she had planned to go over one practice examination question every week in preparation for the mock GCSE examination pupils were going to take in January, focusing upon the topic of *organisms and energy*. The examination required pupils to write extended answers to questions that gained a total of six marks for the first time. She told me that her pupils found the blank space underneath the question that had to be filled in very difficult to complete and off-putting. The need to answer such questions in the examination provided Denise with the opportunity for her to scaffold her pupils' writing in relation to such examination questions through incorporating the modelling, deconstruction and joint construction steps or phases of the LTC into her teaching.

She gave the class the following question to answer on their own as a pre-test piece of writing, undertaken in examination conditions. A diagram showing a magnified section through a leaf was followed by the question:

*Explain how leaves are adapted for gas exchange.*

Denise incorporated phases 2 and 3 of the LTC as outlined in Chapter 2. She reported that this felt like, in her words, 'taking time out'. However, she was encouraged by her pupils' responses to the explicit focus upon language. She saw how beneficial 'taking time out' was in relation to paying explicit attention to the language of cause and effect required by answers to questions in relation to both genre and register features of scientific explanations. Deconstructing, modelling and joint construction activities had helped her pupils to develop and exercise more control over their written expression.

In terms of developing her students' writing, Denise reported an overall improvement in their responses in relation to the post-test answer, written two weeks after the first. For the pre-test, the majority of marks had clustered around three out of six (50%) or four out of six (25%), with the remainder spread between zero, one, two, five and six. In the post-test, the number of pupils achieving between four and six marks out of six rose from 20 to 45%. For example, the following answer had received a mark of three on the pre-test:

> *Gas exchange is when the plants release the gas that they need which is oxygen, and exchange for the gas that they do which carbon dioxide.* (**one mark awarded**). *The leaves are adapted for gas exchange because the stomata allows the gas exchange to take place* (**one mark awarded**). *The stomata are the pores in the leaves which absorb the $CO_2$ from the atmosphere and release the $O_2$* (**one mark awarded**).

In this answer, the pupil began with explaining the process of gas exchange rather than how leaves are adapted for it. This is followed by explaining how leaves are adapted for gas exchange by way of stomata, followed by an explanation of stomata.

On the post-test, the same pupil achieved five marks:

*The leaves are adapted for gas exchange through air spaces* **(one mark awarded)**. *The stomata that lays under the surface allows gas to pass through. Leaves are thin and flat allowing the larger surface area to absorb gas and light energy* **(one mark awarded)**. *The air spaces allow gases such as water vapour to circulate within the leaf* **(one mark awarded)**. *Also, oxygen, vapour and CO2 diffuse in the leaf one mark awarded). And when water vapour evaporates from stomata (the leaf's pores) this is transpiration* **(one mark awarded)**

In this answer, the pupil begins with a hypertheme or topic sentence, summarising the process of exchange. She then goes on to provide the explanations that answer the question, deleting her second sentence in order to explain more clearly what it is about the property of leaves that enables gas exchange to take place before moving on to explain the gas exchange itself and ending with an explanation of the nominalised transpiration. For Denise, what had initially felt like 'taking time out' was, in fact, helping her pupils to write the kinds of answers required of them for this most challenging aspect of the new GCSE examination. She also found that structuring her teaching this way made for more dialogic talk to take place between the pupils when working in groups and between herself and her pupils both as a whole class and when talking to them individually or in groups.

In the next lesson, Denise gave the pupils another practice question:

*Explain why heart rate and breathing rate increase during exercise.*

Together with the class, she deconstructed the wording of the question. This included including identifying the verb/process *explain* (which is a verbal one) followed by *why* which invites discussion of *cause* and *effect: increased heart and breathing rates* as a consequence or effect of *exercise*. Discussion ensued about the genre of the writing, an *explanation*, nominalised from *explain*, and what kinds of information the pupils would include in their answer that qualified as explanations. Although worded as one question, she also explained to the class that actually they were being asked to explain two processes: *heart rates* and *breathing rates*.

Three marks, therefore, were apportioned to the explanation of each of the two rates given in logical sequence. It also followed that equal attention would need to be paid to explaining the effect of exercise on the two rates.

Denise reported that she would have normally prepared her class to answer a practice question in such a way, although would not have drawn as much explicit attention to the verbs/processes contained within the question. Also, as a departure from her previous practice, Denise gave her class the following model answer to the question she had written herself:

> *Heart rate increases during exercise because more blood is needed around the body. Heart rate is a measure of how often the heart pumps blood per minute. During exercise muscles contract more quickly and so require more oxygen to produce energy during aerobic respiration. The blood supplies the oxygen to the muscle cells and needs to do so more quickly as there is greater demand. When the oxygen gets into the cell, it diffuses out of the blood and into the cell during gas exchange and carbon dioxide (being produced in the cell) diffuses into the blood. The body needs to get rid of the carbon dioxide quickly, so the blood has to be sent back to the lungs quickly, so that we can get rid of the carbon dioxide.*
>
> *The breathing rate increases during exercise because oxygen is needed for respiration into muscle cells as the muscles contract. Breathing rate is the number of breaths you take per minute. During exercise you would have to inhale and exhale more frequently to get oxygen into the body and get rid of carbon dioxide more quickly. This causes the rate of gas exchange to increase. This will reduce the build-up of lactic acid in the muscles.*

In groups, the class was asked to discuss any unfamiliar vocabulary and items, chief of which were *aerobic respiration* and *diffuses*. Denise then explained that she had used a three part structure in writing the answer to the question to help her organise her answer in a logical sequence. This was: *hypertheme (sometimes called a macrotheme or topic sentence); definition* and *explanation*. The notion of a hypertheme or topic sentence is a higher level theme (see Chapter 2) than that found in individual clauses. This is because its relation to the text that follows is like the relation of a clause theme to the remainder of the clause. In both cases,

Theme provides an orientation of what is to come. A hypertheme is predictive of forthcoming themes in that it establishes expectations of how the text will unfold. Thus, in terms of the first sentence its theme and rheme structure is:

> *Heart rate // increases during exercise*
> theme rheme
> *(because) more blood // is needed around the body*
> theme rheme

Its position as a first sentence though acts as a hypertheme that sets up what is to be explained in the remainder of the text.

Denise then gave out two tables for her students to complete, in order to locate the structure of the two parts of her answer (Table 3.2).

Following this, Denise explained to the whole class that the sentences which detail the explanation are organised *sequentially in time* in that they happen one after the other and that they are also *causal*: that is, one thing leads to another. She then asked the class in groups to identify the words and phrases that signalled *cause* and *effect* by underlining them, as follows:

> *Heart rate increases during exercise <u>because</u> more blood is needed around the body. Heart rate is a measure of how often the heart pumps blood per minute. When you're exercising your muscles <u>are contracting more quickly</u> and so <u>require more oxygen</u> to produce energy during aerobic respiration. The blood <u>supplies</u> the oxygen to the muscle cells and <u>needs to do so more quickly</u> as there is greater demand. When the oxygen gets into the cell, <u>it diffuses out</u> of the blood and <u>into</u> the cell during gas exchange and carbon dioxide (being produced in the cell) <u>diffuses</u> into the blood. The body needs <u>to get rid of</u> the*

**Table 3.2** Three-part answer structure for science

| | |
|---|---|
| (a) | |
| Hypertheme (topic sentence) | Sentence 1 |
| Definition: what heart rate is | Sentence 2 |
| Explanation: how it works | Sentences 3–5 |
| (b) | |
| Hypertheme (topic sentence) | Sentence 1 |
| Definition: what breathing rate is | Sentence 2 |
| Explanation: how it works | Sentences 3 and 4 |

*carbon dioxide quickly, so the blood has to be <u>sent back</u> to the lungs quickly, so that <u>we can get rid of</u> the carbon dioxide.*

*The breathing rate increases during exercise because oxygen is needed for respiration into muscle cells as the muscles contract. Breathing rate is the number of breaths you take per minute. <u>During</u> exercise you would have to <u>inhale and exhale more frequently</u> to get oxygen into the body and <u>get rid of</u> carbon dioxide more quickly. <u>This causes</u> the rate of gas exchange to <u>increase.</u> This <u>will reduce</u> the <u>build-up</u> of lactic acid in the muscles.*

Finally, the class wrote their own answers to the question as a group activity. Denise had found that scaffolding answers in preparation for the examination in the way that she did encouraged her pupils to write more extensive answers to their questions than they might otherwise have done. As she said: 'I was able to build up the scaffold in ways that could be taken down so they (the pupils) could write the answers for themselves'. Denise, and other members of her department, one of which is discussed further in Chapter 6, have since gone on to integrate LBP across all of their teaching.

## Key Stage 5 English

Bruno, whose parents are both Italian but was himself born in England, was the English teacher who took part in the project. He had a degree in English Literature, an MA in Shakespeare Studies and a PGCE, had been teaching for 14 years, of which the last two had been as an education consultant. This was his first year at Makepeace School where he was responsible for all CPD activity at the school. Because he had to introduce a new syllabus for A level in 2015/2016, he chose his Year 12 class (16- to 17-year-olds) to take part in the project. One of the challenges Bruno faced in teaching his students was their lack of cultural knowledge in regard to Shakespeare's plays, not only in relation to their historical framing and lack of understanding of literary genres in general but any kind of wider general knowledge in relation to English cultural heritage. This places students from predominantly low-income EAL backgrounds such as the ones in Bruno's class at an immediate disadvantage in that their *knower code* as explained in Chapter 2 is underdeveloped for their stage of schooling. The example of a knower code in English literature is that pupils and students are learning, through the literary texts they read, talk and write about in school, a shared set of cultural understandings about life and human behavior that are valued in English society that may not be supplemented by any other readings of English literary texts outside of school. Teaching English literature in the context of Makepeace, meant that Bruno had to be more explicit about articulating the cultural understandings and values exemplified through the literary texts he taught, in this case, the play studied by the class, which was *Hamlet* by William Shakespeare.

Like the geography and biology teachers, he had attended the initial two-hour CPD session that had introduced LBP. He chose to work with his Year 12 class during the latter part of the Autumn term 2015 and into the first half of the Spring term 2016. The Autumn term acts as a transitional one from Key Stage 4 to Key Stage 5 in the UK context, and the concomitant move from the academic level of study expected at GCSE to that expected of A Level. Teachers normally teach the same class throughout the two years of study, and the term is also transitional in relation to teacher and students establishing pedagogic practices and personal relationships.

Christie (2016) in her study of the development of pupils' writing in early to late adolescence in relation to the study of English Literature, has identified the ways in which pupils' and students' written responses to literature are organized in relation to the expression of attitudes and meanings and the development of a knower code. Attention is paid in the first instance to contextual details of character, plot and the temporal and physical background against which events are played out. This is followed by moving onto the construction of abstract generalisations about life. As Christie (2016: 171) points out: 'Mastery of the code requires firstly, an ability to read and interpret the literary piece, and secondly, an ability to create a response to the text, by moving between reference to the literary piece and declarations of what that piece 'shows' and 'reveals'.

Christie has identified how in early adolescence, the texts pupils' write is largely congruent, albeit with reference to abstract ideas such as 'friendship', 'love' and 'racism'. The developmental trajectory here is from *the immediate contextual detail* to *what 'we learn'*. By mid-adolescence, successful writing is characterized by moving between two fields, that of literary critique and interpretation interwoven with details from incidents in the text being studied. The former field becoming increasingly foregrounded and the use of *grammatical metaphor* also increases. In literary studies, the term *metaphor* means the substitution of a word or phrase for a non-synonymous word or phrase, so that attributes of the new word are taken as referring to the original. For example, *Juliet is the sun.* In grammatical metaphor, meaning is construed in a different way through different grammatical construction. The developmental trajectory here is *from reflection on events* to *what we 'we learn'* through to *what is shown.* By late adolescence successful writing becomes dense and grammatically metaphorical.

The kinds of questions asked at this stage establish the abstraction around which an essay is to be written. Abstraction is thus foregrounded with reference to the text serving to exemplify the broad generalizations made. The developmental trajectory here is *from assertion of principle, to exemplification of the principle* through to *a final statement of principle.* Christie's framework for analysis of students' writing in late adolescence is applied to the texts written by Bruno's students in the examples given below.

The text Bruno's class was studying was *Hamlet* by William Shakespeare, written at the turn of the seventeenth century. As a literary text, the play is far removed from many of his students' reading experiences, regardless of whether or not English is an L1 or L2, and poses specific challenges for teachers. Bruno's class was comprised of 100% EAL students, all of whom were of Pakistani heritage. Prior to taking part in the project, Bruno had structured his teaching around phases 1 and 4 of the LTC, with time in class devoted to discussing and understanding both the language and the content of the play followed by writing activities the students would then write individually mainly outside of class time for the purposes of both formative and summative assessment. For the first half of the term, Bruno had focused as usual upon a close reading of the play and taking the students through the unfamiliar Shakepearean language. Bruno's teaching of the contextual and linguistic details of the play was interwoven with identifying its wider themes in relation to the cultural values they displayed or revealed. Homework activities for the first half term thus centred upon reading and learning to understand what the play itself was about. Much of this learning and teaching took place as whole class activity in an atmosphere of dialogic talk as discussed in Chapter 3.

The students first written task focused upon the opening scene of the play, with the title:

*Discuss the presentation of Claudius in Act 1 Scene 2 lines 1–50 of Shakespeare's play Hamlet.*

Students undertook this piece of writing independently as a homework task, with no discussion or scaffolding activities undertaken in class to support the kinds of structure a writing task of this kind entails. As discussed in Chapter 3, The English teachers at the school felt that they already had an explicit focus upon the teaching of grammar. However, this focus was provided through feedback on lexical and grammatical features that was separate from the writing process itself, and applied to completed pieces of written work. Thus, whilst attention to spelling, grammar and some discursive aspects of writing can be said to have been taught in the context of students' writing, it was undertaken solely as part of the assessment process and underpinned by the 'grammar as error correction' paradigm. This attention then came as part of the criterial rules of pedagogic practice, rather than as part of rules of sequencing and pacing that characterize cumulative knowledge building (see Chapter 2). No opportunities were given for discussing the writing process itself through discussion of features of genre and register and no opportunity was provided in class to model, deconstruct and jointly construct written drafts.

In line with the school's assessment policy and practices, Bruno had developed a method of peer assessment for his students' essays. Once the essays had been written individually they were then peer assessed in class in relation to criteria given on an assessment grid (Table 3.3).

**Table 3.3** Assessment grid

| Target | Satisfactory | Achieved |
|---|---|---|
| Spelling | | |
| Key terms | | |
| Punctuation | | |
| Sentence structure | | |
| Syntax (word order) | | |
| C's main clause | | |
| C's subordinate clause | | |
| How Claudius placates all sides | | |
| Use of oxymorons | | |
| How Claudius marginalizes Hamlet | | |

Following peer assessment, Bruno then marked the essays himself. The assessment grid combined a reference to register features of language use with features that were specific to the essay question itself, which the example above illustrates. The focus on the developing students' writing was thus through the iterative cycle of individual writing together with summative peer and teacher assessment on the written piece that also doubled as formative feedback. The assumption underpinning this approach is that students would assimilate and learn from the feedback given and incorporate it into their next written piece. As with most teachers, Bruno had undertaken a 'practice makes perfect' process approach, whereby students produce written work that is given feedback as part of the assessment, with the assumption made that students would take on board the feedback given and show improvement in subsequent pieces of writing without any further support.

Bruno had engaged positively with the two-hour CPD session I had led that had introduced the teachers to both an LBP approach and the design of the research itself. However, although keen to take part, initially he was reluctant to engage with phases 2 and 3 of the LTC, as he admitted that he thought that he would find this 'too boring'. As a teacher, Bruno showed himself to be very goal focused and oriented, concerned much more with the writing tasks his students were required to undertake as product, and not so much with unpacking and making explicit the discursive demands of the register and genre in which the students were required to write and through which they demonstrated their knowledge and understanding.

I had asked the teachers to write their own mentor texts for use with their classes, but Bruno chose instead an essay that had been awarded a top A grade written by one of his previous cohorts of students on the same topic. He gave out copies of this essay to his class, stressing to the students that the one who had written the essay was not any cleverer than they themselves were, but had achieved an A through the ways in which she had expressed her knowledge through her writing. Bruno was aware of the need with his students to balance teaching the demanding conceptual thinking required for understanding the text, with improving the quality of written expression required for higher A Level grades. In other words, aware of needing to make more explicit the move from everyday language to the academic language required to achieve good A level grades. His students had shown through class discussion that they were quick to grasp conceptual thinking and able to express such thinking through their discussion in class, but the quality of their discussion did not translate into that of their written expression.

Bruno had spent time in class explaining contextual background relevant to the play, first of all by talking generally about the conventions associated with Renaissance tragedy, their Ancient Greek antecedents, the three-part structure of tragedy that he compared to the structure of a musical symphony and how that structure is also echoed and used within scenes of the play. He spent time elaborating the themes of the play, particularly discussing the role of women in western society; the notion of patriarchy; the fact that the play is an example of a patriarchal society which in western societies is viewed negatively in attitudinal terms. In addition, he introduced his students to the ways in which the play could link to the work of philosophers such as Hegel and Nietsche that give contradictory views about human nature. and drew upon contemporary literary criticism. He included these latter aspects in his teaching, because it has been his experience that it was these philosophical and literary critical considerations that distinguished assessment grades at the upper end of the scale.

The students' essays at first attempt showed that whilst many of them demonstrated a high degree of conceptual understanding, their written expression of it was in the main undeveloped and unfocused with many inaccuracies in written expression that consequently led to a depression of their marks. Part of Bruno's embracing of an LBP approach was, in a departure to his usual practice, to write key vocabulary and phrases on the board accompanied by explanations, that the students wrote down and were subsequently expected to use in their essays. For Bruno, the value he saw in structuring his teaching around an LBP approach was in paying more attention in class to the development of the students' writing than he had done previously, in order to close the gap between their grasp of concepts demonstrated in discussion and in written expression.

After the students' first essay had been both peer and teacher assessed, Bruno would have normally moved on to discussing the next section of the play and setting the next writing task. Instead, he chose to draw upon LBP by producing a group diagnostic of the students' writing, pinpointing general weaknesses students should work on in their future attempts. Bruno then gave out to the students the model A grade essay again, and asked them in groups to compare it with their own, specifically identifying the register features that had warranted the A grade by first picking out vocabulary, phrases and clauses and encouraging the students to, in his words, 'plagiarise' them or, as used by another teacher put it, to 'burglar bag' them. Bruno then asked the students to write a second draft of their original essay, taking into account the feedback they had been given and incorporating what they had learnt from their deconstruction of the mentor text. A time period of a week had elapsed between writing the first draft and the second draft. In all cases, the students' grades improved, with one girl who had scored an E grade on her first attempt achieving an A grade for her second, and all other essays previously scoring an E grade showing improvement.

When I first interviewed Bruno, it was after the students had been given back their second draft of the essay and after 'dipping his toe into the water of LBP' in Bruno's words, he was keen to develop the approach further. He reported that he had thought going through the mentor text and identifying key phrases and wordings would have been sufficient to significantly improve all students' written performance and had been disappointed that it had not. At the same time, the time he had taken to focus upon developing his students' writing had led to a demonstrable improvement, and made him realize that they appreciated a more direct approach to instruction than he had taken previously. He, thus decided to change his practice from focusing upon language features that an essay in English Literature demanded as part of the assessment to integrating discussion of them as part of lesson content itself. What had prevented him from doing this previously, he reported, had been a twofold concern. He was concerned firstly as to how to go about jointly constructed or guided writing in ways that allowed the girls to write their own words and not ventriloquize his. Second, he had wanted to avoid teaching pupils 'how to write the essay' as he wanted them to learn to do this for themselves through the iterative process described above. However, through engaging with LBP in the way described above, Bruno had come to acknowledge and realize the limitations of such a process-based approach and that his students benefited from a more scaffolded approach in relation to developing their literacy in writing.

Bruno thus decided to incorporate phases two and three of the LTC into his teaching for the first time as part of mainstream classroom activity for the second piece of written work required: *How does Shakespeare develop the presentation of women in society in Act 1 Scene 3 of the play Hamlet?* The first 25 minutes of the class was spent discussing the scene and how women were presented in the play, including discussions of judgement and value. Bruno explained to the girls in his class that the function or purpose of the opening paragraph of their essays is to introduce the notions or ideas that the rest of the essay will explore. In functional terms, this is known as the hypertheme or macrotheme, as discussed in the section above in biology. Where in biology typically the first sentence acts as a hypertheme, in English literature, it is usually the whole of the first paragraph that functions in this way, thereby setting up the structure of the discussion that follows. Bruno explained how the topics for discussion in an essay can be identified through the wording of the question, and the students were asked to give suggestions on what the question was inviting them to discuss. In other words, what did writing about 'the presentation of Claudius' actually mean and what did it invite the students to write about? Discussion ensued on the nominalisation of 'presentation' from the verb 'present' and the elements that work together in presenting and revealing a character.

In preparation for jointly constructing an opening paragraph to the mini essay, he brainstormed key vocabulary with the class, including discussion of its meaning. This generated the following list:

*Patriarchal*
*Symphonic structure*
*Misogynistic*
*Benevolent patriarchy*
*Hypocritical*
*Passive*
*Innocent*
*Submissive*
*Oppressed*
*Ophelia*

These terms can be rearranged in order of semantic density as discussed in Chapter 2: *symphonic structure; misogynistic; benevolent patriarchy; patriarchal* being dense, with *hypocritical; passive; innocent; submissive; oppressed* less dense. *Ophelia* l any women in a misogynistic and patriarchal society of the kind portrayed in the play. Through discussion, Bruno unpacked the semantic density of the identified terms to ensure the class understood them all, followed by the ways in which the character of Ophelia symbolised women in general.

The students were then divided into three groups and asked to spend 5 minutes drafting opening sentences for the essay, incorporating as many of the key terms identified as possible. Bruno went around and checked what the students had written, in order to determine the sequence in which they would be invited read out their paragraphs. The first group then read out their opening paragraph as follows:

Group 1

| | |
|---|---|
| *Shakespeare develops the presentation of women in society in this scene* // | Abstract principle |
| *by displaying **Ophelia** as an **oppressed product** of a patriarchal society* | Abstract principle |

Said as speech, a more congruent grammar might read: *In this scene, Shakespeare uses Ophelia to represent the ways in which women are treated in a society dominated by men.* In the written form, several items expressed through verbs become nouns, such as *represent* becomes *representation* and *women are treated in a society dominated by men* becomes an abstract nominal group: *an oppressed product of a patriarchal society*.

The group were praised for their effort, and Bruno pointed out that although the girls had identified key themes, they had yet to link them to the text itself. Bruno then invited Group 2 to read their draft opening, which was as follows:

Group 2

| | |
|---|---|
| ***The symphonic structure** of Act 1 scene **3*** | Abstract principle<br>Identification of text to exemplify the principle |
| ***shows that Hamlet was written within a patriarchal society*** | Abstract principle |
| *There are two sides of **patriarchy** represented through the characters, Polonius and Laertes* | Reiteration abstract principle<br>Identification of texts to exemplify the principle |
| *Polonius has a **misogynistic** view of women, // whereas Laertes is seen* | Identification of text/abstract principle |
| *to have taken a **more benevolent** approach, whilst talking to **Ophelia*** | Identification of text/abstract principle<br>Identification of text |

The difference in structure between this paragraph and the one above is the inclusion of reference to textual detail, to which Bruno drew the class's attention. The final version came from Group 3:

| | |
|---|---|
| *The presentation of women in Act 1 scene 3 is expressed through **Ophelia**,* | Abstract principle—human<br>Identification of text |
| *// who is **portrayed as submissive and oppressed in a patriarchal society**.* | Abstract principle—human |
| *This is **displayed through the symphonic structure*** | General abstract statement—textual |
| *// which consists of a **first movement**, which introduces **the theme of patriarchy**, between Laertes and Ophelia, //* | Abstract statement clarified<br>Abstract principle—human<br>Abstract statement clarified |
| *the **andante**, which is **benign**, between Polonius and Laertes,* | Abstract principle—human |
| *// and **the third movement, which reinforces the theme of patriarchy**, between Polonius and Ophelia* | Abstract statement clarified<br>Abstract principle—human |

Here, the difference between the extracts groups 1 and 2 had written is the inclusion to the textual structure of the play in addition to identifying the parts of the play through which the abstract principles are presented. In pedagogic terms, such organisation meant that every student in the class participated in the activity which was received affirmatively.

Bruno decided to draw upon the $4 \times 4$ literacy toolkit matrix as developed by Humphrey into, Humphrey et al. (2015) and Humphrey (2015, 2016) in relation to PEEL structure in the context of the lower secondary curriculum for English, which I had introduced in the second CPD session I held with the LBP group. Subsequent to this CPD session, Bruno drew upon the matrix to help his students organise their written responses, both in terms of organising paragraphs through PEE and linking through paragraphs in the conclusion and referencing back to the question as L. By the end of a half term's teaching in this way, the grades achieved by Bruno's students had all improved. Although one would expect progress some progress over this period, the change was more than that expected. Most students' work improved by one whole grade with a student who had failed with a U grade gaining a B grade and one who had started with an E also gaining a B grade. As a consequence of organising his teaching in this way and in the light of the demonstrable improvement his students had made, Bruno went on to incorporate more modelling, deconstruction and joint construction activities in his classes, and getting his pupils to write shorter, mini essays that build up to the main one and are marked formatively with no mark is given.

Bruno also reported on how paying attention to his pupils' writing also extended to changing his practices in relation to the first phase of the LTC. This was particularly in relation to making connections between subject knowledge and language, ensuring that his students developed an understanding of the key concepts and ideas explored by the play. Previously, he had used notes he had written to guide his teaching on background aspects of the play such as historical and socio-cultural contexts which he went through in class, asking the pupils to make their own notes in turn. As a result of taking part in the project, he began to share his notes with the class, giving pupils time to annotate their own copies of the notes as he went through them. Bruno reported how astonished and surprised he was at the increased

**Table 3.4** Assessment Grid: revised

| Target | Satisfactory | Achieved |
|---|---|---|
| Accurate and precise use of technical vocabulary | | |
| Accurate use of grammar and punctuation | | |
| Sequenced and logical expression of thought processes | | |
| Point | | |
| Evidence | | |
| Explanation | | |
| Link back to question | | |
| Convincing and clear argument | | |
| Detailed knowledge of the text | | |

dialogic nature of the interaction between himself and his pupils in relation to level of detail they wanted to explore with him. Far from an LBP approach leading his pupils to plagiarise or ventriloquise his words, Bruno found the opposite to be the case, as their confidence in expressing themselves and grappling with the knower code that characterises the study of English Literature at this level. As this example and the two preceding it make clear, successful writing can only occur once the knowledge building that has gone on through reading and talk has occurred. Bruno became more consciously aware of scaffolding the pupils' learning than he had been before, and now deliberately draws attention to key vocabulary, phrasing, sentence structure and discursive aspects of textual organisation of the responses students are required to write as an integral aspect of classroom activity.

He has also redesigned his assessment feedback sheet in terms of success criteria including and incorporating the PEEL matrix. Such a redesign had the added advantage of being applicable to any written essay he asked his students' to write, rather than designing individual ones each time (Table 3.4).

# Conclusion

Research into the introduction of an LBP approach to language and literacy across the curriculum in England in a secondary context, particularly where EAL pupils are in the majority, demonstrates its potential as a potent resource for their language development in ways that integrate with both subject content and its assessment. LBP is above all an approach that integrates content learning and language development through explicitly paying attention to the linguistic structure of texts and developing pupils' and students' language awareness, knowledge about language and metalinguistic concepts and terminology, including grammar. As the illustrative vignettes in this chapter show and in line with research undertaken in Australia and the USA, an LBP approach to works best when introduced in the context of teachers' day to day assessment and curriculum goals and practices and integrated into them. These, in turn, relates to the individual institutional context in which they work, the nature of the community the school serves and the wider national education context. The research discussed in the first half of this chapter also shows how teachers' own metalinguistic awareness is a key factor. Lack of any explicit knowledge on the teacher's part is not *of itself*, as the vignette in relation to the geography vignette demonstrates, a barrier to adopting an LBP approach.

As a 'grand theory', LBP provides a range of well developed strategies for integrating language instruction in contextualised ways that take into account teachers' own starting points when it comes to explicit teaching about language. The research also indicates how LBP is drawn upon depends upon the needs of both local contexts and regional and national policies if they are to have any chance of success. It also illustrates that adopting an LBP approach relies upon the judgement and professionalism of educators and teachers to translate LBP principles and practices in ways that are appropriate to the pupils in front of them in relation to local, regional and national contexts.

The following three chapters review some of the ways in which LBP has been integrated into all three secondary schools who took part in the second year of the project in English (Chapter 4), the humanities (Chapter 5) and maths and science (Chapter 6), predominantly key stages 4 and 5 and the 14–19 age range.

# References

Anderson, A., & Shattock, J. (2012). Design-based research: A decade of progress in education research? *Educational Researcher, 41*(1), 16–25.

Charmaz, K. (2014). *Constructing grounded theory* (2nd ed.). London and New York: Sage.

Christie, F. (2016). Secondary school English literary studies: An example of a Knower code. In K. Maton, S. Hood, & S. Shay (Eds.), *Knowledge-building: Educational studies in Legitimation Code Theory* (pp. 158–156). London and New York: Routledge.

Fielding, M., Bragg, S., Craig, J., Cunningham, I., Eraut, M., Gillinson, S., et al. (2005). *Factors influencing the transfer of good practice.* http://webarchive.nationalarchives.gov.uk/20130402091155/https://www.education.gov.uk/publications/eOrderingDownload/RR615.pdf.pdf. Accessed August 3, 2017.

Giovanelli, M. (2015). Becoming an English language teacher: Linguistic knowledge, anxieties and the shifting sense of identity. *Language and Education, 29*(5): 416–429.

Glazer, B., & Strauss, A. (1967). *The discovery of grounded theory—Strategies for qualitative research.* New Brunswick and London: AldineTransaction.

Humphrey, S. (1996). *Exploring literacy in school geography.* Sydney: Metropolitan East Disadvantaged Schools Program.

Humphrey, S. (2015). A 4 × 4 literacy toolkit for employment: English language learners for academic literacies. In M. B. Schaefer (Ed.), *Research on teaching and learning with the literacies of young adolescents* (pp. 49–72). Charlotte: Information Age Publishing.

Humphrey, S. (2016). *Academic literacies in the middle years: A framework for enhancing teacher knowledge and student achievement.* London and New York: Routledge.

Humphrey, S., Sharpe, T., & Cullen, T. (2015). Peeling the PEEL: Integrating language and literacy in the middle years. *Literacy Learning: The Middle Years, 23*(2), 53–62.

Murphy, V. (2015). *A systematic review of intervention research examining English language and literacy development in children with English as an Additional Language (EAL).* https://www.bell-foundation.org.uk/assets/Documents/EALachievementMurphy.pdf?1422548394. Accessed December 30, 2015.

Sandoval, W. A., & Bell, P. (2004). Design-based research methods for studying learning in context: Introduction. *Educational Psychologist, 39*(4), 199–201.

Schleppegrell, M. (2015). *Learning to situate SFL-inspired pedagogies in new contexts.* Paper presented at the *Education Semiotics* conference, Aachen, Germany.

Strand, S. (2015). *English as an Additional Language (EAL) and educational achievement in England: An analysis of the National Pupil Database.* https://www.bellfoundation.org.uk/assets/Documents/EALachievementStrand.pdf?1422548358. Accessed December 30, 2015.

Watson, A. (2015). The problem of grammar teaching: A case study of the relationship between a teacher's beliefs and pedagogical practice. *Language and Education, 29*(4), 332–346.

# 4

# Developing Literacy Across the Curriculum for Subject English

## Introduction

In this chapter, I develop LBP in the context of the curriculum for subject English. The chapter highlights how subject English at secondary level (11–18 year olds) has its own distinctive discursive practices that differ from those of other subjects. It identifies the main patterns of *register* and *genre/text type* that characterise the texts that are talked about, read and written across the secondary school curriculum for English. This is particularly in relation to the literary texts pupils and students are required to study. I draw upon examples of schemes of work and/or lesson plans at each of the three key stages of 3, 4 and 5, together with interviews undertaken with teachers and samples of student work, to illustrate how paying attention to language structure can be integrated into the curriculum.

In common with many other English L1 countries, the secondary curriculum for English is underpinned by a set of guiding principles as laid down in a National Curriculum or Common Core. The most recent version of the National Curriculum for English at key stages 3 and 4 provides identical aims for both key stages and state that:

The overarching aim for English in the national curriculum is to promote high standards of language and literacy by equipping pupils with a strong command of the spoken and written word, and to develop their love of literature through widespread reading for enjoyment. The national curriculum for English aims to ensure that all pupils:

- read easily, fluently and with good understanding
- develop the habit of reading widely and often, for both pleasure and information
- acquire a wide vocabulary, an understanding of grammar and knowledge of linguistic conventions for reading, writing and spoken language
- appreciate our rich and varied literary heritage
- write clearly, accurately and coherently, adapting their language and style in and for a range of contexts, purposes and audiences
- use discussion in order to learn; they should be able to elaborate and explain clearly their understanding and ideas
- are competent in the arts of speaking and listening, making formal presentations, demonstrating to others and participating in debate (2014: 13), https://www.gov.uk/government/uploads/system/uploads/attachment_data/file/381754/SECONDARY_national_curriculum.pdf, accessed 9 March 2018.

One of the major changes to the curriculum in this version to that of others is the emphasis upon 'reading a wide range of fiction and non-fiction, including in particular whole books, short stories, poems and plays with a wide coverage of genres, historical periods, forms and authors'. At both key stages 3 and 4, pupils are required to read plays by William Shakespeare: two at Key Stage 3 and one at Key Stage 4, with, as Chapter 3 has discussed, this also being a requirement at Key Stage 5. Pre-1914 literature also figures, as does seminal world literature. Changes to the curriculum have also been accompanied by changes in assessment. For GCSE English Language (taken at 15/16 years of age), there is no longer any assessed coursework component, and reading and writing are assessed by two 100% closed book examination totalling three and a half hours with literature as a component. Speaking and listening, which used to have a fairly high weighting, now has none at all. Typical components of the two examination papers are: one creative writing task; unseen literary non-fiction and non-fiction texts with an emphasis upon analysis and evaluation; synthesis of information from different texts. There is an increased emphasis and weighting on 'technical accuracy' by which presumably is meant accurate grammar, punctuation and spelling. The weighting, however, is given in the context of pupils' own writing and not as a separate task. For GCSE English Literature, compulsory components are: a Shakespeare play, a nineteenth-century novel, poetry from 1789 including the Romantics, fiction and drama from The British Isles from 1914 onwards and a comparison of two unseen literary texts.

An LBP approach and the kind of pedagogic grammar exemplified in Chapter 2 are entirely consistent with such a curriculum. Particularly in relation to the fact that pupils and students are required to: write for a wide variety of range of audiences and purposes; consider how writing reflects the audience and purposes for which it is intended; apply their developing and growing knowledge of vocabulary, grammar and text structure to their writing and also alluding to the LTC by the advice to amend these elements to improve upon it as part of formative planning, drafting, editing and proof-reading rather than as a separate feature of summative assessment. The notion of *register* as explained in Chapter 2 is included. It is also expected that the key stages 1 and 2 Glossaries are also referred to by teachers at these key stages. Thus whilst the NLS may have become defunct, the emphasis upon the importance of audience, context and purpose and the twin notions of *register* and *genre* or *text type* are firmly embedded in the new curriculum. The following extract from the National Curriculum in relation to grammar and vocabulary is as follows.

# English: Key Stage 3

## Grammar and Vocabulary

Pupils should be taught to: consolidate and build on their knowledge of grammar and vocabulary through:

- extending and applying the grammatical knowledge set out in English Appendix 2 to the key stages 1 and 2 programmes of study to analyse more challenging texts
- studying the effectiveness and impact of the grammatical features of the texts they read
- drawing on new vocabulary and grammatical constructions from their reading and listening, and using these consciously in their writing and speech to achieve particular effects
- knowing and understanding the differences between spoken and written language, including differences associated with formal and informal registers, and between Standard English and other varieties of English.
- using Standard English confidently in their own writing and speech
- discussing reading, writing and spoken language with precise and confident use of linguistic and literary terminology.

Teachers should refer to the Glossary that accompanies the programmes of study for English for their own information on the range of terms used within the programmes of study as a whole.

# English: Key Stage 4

## Grammar and Vocabulary

Pupils should be taught to: consolidate and build on their knowledge of grammar and vocabulary through:

- studying their effectiveness and impact in the texts they read
- drawing on new vocabulary and grammatical constructions from their reading and listening, and using these consciously in their writing and speech to achieve particular effects
- analysing some of the differences between spoken and written language, including differences associated with formal and informal registers, and between Standard English and other varieties of English

Spelling patterns and guidance are set out in Appendix 1 to the key stage 1 and 2 programmes of study for English (2014: 16, 19), https://www.gov.uk/government/uploads/system/uploads/attachment_data/file/381754/SECONDARY_national_curriculum.pdf.

The extent to which the English teaching profession has shifted its position on the teaching of grammar is evidenced in recent publications such as Barton (2012), Giovanelli (2014) and Giovanelli and Clayton (2016). A series of papers was also published in 2015 by The National Association of the Teachers of English (NATE); the National Association of Advisors of English (NAAE) and the United Kingdom Literacy Association (UKLA). These papers are called collectively: *Curriculum and Assessment in English 3–19: A Better Plan.* https://www.nate.org.uk/file/2016/04/The-National-Curriculum-for-English-from-2015.pdf. The 11–19 sections of the papers owe a great deal to two books, namely *Grammar Makes Sense: Grammar and Knowledge About Language* (Richmond 2015) and *Curriculum and Assessment in English 11–19: A Better Plan* (Richmond et al. 2017). Richmond's and Richmond et al.'s work is totally in tune with an LBP approach, and also draws upon SFG as outlined in Chapter 2. However, Richmond et al. also argue that knowledge about language should extend beyond grammar to include various elements of The Kingman Model, namely language acquisition and development; the history of language; variety in and between languages as well as language as a system and language and power in society. Whilst of course as an applied linguist I have some sympathy with this, there is a limit to how much content a curriculum can stand. These elements all feature in the programme specification for

English Language A Level and are arguably best left there. The grammar curriculum put forward by the authors of the pamphlets for key stages 1 and 2 laid the foundations for further study at key stages 3, 4 and beyond, in much the same way as discussed in Chapter 2.

Richmond et al. also locate what they call 'text grammar' in relation to genre and register as part of the curriculum for knowledge about language rather than that for grammar. The point of difference between the approach I have taken and that of Richmond et al. is of recontextualising grammar as register, thereby not separating the two and extending the unit of grammatical analysis to the textual level. This is because, as Chapter 3, the remainder of this chapter and the two following exemplify, the extent to which any specific grammatical features are drawn in any written texts pupils and students write depends upon the characteristic patterns of register in which it is written associated with any one given genre or text type.

In all but the first of the case studies given below, teachers chose to incorporate teaching grammatical aspects of English in relation to their pupils writing evaluative responses to literary and non-fiction texts, rather than as part of any creative writing activity. Even where the activity centred upon developing creative writing, the teaching was undertaken in relation to a specific genre, in this instance that of travel writing. In this way, discussion that centred upon identifying any text's grammatical features was accompanied by a discussion of their effects upon the reader, with the structure of their writing guided by the rubric of the question. The degree to which teachers then drew attention to pupils' own use of written expression differed, depending upon the school's context. The example given below from Key Stage 3 was in the context of School C, a selective boys' school where the majority of pupils are white British and for whom English is correspondingly their first language. Here, the teacher's attention was focussed more upon getting his pupils to articulate their thoughts in relation to what the question asked, rather than upon the accuracy of their own written expression which by and large, was not an issue at this school. By contrast, the examples from key stages 4 and 5 are taken from schools A and B, where the majority of pupils and students have English as an AL and where expression of ideas in writing using the appropriate register to develop said ideas is something of a challenge for them. The vignettes all exemplify the ways in which the pacing and sequencing of lessons are determined by the school context, and what takes a certain amount of time in one context may take a different amount of time in another.

## English Key Stage 3: Year 8
## *Touching the Void*—Non-fiction Unit

The teacher, Mary, taught in School C, Farming School, a selective 11–18 boys' school. She had been teaching for 17 years, been educated in the late 1980s early 1990s, had a degree in English Literature and a PGCE in English. As with so many of her contemporaries, she reported that her own knowledge of linguistic terminology was non-existent, and that she had found the thought of teaching it initially 'scary', but was beginning to pick it up as she went along in her teaching. She had taught at two comprehensive schools before joining Farming School in 2006. Mary decided to 'dip her toe' into an LBP approach through incorporating it into her lesson plans centred upon writing a response to a non-fiction text, *Touching the Void*, over the course of two 50 minute lessons. This book (also made into a film) is an autobiographical account by the mountaineer Joe Simpson about his and his partner's Simon Yates' challenging and testing climb of a mountain in The Andes that nearly resulted in Yates' death. In it, Simpson recounts the decision centred upon the moral dilemma he faced where in order to save his own life, he risked that of his partner. The fact that Yates survived the ordeal is nothing short of a miracle, and the power of the book lies in its testimony to the spirit of human endurance in the face of great adversity—in this case, physical as well as mental.

The text was chosen initially to fit into a cross-curricular link to geography on mountains, and because she thought it would appeal to the boys in her class which it did. Like virtually all of the other participating teachers, Mary decided to structure her teaching of grammar in the context of the genre/text type in which her pupils were being asked to write, in this case, a critical evaluation. This genre has been identified as one of the most challenging of all genres/text type to write, but one which pupils need to master if they are to succeed in answering questions about English Literature at GCSE as the new curriculum requires them to do. Mary thus drew upon a textual organisation tool I had introduced in my CPD session with her and her two colleagues. It is one that has come to be used by teachers of English, centring upon the *Point(s), Evidence, Technique, Explain* and *Reflect* (PETER), which is an extension of Point (P) Evidence (E) and Explain (PEE), popularised by the NLS. It is also recommended for use by the GCSE examination board, OCR, for which Mary is also a GCSE examiner. It is freely available as a resource from various sources, including *The Times Educational Supplement*, https://www.tes.com/teaching-resource/peter-paragraphs-how-to-analyse-text-6310603, accessed 10 July 2017.

Depending upon how they are used, such structures can help to develop pupils' writing when they are used as a scaffold as part of the drafting phase of the LTC, to help pupils organise their thoughts into coherent expression in writing. Time and time again, teachers from all three schools reported that their pupils had a tendency to, in Mary's words, 'vomit' words onto a page without any thought as to their coherence. This metaphor is similar to and harks back to Cobbett's simile discussed in Chapter 1, of words being scattered like seeds willy-nilly, rather than being carefully sown. This feature is particularly striking, given the varied linguistic and sociocultural backgrounds of the pupils and students attending all three schools. Expressing thought coherently in writing then is a challenge that cuts across pupils and students regardless of their linguistic and sociocultural backgrounds.

Mary began her first lesson in the usual way, by asking her pupils to read page 35 of the book. In a departure from her usual practice she then, without any prior discussion, gave them 10 minutes to write individual initial responses to answer the question:

*How does Joe Simpson make this description so intense and powerful?*

She asked them to structure their answer around what they could remember of the PEE paragraph structure to which her class had been

## 4 Developing Literacy Across the Curriculum for Subject English

introduced in Year 7. Also as a departure from her usual practice, Mary then went through the extract from the autobiography with the class in a dialogic way, pulling out with them the various language techniques used in the passage and eliciting from her class their effect upon the reader. Normally, Mary would have provided a word bank and vocabulary sheet to accompany and support the written assessment she set. Instead, she asked her pupils to annotate the page they had read and discussed as shown below:

Mary then took the class through the PETER structure, again employing a dialogic approach making sure through her questioning and the pupils' responses that they understood its principles and in what ways it was an extension of the PEE structure to which they had been previously introduced (Table 4.1).

The following lesson was then devoted to the pupils writing two paragraphs in answer to the same question, using the PETER technique. Mary reported that as a result of this exercise, her pupils' confidence in their writing rose, and their second attempts were a large improvement upon the first. For example, in his first attempt one pupil wrote:

> *I think that this extract was really tense and powerful because of the way that it gradually rises in tension. It starts by saying he is 'fumbling', so it makes you think that he has no control of the situation. Then he calls, but there is no response, so then we feel he is alone. Then he does not know what to do. All of these things keep building up the pressure. Then he loses control, which is where it is the most tense, and as he was so close to falling does make it very tense. The fact that he was alone and was not in control made it very tense.*

His second attempt was as follows, with PETER elements identified:

> *Joe Simpson uses different tenses to make this extract so tense and powerful. (P) This is shown here: 'I shouted again but there was no reply. Take a few breaths and get on with it!' (Ev) The verb – shout – creates tension because it shows he is panicking, and the fact there was no reply creates tension too, as it shows that he was isolated. The contrast between the first sentence, which is in the past tense, creates a sense that there may not be a future for Joe, and that adds tension. (T) Joe Simpson talks to himself, which shows that*

**Table 4.1** PETER support scaffold

| Assessment criteria | Above average/expectations | Average/meets expectations | Below average/does not meet expectations |
|---|---|---|---|
| Point(s) | Clear and interesting points made that refer to the question; linking to other paragraphs; clear line of thought running throughout the answer | Clear and interesting points made that refer to the question; linking to other paragraphs | Points made but not very clear and little or no reference to the question; no linking to other paragraphs |
| Evidence | Appropriate evidence chosen, that picks up on subtle meanings; most salient evidence—the best bits—chosen; more than one piece of evidence referred to and interwoven in any one paragraph | Appropriate evidence chosen, that may not pick up on subtle meanings; most salient evidence—the best bits—chosen; more than one piece of evidence referred to in any one paragraph but not interwoven | Limited appropriate evidence chosen; limited interweaving of evidence into any one paragraph |
| Technique | Identification of the whole range of language features and the multiple and subtle effects they create. Explicit comment upon how these features effect the overall reading of the question and the text to which it refers | Identification of a more limited range of language features and less discussion of the multiple and subtle effects they create. Less explicit comment upon how these features effect the overall reading of the question and the text to which it refers | Identification of an even more limited range of language features and little discussion of the multiple and subtle effects they create. Little or no explicit comment upon how these features effect the overall reading of the question and the text to which it refers |

(continued)

Table 4.1 (continued)

| Assessment criteria | Above average/expectations | Average/meets expectations | Below average/does not meet expectations |
|---|---|---|---|
| Explain | Explanation includes looking for multiple meanings; exploring whether or not there is more than one effect on the reader; identifying various interpretations of the text; employing language techniques such as connectives and adverbs to enhance the explanation | Explanation includes looking for multiple meanings but these are more limited in scope; exploring whether or not there is more than one effect on the reader; identifying limited range of interpretations of the text; employing a limited range of language techniques to enhance the explanation | Explanation includes a limited look for multiple meanings; exploring whether or not there is more than one effect on the reader limited to one effect; identifying a limited range of interpretations of the text; employing little or a limited range of language techniques to enhance the explanation |
| Reflect | Refer back to the question, commenting upon the text as a whole. Link back to key themes and show an awareness of how different readers may have different reactions to the text that are different from your own | Refer back to the question, but little comment upon the text as a whole. Link back to key themes and limited awareness of how different readers may have different reactions to the text that are different from your own | Limited or no reference back to the question; little or no comment upon the text as a whole. Little or no link back to key themes and limited awareness of how different readers may have different reactions to the text that are different from your own |

*he is trying to calm himself down, which creates a lot of tension, as it shows he is panicking. This quotation affects the text around it by showing that he has panicked, making the next sentence more engaging, as you know how the fact he has panicked has affected the situation* (Ex) *Joe Simpson uses different tenses and appropriate language to create a tense and powerful atmosphere in this extract* (R).

*Joe Simpson shortens adverbs to emphasise the word, to create a tense and powerful text. "Unexpected, it made my heart leap."* (P) *He shortens the adverb "unexpectedly" to "Unexpected", which puts emphasis upon the word and makes the sentence pass quicker. This suggests that it was not expected at all, which makes the sentence very tense.* (Ev&T) *he also uses imagery in the phrase "make my heart leap."* (T) *This shows that he is fearing whatever is coming, which adds tension to the extract. The whole sentence shows that he is scared, and means that he has to consider if he is safe in the next few sentences.* (Ex) *Joe Simpson uses shortened words and imagery to create a tense atmosphere to this extract* (R).

Mary had undertaken this writing task as formative assessment and did not give a grade, but rather made written comments in relation to the second attempt each pupil had written for where it could be improved. Thus, for example, one pupil wrote in his second attempt: 'The terminology used is to create tension'. Mary had written in the margin: 'verbs' as an alternative to terminology, and her comment at the end read: 'You need to be even more specific about the role quotations have and the subject specific terminology for them'. Where another pupil had written 'statement' Mary wrote in the margin: 'rhetorical question'.

In common with her counterparts at the other two project schools as well as the two other teachers in her school, Mary said that the boys she taught had a tendency to give little thought to the organisation and structure of their writing. Her experience of scaffolded drafting activities of the kind outlined above illustrate how paying attention to the writing process supported by the PETER structure made her pupils think more carefully about how they organised and structured their writing. Far from such a structure preventing her pupils from having sufficient time to think and develop their thoughts, using it as a scaffold helped her pupils to organise their thoughts into coherent expression in writing.

## Key Stage 3 Year 9: Travel Writing

John was a teacher at Farming School, School C, and had been teaching for 18 years, all of them at the school where he was head of the English department. He had been educated in the late 1970s and early 1980s including GCSE Latin, and thus felt he had an excellent grasp of grammatical terminology. He too, has a degree in English Literature and a PGCE in English. He had routinely taught grammar in the context of pupils' reading and writing and his impetus for taking part in the project was to encourage other members of his department and that of others in the school to do the same.

John chose to incorporate aspects of an LBP approach into a scheme of work centred upon travel writing, that aimed to teach his pupils the appropriate style and conventions (in other words, register features) of that literary genre. The lesson plans were ones he had used before, but adapted so that the pupils wrote an initial description of their journey to school before going on to re-draft their work. The lessons were structured and sequenced as follows. Pupils:

- Wrote a basic description of their journey to school
- Identified use of expanded noun and verb phrases in examples of Bill Bryson's writing
- Practised the skill on uncontextualised examples
- Applied the principle first to nouns and then verbs in that original piece of writing.

In the first lesson, the class first wrote a description individually of their daily journey into school, focusing on what they saw, how people behaved, the noises they heard and the way fellow commuters moved, with an upper word limit of 50 words. One pupil wrote:

> *I opened the door. I crossed the road. I waited for the bus. I payed the driver with my bus pass. I heard my friends talking. We waited for the bus to arrive. I walked to school. I herad cars beeping.*

In pairs, the class then found and analysed examples of noun and verb groups in Bill Bryson's work for the second half of lesson one and first half of lesson two. In pairs, they completed discrete examples relating to nouns in the second lesson as given below. Finally, in lesson three, they re-drafted their description with a focus on the nouns and finally repeated the process for verbs.

**From Bill Bryson "Neither Here Nor There"**

I wandered up to the lofty heights of the Gianicolo, where the views across the city were sensational and where young couples entwined themselves in steamy embraces on the narrow ledges. I had an ice-cream and watched to see how many of them tumbled over the edge to dash themselves on the rocks below, but none did, thank goodness. They must wear suction cups on their backs.

For a week, I just walked and walked. And when I tired I sat with a coffee or sunned myself on a bench, until I was ready to walk again.

Having said this, Rome is not an especially good city for walking. For one thing, there is the constant danger that you will be run over. Zebra crossings count for nothing in Rome, which is not unexpected but takes some getting used to. It is a shock to be strolling across some expansive boulevard, lost in an idle fantasy involving Ornella Muti, when suddenly it dawns on you that the six lanes of cars bearing down on you have no intention of stopping.

\*\*\*\*

The bus was crowded—ramshackle charabancs in Yugoslavia always are—but I found a seat three-quarters of the way back and gripped the seat bar in front of me with both hands. When Katz and I had crossed Yugoslavia, it had been nothing if not exciting. The roads through the mountains were perilous beyond words, much too narrow for a bus, full of impossible bends and sheer falls from unimaginable heights. Our driver was an escaped lunatic who had somehow talked his way into a job with the bus company. Young and handsome, wearing his cap at a rakish angle, he drove as if cheerfully possessed, passing on blind bends, driving at breakneck speed, honking at everything, slowing for nothing. He sang hearty tunes and carried on lively conversations with the passengers—often turning around in his seat to address them directly—while simultaneously sweeping us along the edge of ragged roads on the brink of sheerside cliffs. I remember pressing my face to the window many times and

## 4 Developing Literacy Across the Curriculum for Subject English

being able to see no road beneath us—just a straight drop and the sort of views you get from an aeroplane. There was never more than an inch of shoulder standing between us and wingless flight (Table 4.2).

For the second draft, one of the pupils modified and improved nouns as follows:

*I opened* **the gleaming white door.** *I crossed* **the grey, concrete road** *and waited for* **the big double decker.** *I payed* **the old man** *behind the wheel. I heard my friends chatting euphorically. We waited for* **the red double decker** *to stop. I walked to the* **old grand architecture** *that is farming school. I heard* **angry metal machines** *beeping.*

In this redraft, the pupil chose more than five nouns, and in the process altered seven single clause sentences to seven sentences of which one has two clauses. Finally, a third draft of the same task was undertaken, this time picking five verbs to modify and improve, to produce a final, all-round improved version:

*I* slung open **the gleaming white door.** *I* skipped happily *across* **the grey concrete road** *and I* longingly sat *at the bus stop until* **the big double decker** *came. I showed my bus pass to the man behind the wheel.*

Table 4.2 Writing like Bryson: expanding phrases

| Basic | Bryson-Ed |
|---|---|
| I looked at the view | I feasted my eyes on the panoramic vista which was spread out before me |
| The street was busy | |
| I went to sleep during the train journey | |
| I hiked up the hill | |
| I had breakfast at the café | |
| The hotel receptionist was helpful | |
| The shopping centre was difficult to find | |
| I spent a lot of money on the gifts | |
| I enjoyed visiting the zoo | |
| The tour guide was boring | |

> *My ears* pricked up ***to the sound of my friends*** *chatting eurphorically. We got bored waiting for **the red double decker** to **come to a halt**. I strolled up to the **old, extraordinary piece of architecture** that is Farming School. On the way, my ears **were disturbed** by **the angry beeping of the moving metal machines.***

Describing a journey to school must be a classic Year 7 or 8 exercise in subject English, since it is an experience that is familiar to all pupils. Arguably its aim in the context of subject English, as this example illustrates, is to initiate pupils into its discursive practices, where expanded noun and verb groups are valued as part of creative writing activities undertaken in the context of travel writing, and exemplifies what is meant by adopting the appropriate style and conventions—register features—of such writing. Such an approach is also consistent with the ways that the now defunct NLS advocated teaching writing. However, if it is to be anywhere near successful, then teachers to have a grasp of linguistic knowledge of the kind John clearly possesses. This also chimes with Myhill's research findings on teaching grammar for writing where teacher knowledge was one of the factors for success (or not). The point being made here is, that teachers who chose to integrate explicit teaching of grammar as part of an LBP approach did so in so far as they felt confident in their own linguistic knowledge. Those whose confidence was limited, drew upon LBP initially in relation to principles of textual organisation, as discussed in the first example above, rather than with specific features of register, as given in this example. Issues of teacher confidence then, can be overcome and should not *of itself* prevent ways being found of developing their linguistic knowledge and in turn, that of their pupils' and students.

## Key Stage 4 Year 11: Wilfred Owen's Poetry

Emily was an English teacher in School B, Greenford School. She had been teaching for 15 years, six of which had been at Greenford. She had a degree in English Literature and a PGCE in English, and any grammatical knowledge she had, had been gained through her learning languages.

Although the school had engaged in practices advocated by the NLS such as word walls, whole school marking policies and providing writing frames for scaffolding written work, Emily felt that such activities were limited. This was largely due she felt, and as has been discussed earlier, to the limitations of the dissemination model used by the NSLS, in that the way the materials were presented in ways that tended to skim the surface of tackling development in writing, but did not help particularly in getting pupils to achieve control over their written expression.

Wilfred Owen's World War One poetry is often included in GCSE syllabi at Key Stage 4, exposing as they do the horrors of war as seen through a soldier's eyes. A typical essay structure in studying English Literature, particularly in relation to poetry, is to explore a key theme that runs across two poems. In the case of Wilfred Owen's poetry, for a GCSE Year 11 class, Emily chose the theme of *feelings about war* expressed through the question: *In what ways does Wilfred Owen express his feelings about war in the two poems 'Dulce et Decorum Est' and 'Anthem for Doomed Youth'?* She drew from the LBP approach by incorporating explicit reference to the register features associated with writing a critical appreciation as part of preparing her pupils to write one.

The assessment objectives for the series of lessons for Wilfred Owen's poetry were:

- Read and understand poetry
- Understand the poetry in its cultural, historical and social context
- Develop interpretations of Owen's attitudes, ideas and values
- Explain and evaluate Owen's use of language and poetic form.

Emily began her teaching as usual with building her pupils' knowledge and understanding of the poems in relation to their interpretation of the poems. This also included learning about the historical period in which they were written which in this case was that of World War One 1914 to 1918 and about the poet himself. Pupils today and regardless of their sociocultural backgrounds, have little or no previous experience of this period, which means that teachers often spend time making sure they gain an understanding of it. This provided the background for studying each poem, including how language is used to convey attitudes, expression and feelings through its phonological, lexical and syntactic patternings. Emily made sure she integrated discussion of these aspects in the context of other, literary key concepts associated with analysing poetry such as rhythm and rhyme, alliteration and assonance, metaphor and simile. Her teaching also included, in the case of the poem *Dulce et Decorum Est*, involved not only learning to understand Latin and providing an English translation for the final two lines of the poem, but what Latin actually is and its place in the history of Western civilisation. She also drew upon word games to help the pupils with their spelling of the new vocabulary they were acquiring in relation to the study of poetry. For each poem, the pupils completed an information sheet to bring out the key features of each poem, to scaffold their subsequent answering of the question:

- Summarise what the poem is about
- Sounds (phonology)
- Words (lexis)
- Structure (morphosyntax)
- Imagery/Technique.

In a departure from previous practice, Emily spent two lessons teaching the class about the register features of the critical appreciation essay that pupils were to write. To help her pupils identify words and phrases that make links between sentences she drew up the following list:

***Conjunctions link ideas within sentences***

*And*
*In order to*
*Where*
*With*
*through*
*despite*
*that*
*whereas*
*also*
*moreover*

She also explained how conjunctions can be used either to *add* information or to *compare* information:

**Addition**  and, in addition, alternatively, moreover, or, as well

**Comparison**  similarly, likewise, on the one hand…on the other hand in contrast, instead, however

This was accompanied by modelling how sentences could be started:

*Through his use of imagery in this poem….*
*Owen uses imagery here to….*
*Lexical choices in this poem..*
*Use of metaphor in this poem….*

And a list of different verbs/processes (mainly mental and verbal) that link a language feature to its effect:

| *Shows* | *suggests* | | *indicates* |
| *Highlights* | *seems* | *implies* | *presents* |
| *Demonstrates* | *reminds* | *emphasises* | *conveys* |

Emily then introduced an exercise to the class, centring upon four different versions of a paragraph that discussed the ways in which Wilfred Owen uses sound in his poems. She then asked them in pairs, to place them in the order to which each one showed the characteristics of a PETER structure, given above.

> **a) In both poems, one of the ways in which Owen evokes the experience of war is through his use of sounds.** In the poem Dulce et Decorum est, this is achieved through his use of rhythm and rhyme. Alternate lines of the poem rhyme and in the first stanza, he uses lines such as 'knock-kneed, coughing like hags, we cursed through sludge' where the rhythm reflects the slow, painful and laboured way the soldiers progressed through the battlefield. By contrast, in Anthem for Doomed Youth, Owen writes lines such as 'Only the stuttering rifles' rapid rattle' to create an aural impression of the constant sound of gunfire.
>
> **b) In both poems, one of the ways in which Owen evokes the experience of war is through his use of sounds.** Owen uses rhythm and rhyme to do this. In Dulce et Decorum est alternate lines of the poem rhyme and in the first stanza,

he uses lines such as 'knock-kneed, coughing like hags, we cursed through sludge.' In Anthem for Doomed Youth though, Owen uses different techniques with sounds. He writes 'Only the stuttering rifles' rapid rattle.' This is alliteration.

**c) In both poems, one of the ways in which Owen evokes the experience of war is through his use of sounds.** In the poem Dulce et Decorum est, this is achieved through his use of rhythm and rhyme. Alternate lines of the poem rhyme and in the first stanza, he uses lines such as 'knock-kneed, coughing like hags, we cursed through sludge' where the rhythm reflects the slow, painful and laboured way the soldiers progressed through the battlefield. By contrast, in Anthem for Doomed Youth, Owen writes lines such as 'Only the stuttering rifles' rapid rattle.' The alliteration of 'r' and assonance of 'rapid rattle' help to create an aural impression of the constant sound of gunfire. The sharp, short words along with a plosive 'p' sound all serve to foreground the violence and danger of war, as they mimic the sound of a gun being fired.

**d) In both poems, one of the ways in which Owen evokes the experience of war is through his use of sounds.** In the poem Dulce et Decorum est, this is achieved through his use of rhythm and rhyme. Alternate lines of the poem rhyme and in the first stanza, he uses lines such as 'knock-kneed, coughing like hags, we cursed through sludge' to describe how the soldiers were walking. By contrast, in Anthem for Doomed Youth, Owen evokes the experience of war through different sounds and techniques. Here he writes 'Only the stuttering rifles' rapid rattle.' The alliteration of 'r' sounds like guns firing.

Emily reported that her pupils found this exercise challenging, since it forced them to think through the organisation and structure of the written responses. In the class discussion that followed the group activity, c) was identified as having the most characteristics of a PETER since it draws upon quotes from both poems in illustrating how sound evokes the experience of war and, crucially, their effect upon the reader in terms of evoking the images described.

Through activities such as this, Emily was able to show her pupils how to move away from simply 'feature spotting' something like alliteration as in example b), to linking the 'feature spotting' of alliteration to a description of effect, as undertaken in d) and also including assonance in c). However, current GCSE requirements to identify stylistic features in literary texts put pressure on teachers who do not have the requisite linguistic knowledge to teach it. John from School C Farming, is a GCSE examiner for English Literature, and he had found in marking the first set of papers for the new GCSE examination that there was a tendency for 'feature spotting' becoming an end in itself. He expressed concern that such a practice leaves pupils open to the risk of identifying a feature but using the wrong term and/or making no link between any one feature to others and their effect upon the reader.

Finally, Emily gave her pupils a writers' checklist to guide them with drafting their essay (Table 4.3).

Incorporating activities of the kind summarised above into lessons makes explicit to pupils what is meant by evaluating and reflecting upon the interpretation of a text in their own writing, since it is the articulation of these particular aspects that pupils find most difficult. Thus, whilst teaching about imagery, conjunctions, verbs/processes, paragraph structure and so on were not a separate assessment objective for Emily's scheme of work, paying attention to them underpinned and laid the foundations for their successful achievement.

Table 4.3 Writers' checklist

| | |
|---|---|
| Structure | Is there a macrotheme or topic sentence at the start which indicates the language features to be considered? |
| | Do each of my paragraphs start with a sentence that introduces what it is about? |
| | Have I included quotations as examples of each key feature and explained its effect? |
| | Have I used words such as 'conveys', 'demonstrates" shows' to do this (to link examples to effects)? |
| | Have I used conjunctions to link and compare ideas? |
| | Have I used references to link paragraphs? |
| | Do I have an overall reflective paragraph at the end that makes a general point and says what my overall judgement is? |
| Technical terms | Have I used technical language terms from my key word list? |
| Spelling | Is my spelling accurate? |
| Overall | Have I read back over my writing to make sure that it makes sense and flows? |

## Key Stage 5 Year 12: *1984* by George Orwell

The example here is taken from classes taught by the English teacher, Bruno in School A, discussed in Chapter 3 in relation to teaching Shakespeare's play *Hamlet*. After completing their work on this play, the class went on to study George Orwell's novel *1984*. As has become common practice in the school, the learning objectives or outcomes of any sequence of lessons are closely aligned with the assessment objectives which, at Key Stage 5 as at Key Stage 4, are set by examination boards. These assessment objectives in turn, are used as the criteria against which written work is marked.

Bruno thus structured his feedback sheet for his students' work as follows (Table 4.4).

In conversations with Bruno, he said that taking part in the LBP project had helped him to realise that there was, in his words, 'more than one way to skin a cat' when it came to making sure that his students understood what was being asked of them. Initially, as discussed in Chapter 3, Bruno admitted he had been reluctant to pay attention to the drafting process of writing as he thought this was too mundane and pedestrian for him to spend his time upon as well as 'boring'. However, his experience of drawing upon LBP had resulted in him paying more attention to writing as a craft and particularly focussing upon patterns of phrase and clause structure in the texts his students wrote. Until taking part in the project, his approach to the teaching of any literary text followed a similar pattern, which was:

**Table 4.4** Feedback sheet

| Assessment objective | Comments |
|---|---|
| 1. Articulate informed, personal and creative responses to literary texts, using associated concepts and terminology, and coherent, accurate written expression | |
| 2. Analyse the ways in which meanings are shaped by literary texts | |
| 3. Demonstrate understanding of the significance and influence of the contexts in which literary texts are written and received | |
| 4. Explore connections across literary texts | |
| 5. Explore literary texts informed by different interpretations | |
| Student response/evaluation | |

4  Developing Literacy Across the Curriculum for Subject English

- Didactic teaching: providing the sociocultural background of the period in which the text being studied is written; identification of key themes
- Readings from key passages of the text given
- Group discussion of key passages, including annotating the text
- Feeding back group discussion to the whole class.

Prior to taking part in the project, Bruno said he would then ask his students to write an essay as a summative form of assessment, with no opportunities provided for drafting or phases 2 and 3 of the LTC. As a result of taking part in the project, he had begun to give more time to group work in class as discussed in Chapter 3 and setting what he called 'mini essays' that were not given a mark but acted as formative, drafting preparation for the longer, complete essays, which were. He also paid more attention to developing vocabulary than he had done previously. Rather than assuming students would develop this for themselves, in his next lesson he gave the class a keyword list, accompanied by explanations of their meanings, and drawing attention to nominalised forms (Table 4.5).

Table 4.5  Developing vocabulary through nominalisation

| | | |
|---|---|---|
| Totalitarianism | Communism | Contraction |
| Propaganda | Feminist perspective | *Animal Farm* by George Orwell |
| Dystopia | Postmodernism | |
| Pessisim | Stalinism | *Brave New World* by Aldous Huxley |
| Doublethink | Marxism | |
| Distancing (e.g. an emotional distance from character so that we don't over-empathise in the interests of objectivity) | Marxist perspective | Tone (the author's intentions/feelings) |
| | Stream of consciousness (or free indirect discourse) | Mood: the character's intentions/feelings) |
| | Freudian perspective | Form (e.g. realism) |
| | Realism | Sadism |
| Nazism | Satire | Didactism |
| Newspeak | Ingsoc | Socialism |
| Interior monologue | Semantic field | Masochism |
| Fascism | | Blitz |
| Rolande Barthes: 'writerly', 'readerly' | | Psychological landscape |
| | | Linguistic determinism |

He then divided his class into four groups, giving each group a different aspect of the novel upon which to focus, explaining that the primary focus of the lesson was how to achieve successfully assessment objectives 3 and 5. Each group was then set a different objective, centring upon the opening pages of the novel:

- Objective 1: Group 1: To be able to draw direct links between the text and the emergence of totalitarianism in the first-half of the twentieth century
- Objective 2: Group 2: To explore Orwell's satire of the British Labour Party through his invention of *doublethink*
- Objective 3: Group 3: To understand the satirical significance of *Newspeak* and to explore Orwell's *tone* and *form* through his use of this device
- Objective 4: Group 4: To develop an engagement with C20th and C21st critics
- Objective 5: Whole class: To the explore the satirical function of Emanuel Goldstein

In preparation for this group work, the class firstly discussed a picture taken from a German anti-Semitic propaganda children's picture book published in 1936 with the title: *Trust no fox in the green meadow and never trust the word of a jew*, and how this related to the novel *Animal Farm*. The girls then watched a 15-minute anti-Semitic propaganda film, jotting down how the combination of images, music and voice-over, play on the fears and prejudices of the audience. They were then asked to include discussion of the film as they worked in their groups. Other activities were supported by a 15-page booklet that contained explanatory/directed reading activities to support their writing, such as the example given below:

> *A03: from Thomas Pynchon's: The Road to* **1984 From *The Guardian*, Saturday May 3, 2003**
> *Many critics have argued that the novel is too narrow and pessimistic in its outlook to be credible and some have dismissed the novel as a "political horror-comic". (See below). On the other hand. Pynchon finds in the appendix, the key to Orwell's' genuine optimism about the future:*

## 4  Developing Literacy Across the Curriculum for Subject English

> *"Why end a novel as passionate, violent and dark as this one with what appears to be a scholarly appendix? The answer may lie in simple grammar. From the first sentence, "The Principles of Newspeak" is written consistently in the past tense, as if to suggest some later piece of history, post-1984, in which Newspeak has become literally a thing of the past—as if in some way the anonymous author of the piece is by now free to discuss, critically and objectively, the political system of which Newspeak was, in its time, the essence. Moreover, it is our own pre-Newspeak language that is being used to write the essay. Newspeak was supposed to have become general by 2050, and yet it appears that it did not last that long, let alone triumph, that the ancient humanistic ways of thinking inherent in standard English have persisted, survived, and ultimately prevailed, and that perhaps the social and moral order it speaks for has even, somehow, been restored."*

*Now re-read the appendix and answer the following questions, providing Evidence, explanation and link back to the theme of optimism versus pessimism:*

1. *What is the purpose of Newspeak as a function of totalitarianism? (AO1/2)*
2. *Orwell was a journalist. What satirical comment could Orwell be making about contemporary journalism's impact on the English language? (AO4)*
3. *How could the appendix be read as part of Orwell's investment in realism? (AO2)*
4. *How is the subversion of conventional narrative structure (an appendix to a novel) be described as a feature of postmodernism? Realism?*
5. *What other elements of realism are there (see exposition in Chapter 1) (AO2)*
6. *What is the impact on the reader of the of orwell's use of realism? (AO2/5)*
7. *What do you think of Pynchon's argument about the appendix providing a source of hope and the prospect of redemption? (AO3)*
8. *Do you agree the appendix introduces a note of hope for the future in an otherwise bleak novel? (AO1/2)*
9. *Does the appendix potentially change the meaning of the novel from a writerly to a readerly text? (Roland Barthes)? (AO1/2/3).*

When setting a question for his students to answer, Bruno also spent more time than he had previously explained the wording of the question to the students, and how the question related to the structure of what the students were required to write. The mini essay was then marked in relation to identifying the assessment objective/s each paragraph met. Even though the question did not specify relating the novel to other texts, Bruno stressed the importance of referring to other works by the same author; other works related to that of the author and key literary and philosophical theorists. Take, for example, the question: *What is the function of newspeak in the novel 1984 and how does this contribute to its tone and form?* which the activity above supports.

Bruno pointed out this was a two-clause co-ordinating sentence that was essentially asking two questions related to three concepts: *function, tone* and *form*. In order to write about the function of newspeak, the concept of newspeak had first to be defined. One of the students wrote as her first paragraph:

> *Orwell was certain that the decline of a language had political and economic causes. Although he had no solid proof, he presumed that the languages of countries under dictatorships, such as the then Soviet Union or Germany, had deteriorated under their respective regimes. "when the general atmosphere is bad, language must suffer", Orwell wrote in his essay 'Politics and the English Language.' 'if thought corrupts language, language can corrupt thought,' he continues. Here is the very concept behind the invention of Newspeak.*

This example typifies the symbiotic nature not only of the relationship between curriculum and assessment but also between reading, talk and writing and also the ways in which an LBP approach can support language development. Whilst not specifically tied to LBP, an assessment for learning approach such as that practised in School A is consistent with it, since LBP focuses upon:

- making visible the knower code pupils acquire through their discussion and reading in their writing for assessment purposes from the very beginning and at all points of phase 1 of the LTC;
- recognising that mastery of the code requires an ability to both read and interpret the literary piece and to create a response to it;

- recognising that acquisition of the code means knowing how to move between reference to the literary piece and declarations of what that piece 'shows' and 'reveals';
- viewing writing for assessment as a process, broken down into smaller writing tasks;
- modelling and deconstructing the vocabulary and clause structures through phases 2 and 3 of the LTC that in turn involves;
- giving more explicit attention paid to the organisation and structure of the critical appreciation genre and its register features.

# Conclusion

As a curriculum subject, English is the place where learning about grammar is normally situated, as exemplified in the Key Stage 3 example above. Such teaching often occurs in the context of developing pupils' own creative writing, and in English Literature to identifying patterns of language including the figurative in a range of literary texts. Language study in this sense permeates the curriculum for English as it always has done. The difference an LBP approach brings is in making language patterns explicit not only in relation to the creative texts pupils' write themselves and literary texts they write about, but in their own responses to literary texts. The questions pupils and students are given to answer in relation to studying literary texts in English Literature are concerned largely with abstract concepts that characterise the 'knower code' discussed in Chapter 2. In English Literature, such concepts are concerned with the identification of human endeavour, experience and imagination. One of the purposes of writing in English Literature then is not only to identify, evaluate and interpret abstract concepts and principles as given in literary texts but also to construe a certain subject position in relation to them. Independently, the teachers of English in all three participating schools chose to integrate an LBP approach across all three key stages as part of developing their pupils' and students' evaluative and interpretive abilities in relation to writing about literary and non-fiction texts. This was in addition to the kinds of activities related to developing grammar in the context of creative writing. The change to their previous pedagogic practice centred particularly upon developing writing in the context of formative assessment, centred upon phases 2 and 3 of the LTC and paying explicit attention to textual organisation and the register features therein.

Incorporating an LBP approach and its related pedagogic grammar made sense to teachers in that it could be aligned with their own predominantly literary backgrounds, beliefs and practices as teachers of English. It encourages teachers to take include more of a stylistic approach to text analysis, as well as paying increased attention to the ways in which their pupils and students articulate their thoughts and ideas in writing across their whole response to the question asked in ways that are both cohesive and coherent. An LBP approach thus has much to offer in terms of reducing the compartmentalisation of language and literature in schools, particularly given the National Curriculum directive to build upon Key Stage 2 language work in relation to spelling, punctuation and grammar into key stages 3 and 4.

An LBP approach means that attention to language features in the text about which they are writing is accompanied by teachers paying more explicit attention to the quality of written expression which can be beneficial to all pupils and students, regardless of their linguistic and sociocultural backgrounds. It fosters a dialogic approach to talk in the classroom, and makes teachers of English more aware of explaining explicitly the different elements of any textual organisation frame they may use, such as the PEE/L/PETER structure, and what exactly is meant by description or point, evidence, evaluation and reflection in the context of their subject. What felt initially like 'taking the time out' to do this had a positive impact upon the quality of student writing, which in turn resulted in teachers making greater use of LBP in terms of integrating it into and informing lesson planning. In turn, teachers' own confidence in teaching linguistic terminology improved.

The main genre or text type in which pupils and students write in relation to English Literature is that of *critical appreciation or evaluation*, written for a teacher/examiner, in the context and purpose of showing the degree to which they are acquiring and developing the knowledge structures required for critical appreciation of the worlds created in and through texts. Developing control over critical appreciation is a recursive and reiterative process, as the vignettes in this chapter demonstrate. Textual organisation tools such as the PEE/L/PETER structure can prove helpful in terms of providing a support for their written expression, particularly when time is taken to explain and practise various elements of the structure. Such an audience, context and purpose require pupils to develop their command over written expression in standard English that includes developing the appropriate vocabulary and grammatical structures through which their knowledge—in this case, as expressed through critical appreciation—of literary and non-fiction texts.

Register features associated with this genre as evident in the texts pupils and students wrote, especially when writing about literary texts were:

- writing predominantly in the present tense;
- writing predominantly in the third person, particularly when referring to the author of a text but sometimes first or second person, and especially when expressing judgements and opinions;
- subjects of clauses and clause-complexes are normally concepts, characters and events in a text or the author being discussed;
- use of additive and causal conjunctions to signal explanations and to form sentences comprised of two or three clause-complexes;
- all verbal groups/processes drawn upon: behavioural, existential, material, mental, relational and verbal and in critical appreciation mainly relational, mental and verbal;
- use of pronouns as referents to link back to preceding sentences;
- use of modals and mental processes to signal interpretation;
- technical vocabulary to identify stylistic techniques in texts;
- describing/evaluating the effect of stylistic features used in the text being written about through use of verb groups and extended noun groups;
- use of quotes to support developing argument;
- increased nominalisation;
- increased semantic density and gravity.

The list given above is not a recipe that guarantees successful command of writing a critical appreciation of a literary or other non-fiction texts. Rather, it is a list of characteristics that exemplify its discursive practice. What changes throughout the key stages, is pupils' and students growing development of the *knower codes* and *knowledge structures* as evidenced through their developing control of the register features that taken together constitute the discursive practices associated with the genre of critical appreciation. In all three schools, participating teachers who were initially nervous about implementing an LBP approach reported that they had gone on to incorporate it into all their classes across all key stages and also into their approach in teaching other genres or text types such as persuasive writing. What felt like 'taking time out' to begin with, became part and parcel of their pedagogic practice, especially as teachers could see the tangible benefits of taking time to explain about the register features of the writing they were asking their pupils to undertake. In the words of a teacher from School C, '…giving time at the beginning means less mopping up and remedial work needing to be done at the other end'. In this way then, LBP suggests a re-ordering of pacing and sequencing rather than of finding 'extra time'.

A striking aspect of the curriculum for English is that it requires pupils and students at key stages 3 and 4 especially, to engage with the greatest number of genres or text types in their reading and writing when compared to those of other subjects. Arguably what they all have in common is that by and large they are concerned with the world of experience and imagination, rather than with the physical world that surrounds us. This is true even where non-fiction texts are chosen to link in with a cross-curricular theme such as mountains, as with *Stepping into the void* work with Year 8, where the focus is upon the mental and physical challenges climbing mountains brings, rather than with their physical properties which would be the main focus in a subject such as geography or geology. Consequently, the register features that characterise writing in these subjects can be very different, as the next two chapters demonstrate.

## References

Barton, G. (2012). *Don't call it literacy!* London: Routledge.
Giovanelli, M. (2014). *Teaching grammar, structure and meaning: Exploring theory and practice for post-16 English language teachers.* London: Routledge.
Giovanelli, M., & Clayton, D. (Eds.). (2016). *Knowing about language: Linguistics and the secondary English classroom.* London: Routledge.
Richmond, J. (2015). *Grammar and knowledge about language.* UKLA and Owen Education.
Richmond, J., Burn, A., Dougill, P., Goddard, A., Raleigh, M., & Traves, P. (2017). *Curriculum and assessment in English 11 to 19: A better plan.* London: Routledge.

# 5

# Developing Literacy Across the Curriculum for the Humanities: RE, History and Geography

## Introduction

In this chapter I develop the ideas presented in Chapter 4 by extending LBP and its pedagogic grammar in the context of the curriculum for subjects in the humanities, namely religious education, history and geography. I identify the main patterns of register and genre that characterise the texts that are talked about, read and written across the secondary school curriculum for these three subjects. I draw upon examples of schemes of work and lesson plans at each of the three key stages of 3, 4 and 5, together with interviews undertaken with teachers and samples of student work, to illustrate how paying attention to patterns of language structure can be integrated into the curriculum for the humanities.

Although all three subjects tend to sit within the humanities in terms of how schools organise different curriculum/subject areas, the examples below show the ways in which they are different, particularly in relation to geography, where discursive practices and knowledge structures arguably share more similarities with science than with either RE or history. Working with teachers to tease out principles of discourse that include specific patterns of textual organisation can be linked overtly to developing pupils' and students' written expression of disciplinary/subject specific concepts, ideas and knowledge.

Success or otherwise in using frames to scaffold writing then, rests in how they are used by teachers to help and support adolescents to organise their written expression articulately and logically, rather than to constrain and restrict such expression. It has to be remembered that the concept of a frame or framework is an abstract one, derived from the congruent notion of frames that support building structures or parts of such structures such as, for example, windows. Just as no one frame fits every single possible configuration of individual buildings or parts of it such as windows, so too no one frame can support every kind of academic written expression. Which frame a teacher draws upon depends upon the internal logic of the discourse practices associated with a specific subject. A frame that works perfectly well in one subject may not in another.

In the initial CPD session I held with teachers in the three participating schools, I explained that central to an LBP approach was identifying patterns of genres and the register features that characterised writing in their subjects. At all three schools, the first thing I was then asked was to identify a framework or writing frame that would work best for their subjects. I explained that I could not presume to provide such answers. What I was able to do, was to provide examples and to invite teachers to explore whether or not any of them could work for them in relation to their subjects. As has been previously discussed, the notion of frames such as PEE/L and IDEA had seeped into teachers' consciousness to varying degrees through the FTE and NLS initiatives, particularly in English and the humanities. Teachers therefore felt that what I was saying was nothing new to them. For teachers of science, however, the idea of frames was less familiar to them. As discussion in this chapter makes clear, those teachers who had introduced the use of scaffolds such as PEE/L and IDEA, came to realise that in so doing, they had not paid enough attention to explaining and unpacking for their pupils and students what the various elements—in other words main register features—actually entailed.

The sections below illustrates how teachers in RE, history and geography integrated LBP into her revised lesson planning through drawing upon writing frames as a way of supporting their delivery to take account of curriculum and assessment changes.

## RE

Changes in the curriculum for RE first introduced in 2010 were set against a changing demographic in England that has become culturally more diverse. GCSE and A Level programme specifications for RE frame concepts in open-ended ways to allow pupils and students to answer with reference to any religion(s) they have may studied. In this way, RE is more of a knower code like English literature than a knowledge code like history or geography as discussed in Chapter 2. Programme specifications allow for both the study of a single religion—Buddhism, Christianity, Hinduism, Islam, Judaism or Sikhism—or for a combination of any of the specified religions. At the same time, they have increased the amount of subject content and the word count of the writing undertaken for assessment, whilst curriculum time remains the same. The challenge for teachers then in RE alongside those of other subjects, is in relation to issues of pacing and sequencing. That is, how to deliver a curriculum that has expanded in terms of content and assessment requirements within the same timetabled lesson times as before.

## Key Stage 4: Year 10 Prophets

Harjit, the RE teacher in School A, Makepeace, had a degree in political science and sociology, and a PGCE in RE and Urdu which she also taught. She was of Pakistani origin, and had been teaching since 2009. She reported that she felt she had a good grasp of the grammar not only of English but also of Urdu, and held a position as deputy head of the Modern Languages curriculum area. Like many of the teachers who took part in the project, Harjit took to the idea of a writing frame or scaffold to support the development of her pupils' writing, but did not feel that any of the ones I had introduced were suitable for RE. She thus did some research of her own, and found writing frames online that had been developed by The Literacy Trust.

The class Harjit chose to take part in the project was a Year 10 GCSE class. As an initial step, she taught her class a series of lessons centred around the concept of prophets, where after teaching content she set her class a written assessment they completed at home worth a maximum of 15 marks. Below are two examples taken from this homework:

### Do we need another prophet in the 21$^{st}$ century?

**Pupil A** wrote:

*I agree with the statement because another prophet would help us for the better. This is because it would allow people to know what allowed in today society according to Islam. A prophet*
*√ would give us an insight on clear knowledge about a subject. These day because many things things exist now that didn't then people have inconclusive knowledge that might not be correct and might give them bad deeds. The prophet would interpret things in Islam that would be*
*√ easier for us.*

Of a possible 15 marks, the pupil gained 3, for the points made where ticks appear.

**Pupil B**

*I disagree because Prophet Muhammed was the last prophet and he was the seal of the prophet. √ "Muhammed [...] is god's messenger and the seal of the prophets". This quote shows that if there was another prophet there would be a confusion and some people would believe in the √ prophet and some won't.*

*Another reason is that if there is a new prophet there might be another Sharia law and people will get confused and might think that there would be a lot of confusion.*

> *Another reason is that if there was another prophet the schools would be confused too. Also, there would be fewer people who will believe and some will disagree with it.*

This pupil gained marked 8 out of 15, mainly for her use of a quote and attempts to give reasons.

As a result of taking part in the initial CPD session, Harjit paid more attention to the pupils' written expression than she had ever done previously. In common with other teachers, Harjit recognised that the difference between achieving low and high marks as illustrated in the examples given above, lay in understanding what was required in writing their answers as much as in the ideas expressed. For example, the second of the two extracts above uses quotes and tries to give reasons for the opinions given, which the first example does not. Harjit therefore thought that a writing frame of some kind might help her pupils to understand what they needed to include in their answers to achieve high marks: in other words, an understanding of genre and patterns of register associated with it. Rather than engage with the IDEA writing frame advocated by the Head of Humanities as discussed below, Harjit drew upon a framework devised by The National Literacy Trust. This framework identified different aspects of the *process* of reading, interpretation and writing, rather than identifying a specific supporting structure such as IDEA, as given below. The next two topics covered by the class were the notion of destiny as opposed to free will and whether or not Muslims should follow the Quran. Normally, Harjit would have asked her class to answer a question without any further preparatory work, following the pattern given above. In a departure from her usual practice, once she had completed teaching her next topic, she gave her class the sheet given below that focused upon their preparation for writing (Table 5.1).

Once the class had revisited the required reading for the topic, Harjit then devised a further frame to support the organisation of their written responses to a question (Table 5.2).

**164  U. Clark**

**Table 5.1**  Planning writing in GCSE RE

| Read, think and plan |
|---|
| Read the question or title and make sure you understand it thoroughly. Re-read it often. What will it include? |
| Where could you find the information? |
| Plan the writing process. |

| Research and brainstorm |
|---|
| Gather information relevant to the topic. |
| Use: textbooks, notes, ask friends, references from religious text. |

| Check relevance |
|---|
| Check that your information is relevant to the question you have been set. |

| Classify |
|---|
| Use an ordered set of headings or mind maps to sort your information into groups. E.g.,<br>• arguments for, arguments against<br>• reasons 1, 2, 3 etc<br>The categories you will use depend upon the question, so re-read it before you start classifying. |

| Write the question |
|---|
|  |

**Table 5.2** Structuring writing in RE

| |
|---|
| Define the key words: |
| Write whether or not you agree or disagree with the statement. Explain why? Every reason should be justified by giving examples. Reason 1: Reason 2: Reason 3: |
| State that some people would disagree with you. It's an evaluation question so you must give clear reasons. Write why? Reason 1: Reason 2: Reason 3: |

The class were then given a choice of two questions to answer. The same two pupils whose work is cited above wrote the following answers to each of the two questions:

***Every person makes their own destiny. Evaluate this statement considering arguments for and against.***

### Pupil A

*I believe that everyone does have their own destiny because when you are doing things good or bad you do it purely because it is your own choice that is called free will.* √√

*Allah has given us free will to do anything. When a person commits a deed they don't do it because Allah has told them to do it, that is incorrect. Allah has written down everything a person does their whole lifetime before they were even alive, this is written in a book called the loh-e-quran* √√

*Many people think that because it is written down why should they eb blamed for their actions. They think that if all of their actions are written and they are truly in control of what they do? This means can they really accomplish what they want to if it's all just written down for them.* √√

*In the Quran it states 'there is the one who gives, who is mindful of God, who testifies to goodness – we shall smooth his way towards ease.' This shows that the Quran reassures Muslims that they should continue to do good to work towards their destiny because it will make their life easier. It helps guide Muslims and keeps them steadfast in their faith nd belief in Allah.* √√

*However, others believe that because it is written down for them they cannot choose their path so it will not be their fault. They think that maybe if they don't have a choice on anything. The understanding of this comes from the people who think that they are on the wrong path or do bad deeds they justify it with that.* √√

The pupil gained 12 out of 15 marks for answering this question.

Do you agree that Muslims should follow the Quran?

**Pupil B**

*I agree that Muslims should follow the Quran because the message is original and nothing has changed or been corrupted. 'Gabriel – who by God's leave brought down the Quran to your heart.' Mulsims say that nothing has been changed therefore everything in the Quran is still in Allah's words. Also, if it was to change it wouldn't ever happen because Muslims have memorised the whole Quran by heart.* √

*Another reason is that prophet Muhammed was the last prophet and he revealed the Quran. Therefore the Quran should be the best respected and it has all the correct words of Allah. This shows it is because no one has changed the words and they are still the same.* √

*On the other hand, many people may disagree with me because even if the Bible or Toreh have been changed they have been sent down by Allah and it might not have all the truth but it has a little bit of it and they could follow that.* √

*Another reason is that the holy books are our six beliefs which means we have to believe in them even if they have been corrupted (changed). Also, not everything in the holy book has been changed, only parts of it which means most of it is true so you could still follow and it is part of their religion to follow these books.*

This pupil gained 13 out of 15 marks.

Both pupils' writing had improved in that they provided far more explanation in these answers than in the first examples given above. Pupil A showed the greatest improvement, through greater use of connectives other than 'because' such as 'this means that' and mental process verb groups such as 'believe', 'think.' The questions pupils are given to answer in RE such as these also share characteristics with those given in English Literature, in that they are concerned largely with abstract concepts that characterise the 'knower code'. In RE, the concepts are concerned with the identification of the divine as well as the human principles that have been inspired by the divine, but written by humans in constructing religious texts. One of the purposes of writing in RE is not only identify, evaluate and interpret abstract concepts and principles as given in religious texts but also to construe a certain subject position in relation to them. At GCSE, the illustrative examples above show that pupils construct subject positions through use of the first person in their clause structures, thereby constructing interpersonal relationships that are very personal.

## History

In common with other curriculum subjects in England, that of history has also been the subject of recent revision. Revisions have centred upon addressing a central issue identified by Carroll (2016, 2017a, b) amongst others, that pupils entering secondary school did not appear capable of producing complex, developmental narratives over long time periods that the chronological approach typical of historical discourse demands. Lack of such an overview generally results in them not being able to explain adequately key concepts of the discipline. Like others before him, Carroll found that many pupils are incapable of providing an overarching, single track account of the last 2000 years of British history. Moreover, hardly any pupils at all were able to describe history as a complex, developmental narrative. Carroll also points to a wealth of research that has explored how pupils find it hard to engage with the interplay in historical discourse between *depth* and *overview*, finding it difficult to make historical connections across broad time scales.

He attributes this to the lack of an overarching historical framework, wrought about by previous curricula glossing over vast periods of history, such as from the Roman period to the Norman Conquest, and the perception of history not as a continuum, but as a series of events against a background of swathes of time where nothing much happens. Consequently, lack of an overarching narrative framework has resulted in students not being able to apply '…the logical and methodological apparatus of historical enquiry to broader contexts' (2016: 455).

Revisions to the curriculum for history have sought to address the lack of an overarching narrative framework through (re)introducing the teaching of history in a chronological way. The new curriculum encompasses a more complete history of Britain, providing an overview of first civilisations such as Ancient Egypt, The Indus valley or The Shang Dynasty, studying significant individuals who have changed the course of history such as Christopher Columbus, Neil Armstrong and Rosa Parks and the includes study of a non-European society that contrasts with Britain, such as Baghdad or the Mayan civilisation. At GCSE, areas of history include medieval, Early Modern and Modern periods of history, from the year 500 to the present day. 40% of the curriculum is devoted to British history, with the requirement to study the history of the wider world and a thematic study of a period in history that has lasted for at least 50 years on political, cultural, economic or religious themes. At A Level, the chronological range to be studied is that of at least 200 years, with a strong focus on British history. Curriculum changes have been mirrored with changes to assessment, which require pupils and students to write answers of longer length and in examination conditions.

For history the aims of the National Curriculum are:

**Aims**
The national curriculum for history aims to ensure that all pupils:

- know and understand the history of these islands as a coherent, chronological narrative, from the earliest times to the present day: how people's lives have shaped this nation and how Britain has influenced and been influenced by the wider world

- know and understand significant aspects of the history of the wider world: the nature of ancient civilisations; the expansion and dissolution of empires; characteristic features of past non-European societies; achievements and follies of mankind
- gain and deploy a historically grounded understanding of abstract terms such as 'empire', 'civilisation', 'parliament' and 'peasantry'
- understand historical concepts such as continuity and change, cause and consequence, similarity, difference and significance, and use them to make connections, draw contrasts, analyse trends, frame historically-valid questions and create their own structured accounts, including written narratives and analyses
- understand the methods of historical enquiry, including how evidence is used rigorously to make historical claims, and discern how and why contrasting arguments and interpretations of the past have been constructed
- gain historical perspective by placing their growing knowledge into different contexts, understanding the connections between local, regional, national and international history; between cultural, economic, military, political, religious and social history; and between short- and long-term timescales.

https://www.gov.uk/government/uploads/system/uploads/attachment_data/file/381754/SECONDARY_national_curriculum.pdf

The challenge is thus for teachers to find ways to promote students' knowledge and understanding of grand historical narratives across time (overview), whilst also anchoring within any one narrative a specific occurrence (depth) and its impact upon the grander narrative. The remainder of this chapter illustrates ways in which teachers dew upon LBP in terms of addressing this challenge.

## Key Stage 3 Year 9: The Weimar Republic

Joan, a history teacher in School B, Greenford School, had a degree and a PGCE in history. She had been teaching for six years at the time of the project, three of them at School B. Like other teachers participating in the project, she reported that her pupils found it difficult to express the understanding they so clearly showed in class discussion in their writing. She also reported that they also found developing the grand narrative of history a challenge at this key stage. She could not recall ever having been taught any grammar herself, but had been attracted to taking part in the project in relation to developing her pupils' organisation of writing. The question she was preparing her class to answer was: *Why was 1923 such a difficult year for the Weimar Republic?*

In preparation for the topic, she undertook her usual practice of giving her class two separate word lists, as follows, the first of which was vocabulary specific to the Weimar Republic—the historical depth—and the second of which was vocabulary in relation to historical concepts, and historical breadth:

### Weimar Republic

*French and Belgian troops*
*January*
*War guilt*
*Ruhr*
*Hyper-inflation*
*Worthless*
*Closure*
*November*
*Nationalists*
*Beer Hall*

*Passive resistance*
*Reparations*
*Default*
*Inflation*
*November*
*Unemployment*
*Munich*
*Nazis*
*Angry*

### Historical Concepts
- *Significance*
- *Turning Point*
- *Change*
- *Continuity*
- *Impact*
- *Progress*
- *Regress*

She also used the IDEA frame, mapping it onto assessment gradings (Table 5.3).

Table 5.3 IDEA in history

| |
|---|
| I = identify (emerging—grade 1–2)<br>• Identify the key ideas<br>• Use who? Where? What? When?<br>• Give brief examples |
| D = description (developing—grade 3–4)<br>• State your evidence<br>• Write about the idea in detailed sentences<br>• Use your description to answer the enquiry question<br>• Cover as many of the 5ws as possible (why, where, when,) |
| E = explanation (secure—grade 5–6)<br>• Explain your ideas, and say 'why'<br>• Link back to the enquiry question<br>• Focus on 'how' and 'why' |
| A = analysis (excellence—grade 7–9)<br>• Use the 'x'tra factor by incorporating words from the second list<br>• Write a conclusion not a summary<br>• Make sure that you give your judgement about the enquiry question |
| In history, the interpersonal element of their writing rests in pupils' being asked to give their judgement about a particular topic, such as: *'The British Empire was good.' How far do you agree with this statement?* Or the one about the Weimar Republic she was preparing her class to write about. In addition to mapping the IDEA framework onto assessment criteria, she also provided explanations of each of the four elements:<br><br>• **Identify**: A topic sentence at the start of a paragraph identifying the key judgement that the paragraph will explore.<br>• **Describe**: Descriptive sentences which cover the 4Ws Who? What? When? Where?<br>• **Explain**: Give judgements in relation to the 4Ws on the question. E.g. *This means/shows that the British Empire was bad because….*<br>• **Analyse**: Relate the question to explain its broader and wider significance: E.g. *The impact of this was…. The significance of this was… This was a turning point because…* |

In a departure from her usual practice and in preparation for writing the answer to the question: *Why was 1923 such a difficult year for the Weimar Government?* Joan asked her class in pairs to write an introductory paragraph, drawing upon the IDEA framework and the vocabulary she had gone through with them as given above. One pair wrote:

> *1923 was a difficult year for the Weimar Government because they faced three crises. Firstly, they defaulted on the reparations payments which had been imposed on them by the Allies through the TOV. They had been made to pay them because Germany was deemed to take the blame for the war. This was known as war guilt. This led to the French and Belgian troops occupying the Ruhr, the industrial heartland of Germany.*

Joan talked through the example with the whole class, asking for pupils to give their ideas on ways in which the paragraph could be improved. Through discussion, the guided her pupils to see that in an introductory paragraph where a first sentence had identified three crises, subsequent sentences should follow on like the second one in the extract above, to identify all three crises, before going on to discuss each in turn. This vignette illustrates one way in which one teacher, Joan, drew upon LBP in paying attention to aspects of genre and register in history, focusing upon textual organisation, subject-specific vocabulary and some of the register features in relation to the structure of sentences that answer questions related to *who, what, where* and *why*. Joan, in common with all teachers who participated in the project, reported that as a result of participating in it, integrating literacy aspects into her teaching—especially paying explicit attention to textual organisation and vocabulary in particular and modelling and deconstructing paragraphs—became something that she now paid attention to as a matter of course, where this had not previously been the case.

## Key Stage 5 Year 12: Mao's China

Claire was a teacher in School A, Makepeace, with a degree in history and a PGCE, had spent her first few years as a teacher teaching English in China, and therefore had a great deal of experience teaching English in an L2 context. She prided herself on understanding that her students from EAL backgrounds would have little, if no, background knowledge of the history of China, thereby relying almost entirely upon her teaching and guided independent study outside of the classroom to make sure knowledge and understanding of the topic was covered. She chose a Year 12 A Level class to participate in the project, following the newly revised A Level history syllabus, on the topic of Mao's China. The syllabus required students to demonstrate a breadth of Chinese history, beginning in 1911 with the ending of 2000 years of Dynastic Rule to the present day. Depth is provided in the form of the 1957 Hundred Flowers campaign, ostensibly designed to lift the restrictions imposed upon Chinese intellectuals, thereby granting greater freedom of thought and speech than had previously been allowed.

A key feature in the history curriculum in the UK at A level, is the emphasis placed upon the interpretation of source material relevant to the question being asked. The topic Claire was teaching was in relation to answering question based upon four source extracts: *How far do extracts 1 - 4 concur or differ in their interpretations of Mao's motives for introducing the Hundred Flowers campaign in 1957?*

The question then, assumed knowledge of Chinese history in breadth against which to set discussion in depth of the hundred flowers campaign. Claire focussed her preparation on answering the question with knowledge building activities centring upon the rise of Communist China in the twentieth century following 2000 years of Dynastic Rule, the rise and defeat of the warlords, the rise of communism under Mao, the cultural revolution of 1966–1976 and the part played within it of the hundred flowers campaign. Her class of predominantly EAL students necessitated a great deal of input in terms of coming to understand the 'grand narrative' of Communist China and Mao's place within it. After a series of input lessons centering upon topic content, Claire asked her students to independently write the answer to the question above.

Claire reported to me that despite feeling that she had prepared her students adequately to answer the question, when she marked her pupils' written work, she was disappointed. As with Harjit in the RE example above, Through her marking of the written work, it became evident to her that her students had difficulty in first, interpreting each individual source they had been given and second, integrating and interweaving their interpretations of each source against one another. She thus decided to spend time in class deconstructing each individual source and also comparing them against one another. The words/phrases/clause/sentences that appear in bold below, are ones that Claire identified would most need to be explained to her class.

### Extract 1
*From Jung Chang and Jon Halliday, <u>Mao: The Unknown story</u>, Jonathan Cape <u>2005</u>, p. 435*

Few guessed that Mao **was setting a trap**, and that he was **inviting people** to speak out so that he could use what they said as an excuse to **victimise them**. Mao's targets were intellectuals and the educated, the people most likely to speak up.

### Extract 2
*Lee Feigon, <u>Mao: A Reinterpretation,</u> Ivan R. Dee, <u>2002</u>, p. 112*

By giving scientists and engineers the freedom to express their ideas, Mao sought to prevent party **bureaucrats** from interfering with **technical decisions**. He wanted intellectuals to expose and attack corruption and *bureaucracy*. He also wanted peasants, students and workers to speak out and even demonstrate to prevent government bureaucrats from running *roughshod* over their rights.

### Extract 3
*From Yves Chevrier, <u>Mao and the Chinese Revolution,</u> Interlink Books <u>2004</u>, p. 123*

From 100 Flowers turned out to be the eye of the cyclone that would bring the **Great Leap**, itself a precursor of the **Cultural Revolution**. This moment of open debate when **contradictions** were openly discussed for the first time in years, was like a carnivorous flower, ready to **close upon its prey.** It enabled Mao's **political comeback** within the party leadership.

### Extract 4
*Jonathan Spence, <u>The search for Modern China</u>, W.W. Norton, <u>1990</u>, p. 574*

It was rather a muddled and inconclusive movement that grew out of **conflicting attitudes within the CCP leadership**. At its core was an argument about the pace and development that was best for China, a debate about the nature of the First Five – year plan and the promise for **further growth**. From that debate and the political tensions that accompanied it sprang the Great Leap Forward.

In a departure from her usual practice, Claire focussed her attention upon the wording of the four source extracts to make sure her students understood all of them. This was followed by an activity that identified key points across all four sources. The class brainstormed the key factors associated with the question, which Claire put into a grid along the left handside with the extracts given across the top plus an extra column for students' own knowledge. This blank table was given to the class and in pairs, they were asked to complete it by identifying quotes from each source in support of the factors identified. They then completed the grid as a class as follows (Table 5.4).

Claire then wrote a mentor text for source one to show ways in which to interlink source material and subject knowledge, as follows:

*Example:*

***Source one is an extract written in 2005 which is long after the death of Mao.*** *It is written by Jung Chang, who is Chinese.* **He** *explains the negative viewpoint of the Hundred Flowers Campaign. He describes how very few had guessed that Mao was setting a trap for the people, only so that he could later use this as an excuse to victimise them. This shows that Jung was aware of Mao's* ***ill intentions which were not very common, despite the fact that it was in the year 2005. This is because even today, the majority of China's remains ignorant of Mao's destructive acts. They still see him as a godly figure***.

Claire then asked her class to work on ways to improve on the answer, which resulted in the following paragraphs:

*Example*:

*Class improved answer:*

*It can be argued that Mao had many motives behind introducing the Hundred Flower Campaign; one of which is setting the trap for political rivals. Extract one – four appear to agree with this notion. Extract one we establish that Mao attempted to set … "a trap" for political rivals and intellectuals and these posed the greatest threat to his leadership. This view can be further supported by extract two "He wanted intellectuals to expose and*

**Table 5.4** Interpreting sources in GCE history

| Factor | Extract 1 | Extract 2 | Extract 3 | Extract 4 | Own knowledge |
|---|---|---|---|---|---|
| Mao wanted to set a trap for opposition in and out of his party | ✓ "Mao was setting a trap" | ✓ "He wanted intellectuals to expose and attack corruption" | ✓ "close upon its party" | ✓ "conflicting attitudes within the CCP party" | Unhealthy man: paranoid by nature; Zhou Enlai plane crash; Terror campaign: Gao Gang and Rao Shushi |
| Political freedom | ✓ …intellectuals and the educated, the people most likely to speak up | ✓ he wanted intellectuals to expose…and bureaucracy | ✓ contradictions were openly discussed for the first time in years, was like a carnivorous flower | ✓ debate and political tensions | The cult of personality; Centralism, democracy: Politburo, Chinese Communist Party Congress; The little red book; Authoritarian figure |
| Further economic growth | X | ✓ scientists and engineers the freedom to express their ideas | ✓ by the eye of the cyclone that would bring the great leap | ✓ promise for future growth | Lysenkoism: use new breeds and seeds, plant closely, plough deep, increase fertilisation, use new farm tools, improve field management, pests, increase irrigation; Great leap forward with USA and Britain; Paying back USSR loans with grain |

(continued)

Table 5.4 (continued)

| Factor | Extract 1 | Extract 2 | Extract 3 | Extract 4 | Own knowledge |
|---|---|---|---|---|---|
| Political comeback | X | √ to prevent government bureaucrats from running roughshod over their rights. | √ enabled Mao's political comeback within the party leadership | √ muddled and inconclusive movement that grew out of conflicting attitudes within the CCP leadership …political tensions | Swam the Yantze river, joined by peasants in support which showed health and fitness; Balmed corrupt/weak CCP officials for the failure of collectivisation/the great famine; The Great Leap Forward |

attack corruption" From my own knowledge I know that Mao used a reign of terror throughout his leadership, an example of this could be Gao Gang and Rao Shushi who were publicly humiliating and denounced from the party. Extract three supports this opinion by claiming that the campaigned allowed Mao the opportunity to "close upon…prey". The land Reforms of 1950 and collectivisation resulted in conflicting attitudes within the CCP leadership". Therefore Mao used the campaign as an opportunity to purge any political rivals or conflicts.

*Example*:

*Class improved answer:*

*A historian could make use of Sources B and D together to investigate the response of the Chinese people to the introduction of the Great Leap Forward. This is because both sources show the support of the peasants "Iron smelting and steel making in Shaoyang, Hunan Province, are rapidly developing on a mass scale" This tells me that the majority of the Chinese population was in favour of and supported the Great Leap Forward by building their backyard furnaces at a fast rate. This view can be further supported by, "This movement has been spontaneous and started by the mass of peasants on the basis of great socialist consciousness". This means that government intervention was minimal and it was in fact of peasant thinking and enthusiasm that communes and steel production were a direct response to the Great Leap Forward.*

*On the other hand however one also needs to take into account the limitations of the evidence. Sources B and D are not useful to historians to investigate the response of the Chinese people to the introduction of the Great Leap Forward because…….*

Upon marking her students' second attempt at answering this question, one girls' mark went up from a grade E to a grade A, and another's also from grade E to borderline AB. It was clear from their writing that the pupils had not only in their first attempt misunderstood the sources, but also how to integrate and refer to them in comparative ways.

Claire was thus able to focus her attention on making sure her students were aware of the organisational structure required by the answer to a historical question, focusing upon answering it that required analysis and evaluation rather than simply describing their subject knowledge. Her strategy for comparing sources as given above had clearly worked, in relation to pupils' understanding of the source extracts and how to integrate them with their own knowledge to develop successful arguments. Claire also integrated oral rehearsal of written answers into her discussions with the class, where students, having teased out a particular point, rehearsed orally how they would write what they had just said. Claire has gone on to incorporate the strategies discussed above throughout her teaching, providing greater exemplification of the IDEA framework as discussed above and focusing upon explaining key relational concepts in historical discourse such as cause and consequence; change versus continuity, similarity versus difference, expressed through clauses such as *It can be argued that...; Some historians believe....*

Students' interpersonal subject positions in history are taken up in relation to the weighing of evidence as expressed through historical texts, through extending their understanding of grand historical narratives, and how specific historical events relate to the broader narrative. Like writing in English Literature, in history such subject positions are evoked through the use of writing in the third person 'A historian could make…' and the pronoun 'one', rather than the 'I' characteristic of writing in RE. Such subject positioning, even though construed more personally in relation to the subject matter being studied, has the effect of distancing the interpersonal relationships between the writer and the texts about which they are writing in ways that are characteristic and typical of academic discourse in these subjects.

## Geography

Green and Lee (1994) in their study of the role of geography in literacy, identity and schooling, explore the relationship between school writing and student learning in terms of self-production and social formation. They locate their discussion in the general point that the different ways in which various curriculum identities are both constructed and subsequently maintained, through the positions writers take up in relation to the range of discourses associated with the text's production. They also point out that within any one disciplinary/school subject there is not one single subject position but many. This means that writers are constantly negotiating their way through those that are available to them, of which some are more accepted than others.

> **Quote**
>
> To learn and succeed at geography means learning how to take up an authoritative position within a particular scientific-rational discourse. It means to consent (rather than resist) the performance, display and resultant (re)production of official curriculum versions of geographical facts and interpretations and their associated forms of intertextuality. It also necessarily means to suppress whatever does not fit into that category...all students must acquire a critical dimension to literacy, one that allows them to adopt various authoritative positions within a discourse or subject area field, yet not assume 'identity' with these positions.
> (Green and Lee 1994: 220–221)

The ways in which pupils construct subject identities then and the nature of the interpersonal relationship between the audience, context of purpose of writing in geography is very different from that in other school subjects. As Green and Lee point out, writing in geography requires pupils to take up scientific, interpersonally 'distancing' subject positions that allow them to engage with geography's discursive practices by adopting authoritative positions without assuming identity with them. These positions are different from those they are required to take up in subjects such as English, RE, and history, where subject positions are construed more personally in relation to the subject matter being studied. Interpersonal positions are achieved discursively through the linguistic patterning associated with geography texts, to show the extent to which pupils and students have understood key conceptual terms and interpretation of data and sources of differing kinds.

In a 'think piece' written for the Geography Association, Butt wrote:

> **Quote**
> Geography, like any other subject discipline, has a very specific language and we should use the particular forms of language and literacy best suited to posing and answering geographical questions. Simply bolting on generic, cross-curricular 'literacy strategies' may not always promote geographical understanding – such strategies need to appreciate the language, concepts, structures and aims of the subject to ensure that geographical thinking and understanding are advanced. Therefore, if sensitively applied, literacy strategies – such as writing frames, card sorts, DARTs etc. – may only marginally improve children's understanding of the subject.
> https://www.geography.org.uk/download/ga_tp_writing.pdf

Butt was taking issue in the quote above with the ways in which activities promoted by the NLS in the 1990s and 2000s emphasised the skills aspect of writing at the expense of writing that developed and expressed conceptual thinking and understanding. Also in geography, the concept of text is multi modal and includes charts, diagrams, geo-spatial representation of information, graphs, maps and other pictures, both static and animated. Assessment in geography often requires answers based upon a visualisation of some kind such as a map, graph or chart representative of the physical world that pupils are asked to interpret. Geography thus requires a high level of numeracy as well as literacy in relation to pupils' interpretations of geographic texts. Although the writing required for assessment has become longer in length, it is still relatively short when compared to the kind of writing that occurs in subjects such as drama, English, history and RE, and is more akin to that which takes place in subjects such as science and PE. As such, it makes different demands upon literacy and numeracy skills, that generic literacy strategies of the kind exemplified in the quote above do little in and of themselves to promote subject knowledge and understanding, as also discussed in Chapter 4.

The stance I have taken when talking to teachers, either as a group as part of CPD or in individual conversations, has been that I make no claim to being anywhere near as expert as any one of them in relation to their own subjects, but that I am expert in language and discourse/text analysis. By the very virtue of them being a teacher of a specific secondary school subject, teachers are expert in the discursive practices that characterise their subjects. Through sharing their lesson planning and student work with me, I saw my task as primarily that of identifying the discursive features of genre and register with which teachers are familiar, and helping them to identify them so that they can be made explicit in their teaching. As the geography example in Chapter 3 has illustrated, teachers do not need to have a great deal of input to help them to do this, particularly when such input is focused and targeted upon their own discursive practices.

The examples given below illustrate further the features of genre/text type and register that characterise writing in geography. One striking feature is that their range, as with those in RE and history, is limited, characterised by explanations that include analysis, evaluation and interpretation as well as description of the contemporary physical world of the here and now. This is in contrast to explanations given in history that deal with the intangible past reconstructed through surviving texts and relics and different again from RE and English Literature that are more concerned with the spiritual world and that of the imagination. Thus, whilst a genre or text type may occur across several subjects, the interpersonal relationships construed within them can be very different.

Most recently, criticisms of the national curriculum for geography in the UK (as elsewhere around the world) have centred upon the perception that secondary geography had focused for too long upon new pedagogic technologies, classroom techniques and alternative modes of student assessment as a predominantly skills-based curriculum, disconnected from the wider academic discipline. Changes to the curriculum have sought to redress this with a greater emphasis upon its conceptual and knowledge based.

> **Quote**
> Geography is, as Alistair Bonnett says, one of humanity's big idea (Bonnett 2007). It is concerned with producing and communicating knowledge about the world: its places, its morphology, its features and patterns.

> Thinking geographically provides us with a deeper understanding of the human occupation of the earth. All children and young people deserve the best geographical education, therefore, as it contributes significantly to their knowledge and understanding of their place in the world. It teaches us about human relationships across the globe, and the interaction of people with the physical environment.
> (Lambert 2011: 245)

It is not the place of this chapter to rehearse or recap the controversies and debates surrounding recontextualisations of geography in recent years. Rather, its focus is upon the specific features of its discursive practice. The symbiotic nature between developing knowledge and understanding and expressing required knowledge and understanding is made clear in the aims of the revised the National Curriculum aims for geography which at Key Stage 3 are:

**Quote**

**Aims**

The national curriculum for geography aims to ensure that all pupils:

- develop contextual knowledge of the location of globally significant places – both terrestrial and marine – including their defining physical and human characteristics and how these provide a geographical context for understanding the actions of processes
- understand the processes that give rise to key physical and human geographical features of the world, how these are interdependent and how they bring about spatial variation and change over time
- are competent in the geographical skills needed to:
- collect, analyse and communicate with a range of data gathered through experiences of fieldwork that deepen their understanding of geographical processes
- interpret a range of sources of geographical information, including maps, diagrams, globes, aerial photographs and Geographical Information Systems (GIS)
- communicate geographical information in a variety of ways, including through maps, numerical and quantitative skills and writing at length.

https://www.gov.uk/government/uploads/system/uploads/attachment_data/file/381754/SECONDARY_national_curriculum.pdf

Although in the UK geography is located within humanities curriculum areas or departments/faculties, the subject is arguably more closely aligned with those that characterise the sciences. Wignall, Martin and Eggins in their chapter in the seminal 1993 book *Writing Science: Literacy and Discursive Power*, edited by Halliday and Martin, argue that the discourse of geography is indistinguishable from that of science, with the main difference being the lack of experiments to demonstrate a scientific world view, a conclusion they drew an analysis of lower secondary geography textbooks:

> **Quote**
>
> Our analysis here suggests that in the discourse of geography, language is used in three distinct ways, which correspond to the three tasks geography sees itself as fulfilling. First, language is used to 'observe' the experiential world through the creation of a technical vocabulary: a process of dividing up and naming those parts of the world that are significant to geographers. Second, language is used to order the experiential world, through the setting up of field-specific taxonomies. And third, language is used to 'explain' the experiential world, through the positing of implicational relations among natural or manmade states.
>
> In the language of geography only the functions of classifying and explaining necessarily involve a shift from the common or everyday use of language. Ordinary, everyday language can be used to observe and describe things. For example a landform could be described as a kind of hill with steep sides and a flat top. But by naming the landform a mesa, the geographer has created technical name for the landform and at the same time placed it into a set of taxonomic oppositions with other landforms, for example, mesas and butts.
>
> --------------------
>
> In science, the move from describing to classifying is a move from the everyday to the technical; and the move from classifying to explaining is a move from talking about things to talking about processes.
> (Wignell et al. 1993: 152)

The following vignette taken from School C, illustrates such a move from the everyday to the technical, and how geography shifts from talking about things to talking about processes.

## Key Stage 3: Year 8 Life Expectancy Around the Globe

Beth, the geography teacher, had a Ph.D. in Geography as well as a PGCE. She had been teaching for four years, all of them at School C. She could not recall ever having been taught any grammar herself, although she was aware of the importance of textual organisation as part of the process of writing of her Ph.D. thesis. Prior to taking part in the project, she had never given much thought to drawing explicit attention to the language of geography. Like many other teachers participating in the project, after the CPD group input session she felt more comfortable drawing upon and integrating aspects of LBP in relation to features of genre/text type in the context of her pupils' own writing tasks, rather than specific features of register. The sequence of lessons she chose to take part in the project was on the topic of contemporary, differing patterns and trends associated with life expectancy around the globe. Beth began her sequence of lessons in the usual way, developing the concepts and associated knowledge and understanding of the topic. She followed her usual pattern of sequencing and pacing her classroom practice, by asking her class to write their own, independent answer, centred upon a graph showingin diagrammatic form the relationship between life expectancy and income per person in a range of divers countries from around the world in 2013 such as the USA, India, Vietnam and South Africa. The task she set was:

*Describe the trends/patterns in the graph (4 marks).*

Normally, the sequence of lessons would have ended there with Beth marking the pupils' work and moving on to another topic. However, in common with all participating teachers, the focus upon textual organisation and structure that was the focus of the CPD session I ran in school C led Beth to pay more attention to this aspect of her pupils' written work. In common with the RE and history teacher discussed above, the impact of that CPD session was that Beth paid more attention to the language through which her pupils' answered the question, and brought to light for her a thread running throughout the project. This was, that pupils struggled with giving coherent and logical expression to the assimilation of their thoughts as gained through their reading and subsequent discussion. Like the pupils in schools A and B, those in School C Beth said, tended to splurge (or vomit, in her words) their ideas onto paper in unfocussed ways that bring to mind Cobbett's analogy of throwing seeds willy-nilly onto a field as discussed in Chapter 1. Thus, despite the varying economic, linguistic and socio-economic backgrounds of the pupils and studnets in all three schools, a common theme emerged of their struggles to engage with discursive practices and the subject positionings therein of different curriculum subjects.

Beth could thus see the potential benefit of introducing her class to a writing frame that could support their writing. However, she did not think that any of the ones I had outlined at the CPD session however suited her purposes, and she thus sought advice from her colleagues in geography. One of them introduced her to a frame (that he had found on Twitter) based upon **T**rend (pattern); **E**xample (statistic) and **A**nomaly (TEA). Beth would normally have gone and begun another topic with her class, but in a change from her usual practice, she introduced a lesson centred upon the register patterns in which she was asking her pupils to write, and gave the class an exemplar answer or mentor text she had written herself:

> *The general **trend** of the graph is that the higher the GDP per capita, the longer the life expectancy. Some **examples** are the Central African Republic with a GDP of around $500 and a life expectancy of around 53. Another **example** is Kuwait with a GDP of over $40,000 and a life expectancy of around 80. However, there are some **anomalies** such as Swaziland with a GDP of around $9000 and life expectancy of around 49.*

As part of the discussion with her class, Beth pointed out how she could improve on this first attempt, by saying what kind of trend is evident and offering an explanation for anomalies:

*The general **trend** of the graph is that the higher the GDP per capita, the longer the life expectancy **(linear or exponential?)**. Some examples are the Central African Republic with a GDP of around $500 and a life expectancy of around 53 (units). Another example is Kuwait with a GDP of over $40,000 and a life expectancy of around 80 (units). However, there are some **anomalies** such as Swaziland with a GDP of around $9000 and life expectancy of around 49 (units).' (**Why is this an anomaly?**)*

She asked her class in pairs to answer the two questions she had incorporated into the mentor text and to give reasons for them, followed by discussion by the class as a whole. In preparation for writing the answer to the question a second time, she provided the class with a key word bank for describing graphs:

– *Overall*
– *Increase/decrease*
– *Stable*
– *Rapid/quick*
– *Exponential/linear*
– *Slow/Steady*
– *Gradual*
– *Biggest/smallest*
– *Faster/Slower/More/Less*
– *By ……. %/By …….million*
– *From…….to…….*
– *Highest/Lowest*
– *Whereas/however*
– *Similar/different from*

*Don't forget data and units!*

The class then answered the same question again. As a result, one pupil who had written the following:

*Most of the countries go up diagonally. However, there are a few anomalies such as Swaziland and other countries I have circled. Most of the big countries are higher up than the small ones.*

0 marks

On his second attempt wrote:

*The general trend of the graph is the higher the income per person, the higher the life expectancy. The examples include USA which has a life expectancy of over 80 years and an average income of about 40,000 dollars. Another example is India which has an average life expectancy of 65 and GDP of 5000. I chose these because they are different. (teacher comment: how?) The anomaly is Swaziland because it has an income per person of 7,00 but a life expectancy of 50 (fairly low).*

4 marks

The change from the first attempt to the second lies mainly in how noun and verb groups are constructed. In the first attempt, the pupil wrote: *Most of the countries* go up *diagonally*. This gained him 0 marks. In the second attempt, this sentence became: *The general trend of the graph* is *the higher the income per person, the higher the life expectancy*. This reformulation meant that the pupil gained a mark for this. Although still a single clause, the noun groups of both subject/participant and complement/circumstance have been expanded to firstly, alter the focus of the subject from the countries themselves to the graph and secondly, to explain in more detail what was meant by *diagonally* and to what it referred in the first attempt. The noun group that makes up the subject position in the first sentence relates to information as given in the graph, in turn related through the relational verb/process *is* as to the interpretation of that information. As discussed in Chapter 2, the complexity of the sentence lies not in its grammatical structure (present tense, single clause), but through its noun grouping. The next vignette illustrates this point further.

## Key Stage 3 Year 9: The Geography of Disease

Faye was a teacher in School A, with a degree and PGCE in geography, who has already featured in Chapter 3. She had been struck by the processes of nominalisation I had introduced in my first CPD session at the school, whereby words used to express actions or events through verbs or verb groups into things and concepts as nouns or noun groups. Faye recognised that nominalisation was a key feature of writing in geography. She grasped the concept immediately, that also led her to understand the concepts of verb and noun groups. She chose a Year 9 class to take part in the project on the topic of the geography of disease. After her usual sequence of lessons teaching topic content and field, in a departure from her normal practice, Faye prepared the following worksheet for her class (Table 5.5).

Below is an exemplar answer to 2 and 3 above written by one of the pupils.

2.
*People may get infected if they come into contact with a victim of Ebola.*

*People who are vaccinated are most likely to become ill with a deadly disease.*

*People should take caution and prepare for when they go abroad to hot places where there are mosquitos.*

*An infection can occur if a person comes into contact with a person infected with the Ebola virus.*

*People who have the vaccination are most likely not going to become ill with a deadly disease.*

*People should make preparations for when they go abroad so they are less likely to be bitten by a mosquito.*

3.
*The UK has been making preparations for the outbreak of Avian flu. To avoid infection farmers have made preparations such as keeping flocks of sheep away from wild birds who may spread the disease, watering them indoors and keeping them indoors if necessary to make sure the possibility of infection is low. Tests have to be carried out on wild birds to check for any signs of avian flu.*

*The treatment for avian flu needs a vaccination and the government has bought 120 million doses of a vaccine called Tamiflu. A combination of taking measures to avoid infection and vaccinations being made available should anyone contract the disease are two ways that the UK is making preparations for the outbreak.*

**Table 5.5** Nominalisation in geography

---

Year 9 The Geography of Disease

**Nominalisation**

Nominalisation is an important feature of expressing facts and concepts in geography. It is the name given to the ways in which English changes words used to express actions or events through *verbs* or *verb groups* into things or concepts as *nouns* or *noun groups*.

---

1. Underline the **verb group** in the first set of words on the left, and its **nominalisation** on the right. The first one has been done for you.

| | |
|---|---|
| Avian flu <u>breaks out</u> | Avian flu <u>outbreak</u> |
| People may get infected | the possibility of infection |
| People prepare | make preparations |
| Try not to get infected | avoid infection |
| To treat Avian flu | treatment of Avian flu |
| People who are vaccinated | people who have the vaccination |

2. Write **three sentences** of your own that use verbs or verb groups related to this topic and write as many of them again as you can into nominalisations.

For example

Verbs: The UK *is preparing* for avian flu *breaking out* by banning chickens *coming into* the country from places where avian flu *has happened*.

Nominalisation: The UK is making *preparations* for an avian flu *outbreak* by banning the *importation* of chickens from places where avian flu has happened.

3. Now write **two paragraphs** using the nominalised phrases above about how the UK is preparing for an outbreak of avian flu.

Faye felt that focussing upon nominalisation in this way helped her pupils to both understand geographic concepts and to achieve subjective distance that geographic discourse demands. The vignette above was Faye's first attempt at integrating an aspect of LBP into her teaching, and encouraged by the result, has gone on to focus on nominalisation in all her classes. She has also gone on to spend more time on drafting activities with her pupils in preparation for writing a summative assessment. She has gone on to write mentor texts for her pupils using the PEEL framework, spending time on deconstructing the mentor texts and giving time to group and individual drafting activities and more personalised feedback. Far from feeling as if such activities take 'time away' from teaching geography Faye, like so many other teachers, said that they save time, since pupils are far clearer and more aware of what counts as successful writing in geography. The pacing and sequencing of her lessons then, has changed to incorporate attention to the language of geography, without in any way sacrificing acquisition of subject knowledge.

## Conclusion

In humanities subjects such as RE, history and geography, and in common with that of English Literature, one of the key challenges facing pupils and students in writing for assessment purposes is how to organise and structure their ideas and thoughts in the appropriate register patterns of each subject and within the overall textual patterning of the genres they write. Writing frames centred upon mnemonics in these subjects such as IDEA, PEE/L and TEA are some of the ways in which pupils can be scaffolded into expressing their thought in writing in coherent and logical ways. The teachers of RE, history and geography in all three participating schools drew upon an LBP approach initially in relation to making explicit and visible aspects of textual organisation and paying more attention to ensuring that pupils understood subject specific vocabulary, and in the last example given, a specific feature of register, that of nominalisation. All have gone on to embrace further aspects of LBP with all classes that they teach. The focus upon textual organisation was something to which all the teachers could relate, and helped to boost their confidence in relation to addressing literacy aspects of their subjects in the context of their pupils' writing. This chapter illustrates ways in which two of the assumed obstacles to an LBP approach, namely lack of teacher confidence in grammar and paying attention to language taking time away from the development of subject knowledge, can be overcome when it is embraced as part and parcel of that development. In a very short space of time, teachers brought the discursive practices associated with their subjects to the centre stage of their teaching, particularly in relation to not only writing but also in developing their pupils' reading comprehension and giving more time in class to discussion. The pacing and sequencing of lessons were revised to make space for this.

Discussion in this chapter as in the previous one, points to the symbiotic nature of the relationship between grammar, punctuation, vocabulary and textual organisation in relation to subject specific discursive practices. It also illustrates ways in which attention to literacy through such a pedagogic grammar is not a 'bolt on' or an afterthought, something to be paid attention to and commented on *after* a piece of writing is complete. Rather, it is integral to formative activities in relation to the whole process of knowledge acquisition and development. Though the project focussed upon LBP and the LTC in relation to writing, writing would not be possible without its foundations in the reading and talk through which pupils construct their knower codes. As one teacher identified:

- Teaching pupils how to structure their work is crucial. We can't expect pupils just to know what to do, they have to be trained and they have to keep practicing.
- Being consistent in the approach every lesson is crucial.
- Using the structure throughout the lesson in lots of different ways e.g. objectives, key words, content, pupils' written and oral work.
- Paying attention to developing their comprehension of the texts they read and understanding key vocabulary.

What is most striking about the kind of writing pupils undertook in the three subjects discussed in this chapter, is how that undertaken in RE and history shares features that are more in common with English literature than geography. Teachers may use genres or text types such as newspaper or magazine articles as a way of helping pupils bridge the move from everyday genres to academic ones, but writing for assessment is in the main that of critical interpretation and evaluation in relation to abstract concepts in RE and past events in history that centre upon people and texts.

Register features in RE and history include:

- single clause or clause complexes, usually co-ordinating linked by *and* and *because* that give reasons for opinions through conjunctions such as *because; despite, by, therefore, however*
- use of pronouns as referents to refer back to nouns in previous clauses
- verb processes mainly mental, verbal and relational
- participants/subjects are first person, people, ideas and texts
- complements/objects are ideas, groups of people, people, texts
- use of expanded noun groups and nominalisations
- less use of adverbials and adjectives
- subject specific vocabulary, with increasing semantic density and gravity
- interweaving of abstract principles with textual references to religious texts (RE) and sources (history)
- extended writing through the use of paragraphs to write essays based upon critical argumentation, evaluation and interpretation.

Register features for geography include:

- single clause or clause complexes of usually co-ordinating clauses linked by conjunctions *and, because* that give reasons for opinions and others such *despite, by, therefore*; relative clauses
- verb groups/ processes: mental, material and relational
- participants/subjects are people, animals, physical phenomena
- complements/objects are ideas, groups of people, people
- use of expanded noun groups and nominalisations
- less use of adverbials and adjectives than in English, RE and history
- subject-specific vocabulary
- use of maps, graphs, diagrams, photographs and illustrations that require prose interpretation
- short paragraph answers as explanations and interpretations.

Thus whilst RE, history and geography share patterns of register, the key difference is in the nature of the subjects/participants of clauses; less use of adverbials and adjectives in geography in addition to maps, graphs and other visualisations; less use if any of verbal groups/processes. Shorter writing in geography characterised by increasing semantic density and gravity with a greater proportion of noun groups and nominalisation.

# References

Carroll, J. E. (2016). Exploring historical 'frameworks' as a curriculum goal: A case study examining students' notions of historical significance when using millennia-wide time scales. *The Curriculum Journal, 27*(4), 454–478.

Carroll, J. E. (2017a). 'I feel if I say this my essay it's not going to be strong': Multi-voicedness, 'oral rehearsal' and Year 13 students' written arguments. *Teaching Hoistory: The Secondary Education Journal of the Historical Association, 167*, 8–16.

Carroll, J. E. (2017b). From divergent evolution to witting cross-fertilisation: The need for more awareness of potential inter-discursive communication regarding students' extended historical writing. *The Curriculum Journal, 28*(4), 504–523.

Green, B., & Lee, A. (1994). Writing geography: Literacy, identity and schooling. In A. Freedman & P. Medway (Eds.), *Learning and teaching genre* (pp. 207–224). Portsmouth, NH: Heinemann.

Lambert, D. (2011). Reviewing the geography curriculum two decades on. *Curriculum Journal, 22*(2), 243–264.

Wignall, P., Martin, J. R., & Eggins, S. (1993). The discourse of geography: Ordering and explaining the referential world. In M. Halliday & J. Martin (Eds.), *Writing science: Literacy and discursive power* (pp. 151–183). London: Taylor & Francis.

# 6

# Developing Literacy Across the Curriculum for Science and Maths

## Introduction

In this chapter, I develop the ideas presented in Chapters 3–5 by further extending an LBP approach and a pedagogic grammar for English in the context of the curriculum for subjects in the sciences and maths. It identifies the main patterns of register and genre that characterise the texts that are talked about, read and written across the secondary school curriculum for science. In maths, register is considered in relation to the rubric of questions and the writing of prose answers. As with Chapters 3–5, I draw upon examples of schemes of work and lesson plans at each of the three key stages of 3, 4 and 5, together with interviews undertaken with teachers and samples of student work, to illustrate how paying attention to register patterns can be integrated into the curriculum for the sciences and maths.

Science and maths did not escape the scope of the now defunct NLS, with many materials written to support literacy in these subjects. For example, a Department for Education website, www.stem.org.uk, contains an overview of modules that linked literacy in science. As Chapters 4 and 5 have already discussed, NLS materials suffered from a poorly designed dissemination model, with no demonstrable impact upon pupil achievement over their life span. Nevertheless, the NLS did have an impact in generally raising the consciousness of all secondary teachers to the importance of language and literacy for developing learning in all school subjects. Adams and Pegg (2012) make the point that little is known about how teachers shape and use particular literacy strategies, although they are clear that their use needs to be aligned with subject-specific discourses:

> **Quote**
>
> Contemporary perspectives on content literacy indicate the need to consider the nature of subject-specific discourses. To learn subjects such as mathematics or science, students 'need to be exposed to the use of the domain's conceptual tools in authentic activity'…. Science and mathematics disciplines have each developed their own ways of generating new knowledge. In science, claims are made and supported by empirical evidence, using scientific arguments. In mathematics, new knowledge is generated via proof and justification, using laws of mathematics and logic…. therefore, literacy serves the learning process by supporting engagement in discipline-based practices and using those practices to develop understanding of content concepts of the discipline.
> (Adams and Pegg 2012: 152)

Adams' and Pegg's research was undertaken in an American context, where they examined the nature of 26 science and mathematics teachers' use of content literacy strategies over two years, who taught from grades 6–12 (11–19 years of age) equivalent to the UK's Years 7–13 in high-needs districts. They found, like the research discussed in this book, that the ways in which teachers incorporated literacy strategies varied. More importantly, though, they found that teachers did not allow enough time to discuss and reflect upon what they had learn to support the development of conceptual understanding. One of the benefits of an LBP approach over the kinds of interventions Adams and Pegg used, is that literacy activities are not only linked to content but also to pedagogic practice in relation to the pacing and sequencing of lessons, especially through the LTC. The vignettes discussed in this chapter, like those of preceding ones, show how not only content and literacy can be integrated, and how content and literacy intersect with pedgagogic practice.

## Science

In the sciences, just as in all other curriculum subjects, language is a fundamental tool, used to classify, explain and recount experiments and investigations which form the basis of a scientific view of the world. Martin (1993: 220) makes the point that: 'Most significantly, it follows that science cannot be understood 'in your own words." Over centuries, science has evolved its own specialist and technical vocabulary in order to interpret the world in scientific, rather than common sense, terms. Moving pupils from everyday, ordinary registers of language to the academic and theoretical registers associated with scientific discourse, is perhaps most challenging in the sciences than in any other subject. Thus, whilst we all may have a commonsense view of the world, this is not the same as a scientific view of the world.

Martin (1993) wrote, in relation to a common-sense view of the universe:

> **Quote**
>
> The common sense view depends upon careful observation with the naked eye. Science augments this with observatories, radio telescopes, space ships, studies of meteorites (meteors which make it to the ground) and other types of information gathered in various ways and accordingly produces a very different picture. Rather than saying that science is right and common sense is wrong (or vice versa when religious beliefs are introduced as evidence), it is more important to understand common sense and science are different pictures of reality, based on different organizing criteria. The function of science then is to construct an alternative interpretation of our world t that provided by common sense. In our culture, this is its job.
>
> This has important implications for teaching practice. It means that common sense knowledge can be a useful *starting point* for learning science, since it organizes the world in ways that can be clearly related to scientific understandings. At the same time it is clear that common sense understandings differ from scientific ones and schools have a crucial

> responsibility to induct students into the alternative scientific world views. Teachers need to be constantly aware of the dangers of stranding students in their own words. This guiding role, bridging across common sense and science, is put very clearly by Britton.
>
> Surely it is the links between 'commonsense' and 'theoretical' concepts, the links between 'ordinary language' and 'theoretical language' that make learning possible – whether in school or out – and it is the ability to move back and forth across that continuum that characterises thinking at any mature stage.
> (Martin 1993: 188–189)

One metaphor drawn upon in relation to scientific writing is that of *distillation* as a way of accounting for a technical register in that such language both compacts and changes the nature of everyday words. This concept has been explored further in later research discussed in Chapter 2 in relation to those of semantic density and gravity. Martin's warning about the dangers of stranding pupils in their own words relates not only to science but to the subject-specific vocabulary that has evolved in all subject disciplines. To deny pupils access to such vocabulary is, however well meaning, to risk imposing limits or placing restrictions upon pupils' worlds that in turn, trap and strand them into lower achievement bands in high stakes public examinations.

The revised national curriculum for science, states that: 'Pupils should develop their use of scientific vocabulary, including the use of scientific nomenclature and units and mathematical representations'. However, learning scientific vocabulary is not of much use without understanding to what it refers and thus what it means. Developing literacy in science requires developing both knowledge and understanding, as Osborne (2002) argues.

> **Quote**
>
> My argument then, is this, that given the complexities of scientific language, its study is not some marginal adjunct to engaging in its practice, rather it is central to the development of *any* understanding. In short, science cannot be understood without an exploration of its language. On the one hand, that does require some knowledge of its technical

> vocabulary. To be literate in science requires that the individual knows the concept or object represented by words such as mitosis, neutron, phenolphthalein, electron donor, gene and the myriad other words that populate the scientific universe. That much is not denied. But science is more than its vocabulary; words have value only when used as referents or to represent meanings. Knowing the vocabulary of science without understanding how it is used, or why, is akin to knowing the words of a foreign language with no understanding of its grammar or standard modalities of expression.
> (Osborne 2002: 212)

One of the key ways curriculum change is disseminated in the UK following the demise of local authority based support has been through subject associations. The Association for Sceince Education, like that of geography and others, has also paid attention to literacy in science. In a research focus article published 2011, Kearton points out that:

> **Quote**
> Attempting to write, read, speak, debate and actively listen using the sepcialised vocabulary and the technical style of reporting can be a significant challenge for those inexperienced in science. Not least because the language used in science is not like language used in everyday conversation.
> The same words are used differently in science and everyday life, e.g. *incident, factor, force, conductor*; some words even have different meanings in different sciences, e.g. *cell, nucleus, molar* in chemistry and biology.... These problems leave some students unable to easily understand scientific texts or readily write about science in an informed and appropriate way.
> (Kearton 2011: 2)

One of the key ways in which the language of science differs from that of other subjects discussed in this book is the complexity of its vocabulary, particularly noun groups and grammatical metaphor as expressed through the process of nominalisation. Martin (1993: 186) pointed out that to be literate in science involves understanding its technical vocabulary. Lakoff and Johnson's seminal book *Metaphors We Live By* (1980), points to the ways in which metaphor, normally thought of as a term that belongs to the realm of literary study, pervades language use in general. Whilst literary metaphor expresses one noun group in terms of another, technical and scientific writing in particular, relies heavily upon grammatical metaphor. To take an example from Devrim (2015), a sentence such as *Because technology is getting better,/ people are able to write business programs faster* becomes *Advances in technology are speeding up the writing of business programs*. A sentence that comprised two clauses becomes one, with the 'doer', the subject of the first sentence, 'people,' being replaced by the nominalised 'advances in technology'. Such nominalisation reduces the total number of clauses in any one sentence with more information packed into each nominal group, which allows writers, when writing science, to refer to recurring abstract ideas. A single clause then, can encapsulate several complex abstract ideas. Studies such as Kazemain's et al. (2013) into grammatical metaphor in a small corpus of 10 science texts totalling 6100 words, all point to the ways in which nominalisation is essential in producing the informationally dense structures characteristic of scientific writing.

Biber and Gray (2016) in their corpus-based analysis of the three written genres of fiction texts, newspapers and science prose from 1750 to 1990, point to the fact that there has been a change in general in written genres, particularly in narrative. This has been towards an adoption of spoken forms and oral styles in writing that other research such as that by Cambridge Assessment in relation to GCSE English (Eliot et al. 2016) also bears out. One has only to compare a nineteenth century novel written by Charles Dickens or George Elliot with one written in the late twentieth century to also observe this phenomenon. However, such an adoption has not occurred in academic genres, which tend to be more static (or 'uptight' as Biber and Gray call them) in contrast to the more agile registers and genres of newspaper writing and prose fiction. In their register analysis of scientific writing, they also found that use of finite relative clauses fell away sharply in the last half of the twentieth century. Embedded dependent clauses, such as the example used in the National Curriculum for English discussed in Chapter 2, were used hardly at all. Grammatical structures in writing science then are thus relatively simple in that clause structure tend towards single and coordinate. It is also at times telegraphic, such as giving definitions and descriptions in biology (Martin 1993). The most significant aspect of change in writing science is in its elaboration of vocabulary, particularly in the use of nominalisations, expanded noun groups and use of noun modifiers. It is a feature of English that one can take any noun and place it in front of another to make a noun modifier to form two, three, four or even five noun group sequences such as *endopasmic reticulum; peripheral membrane proteins* or *time-dependent density functional theory.*

Findings such as those of Biber and Gray all point to the fact that the discourses of different disciplines have their own distinctive patterns of register and genre. Moreover, patterns of register particularly may change over time, with those of academic discourse remaining more static in relation to those of newspaper writing and prose writing. Even though technology has change the medium of writing, particularly for assessment by coursework from pen and paper to word processing, and brought forth a host of new genres such as online messaging, the change has not of itself affected the structure of genres associated with academic writing nor their related register features. It is also misleading to make sweeping generalisations about register features in relation to clause structure, for example, such as the assumption that the more clauses a sentence has the more complex the ideas being expressed. Writing in science does not bear this out. The importance of noun groups and nominalisation in science and also geography, may also explain why participating project teachers of science and geography particularly found paying attention to these particular aspects of the pedagogic grammar. An LBP approach thus affects the pacing and sequencing in lessons as teachers spend more time in planning and carrying out activities in class to overcome identified barriers to successful outcomes in learning. The examples below from the sciences and maths show further examples of this.

The examples given below are taken from the work of the same teacher as discussed in Chapter 3, Mary Jane from School A. They demonstrate how the same structural principles of pacing and sequencing lessons in a format that is regularly repeated, together with the scaffolded reading and writing activities that underpinned her teaching at key stage 3, can transfer to key stages 4 and 5. In this way, knowledge building in science can follow recursive patterns that build upon and consolidate knowledge in ways that mitigate against the 'bitty' and incremental nature of some teaching, as discussed in Chapter 2.

Changes to assessment at both GCSE and A Level in science, as Chapter 3 has already discussed, came into effect from science from September 2016. Changes to the curriculum had introduced more subject content in relation to the three sciences of biology, chemistry and physics, and changes to assessment mean that pupils are having to answer questions at double the length they had previously, from a maximum of 3 marks to a maximum of 6. Such a change, therefore, requires pupils to write at double the length than previously, thereby expanding the range of scientific knowledge they are required to demonstrate in response to any one question. For pupils in schools such as Schools A and B in particular, this poses a significant challenge.

## Key Stage 4: Moving from the Everyday to the Abstract

Mary Jane is a teacher in School A, Makepeace. She too, like the teachers discussed in the preceding chapters, took to LBP in relation to textual organisation, particularly as changed GCSE assessment requirements meant pupils had to write answers that were double the length of those previously written since the number of marks awarded per question had doubled from three to six. She noticed that her pupils at Key Stage 4 not only had difficulty writing extended answers, but that the answers they wrote were not the one required by the question, but answers to a completely different one. In other words, the information they gave was accurate, but answered a different question from the one they were set. Initially, she drew upon LBP with a Key Stage 4 Year 10 class, in order to scaffold the complete answer pupils would be asked to write in examinations, as discussed in Chapter 3, that she has since gone on to use throughout her teaching at all key stages. She devised the following activity with a Year 10 class to make her pupils aware of the differences between talking about *structure, function* and *appearance* based upon a chair, as a way of using an everyday example to illustrate more abstract concepts.

She gave her class a worksheet with the descriptions given below repeated three times above pictures of chairs, and asked her class to match the description to the three concepts given above.

A. *A chair is a piece of furniture consisting of a seat, legs and back. The seat has a glossy bright blue colour and the legs have a shiny silver colour (appearance).*
B. *A chair is a piece of furniture that you sit on. Chairs can be used in homes, schools and offices and are designed to accommodate one person. They are usually very comfortable (function).*
C. *The chair seat is made of hard plastic which has a bent rectangular shape and the legs form a frame which is made of metal (structure).*

Mary Anne reported that such a starter activity was a good way of making her pupils conscious of the different *nouns* that can be used in questions, and understanding that the meanings of these nouns are key to the interpretation of questions. It also helped to make them conscious of the fact that an answer can contain factual information that may not necessarily be relevant to the question itself, and hence would gain no marks. She thus drew explicit attention to the nouns in the question as well as the instructional verbs/processes in order to make her pupils aware that to maximise their marks, they needed to concentrate on writing information in so far as it was relevant to answering a specific question. This exercise also included making her pupils more conscious of the fact that they needed to give detailed, complete clause answers and not simply to answer a question with just one word or phrase. The activity outlined above had developed over a period of eighteen months or so, during which Mary Jane had devised an LBP informed structured pattern to her lessons tied to a scheme of work or topic that also took into account other whole school literacy strategies such as peer marking and a standardised marking policy. The structure she had developed was as follows:

1. *Starter—Use of nouns in exam questions.*
2. *Revise key concepts, e.g. by watching a video (Optional).*
3. *Do an exam question (15 Min).*

4. *Teach pupils three-part textual organisation LBP framework for answering six mark question and emphasize the importance and benefits of using it.*
5. *Do two generic examples where pupils have to identify hyper theme, definition and explanation.*
6. *Do whole group answer collaboratively.*
7. *Re-test using same questions using the framework (15 Min).*
8. *Mark both papers simultaneously by peer marking.*
9. *Pupils make corrections on the work with a green pen and feedback.*
10. *Pupils compare marks.*

Mary Jane was convinced that a repetitive structure of the kind given above supported her pupils' learning in that it provided a scaffolded framework for making visible the discursive practices associated with science and developed their scientific knowledge in a logical way. She incorporated the LBP textual framework discussed in Chapter 3 in homework and worksheets by inserting the framework in the space for them to answer the question. She also used the same framework on end of topic summary sheets as a form of revision. In addition, she used six mark question starters at the beginning of each lesson to review the previous lesson on a regular basis, not just close to pupils' exams as she had been used to doing previously. Strategies such as these enabled pupils to routinely practice answering questions by using the scaffolding framework so that they became second nature to them and helped them to structure answers to unseen examination questions. Other LBP supported literacy activities Mary Jane had also identified were:

1. *Keyword leads—Giving pupils questions and a list of specific key words that they have to use for each question.*
2. *Use keyword checklists to ensure that they tick off when they are confident that they know the keywords and to refer to the list while practising to answer exam questions.*
3. *Producing six marks extended questions booklets and allow pupils to self-assess when completed so they can see where they have gone wrong.*
4. *Using the framework grid for answering question in lessons.*
5. *Having 'command word' (verbs/processes in examination questions) sheets or giving pupils verb processes to use when practising exam questions.*

The school had focused upon the language of examination questions and had identified the importance of drawing pupils' attention to what the teacher in charge of the initiative called 'command words' that the teachers taking part in the project recognised as verb groups/processes, normally verbal ones, such as *explain, describe, show, compare* and so on. Mary Anne's incorporation of LBP informed activities together with incorporating other whole school initiatives exemplifies ways in which teachers of science can draw upon a 'grand theory' such as LBP in ways that integrate literacy aspects of science in recursive ways, embedded throughout teaching of all lessons in all key stages. LBP had provided the structure that she felt has provided an anchor for her pupils' developing knowledge and understanding in science, as the following sections exemplify further. An LBP approach thus does not seek to exclude, or replace other whole school initiatives as the example above also illustrates, but rather can be integrated with them. The following vignette demonstrates further how Mary Jane developed LBP informed activities to develop her pupils' understanding of, in this case, biology.

## Key Stage 4 Year 10: Ecosystems

This vignette is also taken from teaching undertaken by Mary Jane in School A, on the topic of ecosystems. In common with teachers of other subjects, Mary Jane had also noticed that her pupils did not find it easy to map the marks awarded onto answers to questions. After teaching the content of the topic, and in a strikingly similar way to the English teacher discussed in Chapter 4, Mary Jane wrote a sequence of examplar mentor texts in answer to a six mark question, each of which answered the question to varying degrees. She then gave the texts out to the pupils given below, with the task of marking them using the mark scheme. Such an activity also focuses upon developing and scaffolding pupils' reading comprehension skills, further developed through talking about each of the mentor texts and the extent to which information was or was not given in relation to the question being asked (Table 6.1).

Following this activity, Mary Jane asked her pupils to individually complete the following reflection (Table 6.2).

**Table 6.1** Structuring GCSE biology examination question answers

ECOSYSTEMS
**Explain how the distribution of organisms within the ecosystem can be affected by at least three abiotic factors**
1. Read through all five answers, mark them using the mark scheme and give them a score out of six
2. Which answer got the highest score? Explain why
3. Comment on why the other answers did not get full marks

| Answers | Score/6 | Comments |
|---|---|---|
| Abiotic factors are factors which are non- living or non- biological. They can be either physical or chemical. Physical and chemical factors are like light, temperature, water (moisture), humidity, pH and the presence of substances in the soil for example pollutants. Light comes from the sun. Plants use the sun to photosynthesize. Photosynthesis is the process whereby plants make food using the energy from sunlight. The plant also uses raw materials such as water and carbon dioxide for photosynthesis. The process of photosynthesis makes glucose and oxygen. Plants use this glucose to grow. Temperature affects photosynthesis. As the temperature increases the rate of photosynthesis increases. The more water that you have available the greater will be the rate of photosynthesis | 3 | Did not answer the question; no paragraphs; only explained one point; gave examples of how factors that affect the organisms |
| Abiotic factors affect the number and distribution of organisms within the ecosystem. The distribution of organisms is where they are found in an ecosystem. Abiotic factors are non-living factors such as temperature, light and water<br>Light affects the distribution of plants because the more light there is the more plants that will be present. This is because plants need light energy from the sun to make their own food (photosynthesise). If there are more plants present then you will have more animals there as well because they will have more plants to eat<br>The amount of water present also affects the number of organisms. The more water there is available in the environment the more organisms you would find however, if there is too much water for example during flooding the plants can die as well and this can affect the animals as well. If there is too little water the plants can also die as they need water for photosynthesis and hence to grow<br>Temperature also affects where organisms live. Some organisms are adapted to live in cold climates however they cannot survive in warmer climates, for example polar bears. Some plants like cacti would not be found in cold climates as they are not adapted to survive there | 6 | Split into paragraphs: first an overview, other three relate to each factor, with each explained |

(continued)

## 6  Developing Literacy Across the Curriculum for Science and Maths

**Table 6.1**  (continued)

| Answers | | |
|---|---|---|
| Abiotic factors are the organisms in an ecosystem that affect that the distribution of other organisms. They affect other organisms by competing with them and being their predators. Plants compete for space, light, minerals and water. Animals compete for food, water, mates, territory or shelter. The less of these resources there are the greater the competition and this will decrease the number and distribution of organisms in the environment. Some animals are predators and feed on other animals so the numbers of organisms will decrease if there are a large number of predators | 0 | *No paragraphs, off topic* |
| The distribution of organisms is where they are found in an ecosystem. Examples of abiotic factors include light and water<br><br>The more light there is the more plants that will be present. This is because plants need light energy from the sun to make their own food (photosynthesise)<br><br>The amount of water present also affects the number of organisms. If there is too little water the plants can die as they need water for photosynthesis and hence to grow. This will affect the animals as they will not have enough food to eat and they will die as well. The animals can also become dehydrated | 4 | *Very basic, only mentioned two points* |
| Some factors that affect organisms are light, water and temperature. They all affect plants and animals. The higher these factors are the more organisms you will find in the ecosystem | 1 | *Brief. Needed more points* |

**Table 6.2**  Reflecting upon answer structure

| <u>Reflection.</u> What lessons have you learned from this exercise? Write down three things that you should always do when answering questions and three things that you should not do. | |
|---|---|
| Do's | Don'ts |
| 1. Use paragraphs<br>2. Develop points<br>3. Have more than one point | 1. Go off topic; not explain<br>2. write in only one paragraph<br>3. have only one point |

**Table 6.3** Three part answer structure

| | |
|---|---|
| Hypertheme (topic sentence) | The distribution of organisms within the ecosystem can be affected by three abiotic factors |
| Definition (what it is) | The distribution of organisms is where they are found in an ecosystem and abiotic factors are environmental and non living |
| Explanation (how it works) | Light is essential for plants to grow on land. Light is emitted within forests. In dense forests few plants can grow on the floor as little light gets through |
| | Pollutants cause pollution and release pollutants. These can poison organisms or cause harm to organisms in other ways (such as plastic getting eaten by fish and other organisms). Therefore where there are lots of pollutants there will be less organisms present |
| | Temperature also affects the distribution of organisms. For example, polar bears are adapted to the cold and cacti are adapted to living in hot deserts. If the plants die so will the animals because animals eat the plants |

Having undertaken the preparatory work, the class wrote their own answers to the question, using the three-part textual organisation tool discussed in Chapter 3, of which the text below is an example (Table 6.3).

The writing in this text is all in the present tense with mainly single clause sentences, and with complexity lying in the vocabulary, which is highly technical, abstract, and with a high degree of nominalisation and use of extended noun groups (*the distribution of organisms; pollutants; three abiotic factors*).

As a result of taking part in the project, Mary Jane has gone on to pay far more attention to both the grammar and vocabulary of examination questions. For example, take the question: *Global diversity is in decline. Human population growth, agriculture and climate change each have an effect upon biodiversity. Explain how each of these factors contributes to the decline in biodiversity (6 Marks)*. Like the one on ecosystems above it follows a similar pattern, in that three factors are in this case named that relate to the phenomenon being discussed. To gain full marks, attention needs to be paid to explaining each of these factors in turn with the same amount of detail in order to gain the maximum two marks for each explanation. Through paying explicit attention to this structure and the ways in which clause structure of the question related to it, Mary Jane reported not only increased her pupils' chances of gaining good marks, but also their confidence in relation to answering examination questions.

## Maths

The following vignette is also taken from School A. The school had invested in a maths programme developed in Singapore and Shanghi called *mathematics mastery*, based upon a model that also underpins revsions to the national curriculum for mathematics in England. *Mathematics Mastery* is aimed particularly at closing the attainment gap of pupils from low-income families and their peers, designed to deepen and develop pupils' understanding of mathematical concepts as a long-term approach with impact built up over time. This programme is based upon a whole school approach that has problem solving at its heart. Principles of the 'mastery' approach as summarised by the National Centre for Excellence in the Teaching of Mathematics could also serve as the principles underpinning LBP. Paying attention to the language of maths is also central within the programme.

> **Quote**
> - Teachers reinforce an expectation that all pupils are capable of achieving high standards in mathematics.
> - The large majority of pupils' progress through the curriculum content at the same pace. Differentiation is achieved by emphasising deep knowledge and through individual support and intervention.
> - Teaching is underpinned by methodical curriculum design and supported by carefully crafted lessons and resources to foster deep conceptual and procedural knowledge.
> - Practice and consolidation play a central role. Carefully designed variation within this builds fluency and understanding of underlying mathematical concepts in tandem.
> - Teachers use precise questioning in class to test conceptual and procedural knowledge, and assess pupils regularly to identify those requiring intervention so that all pupils keep up.
>
> (https://www.ncetm.org.uk/public/files/19990433/Developing_mastery_in_mathematics_october_2014.pdf, accessed 30 July 2017)

O'Halloran's work discussed in Chapter 2 has explored the ways in which the abstract nature of mathematical signs can be viewed semiotically as a language. Instructions on how to answer mathematical questions, however, are given in prose. Some questions also include a part that requires answering in prose, and understanding how a question is structured in terms of what is required in answering is thus every bit as important in maths as it is in every other subject.

## Key Stage 5 Maths: Year 12

Sameera, the maths teacher, was a Newly Qualified Teacher (NQT) in School A and thus in her first year of teaching. She had a degree and a PGCE in mathematics. In common with other teachers participating in the project, she had never given much thought to language in relation to maths. However, she had noticed when teaching statistics, that in answering past examination papers, her students often left out the last part of a question, which asked them to provide a prose explanation of what their statistical analysis revealed. Consequently, this decreased the maximum amount of marks they could be awarded to each question. Not answering this part of the question can thus significantly reduce students' chances of being awarded top marks for the examination paper. Sameera decided to draw upon LBP in relation to paying more attention to the wording of questions students were required to answer.

As a result of taking part in an initial LBP CPD session, Sameera decided to introduce maths exercise books for her class to use. The use of exercise books would provide space for not only showing how pupils solved the problems set, but also for including work on the language of mathematics. Pupils wrote down keyword definitions and identification and definition of instructions in examination questions. This was in line with the whole school focus on the understanding the vocabulary of examination questions, particularly the instructional verbs/process. This also allowed her to give space to pointing out to her pupils that answering the final prose part of a question was part and parcel of answering the whole question. Questions in mathematics at A level are generally split into several parts, with new information sometimes being added in between various parts, as the examples below show. Sameera explained that she thought that taking a holistic approach to answering all parts of a question would help her pupil to understand the relationship between them all, and the function of the final part of a question in relation to those that had preceded it. Rather than honing in on an identified problem then, Sameera approached rectifying it in the context of answering a question in its entirety. In the literacy books and in preparation for writing their answers, pupils wrote the keywords and their definitions associated with each topic they covered. As in other subjects, Sameera's participation in the project had drawn her attention to making sure her pupils understood the concepts expressed through mathematical vocabulary, particularly through comprehension activities of this kind. Following this activity that focussed upon pupils reading and understanding of key vocabulary, each pupil then stuck into their exercise book the practice exam question paper. In order to ensure that her pupils had both read and understood all parts of the question being answered, she asked them to identify and highlight the instruction words of each part given in the question that they were required to answer, and to provide definitions on the page opposite.

For example, one question centred around a table summarising the different measurements of foot lengths of a random sample of 120-year-old children. The questions following the summary table were:

a. Use interpolation to estimate the median of this distribution. (2)
b. Calculate estimates for the mean and the standard deviation of these data. (6)
One measure of skewness is given by
$$\text{Coefficient of skewness} = \frac{3(\text{mean}-\text{median})}{\text{Standard deviation}}$$
c. Evaluate and comment on the skewness of this data. (3)

Greg suggests that a normal distribution is a suitable model for the foot-lengths of 10-year-old children.

d. Using the value found in part c., comment on Greg's suggestion, giving a reason for your answer.

One student wrote the following definitions for the keywords identified:

*Estimate—rough/approximate calculation of judgement of the value, number, quantity etc.*
*Calculate—using numerical data to determine an answer.*
*Evaluate—workout the value of something.*
*Comment—describe what a calculation shows.*
*Give a reason—justification or explanation for an action or an event.*

In answer to part d of the question, the pupil wrote:
*There's no skewness in the data as the answer is zero hence it's possible for it to be a normal distribution. Also it (the data) is symmetrical, so it <u>can</u> have normal distribution.*

Another question measured the time each of 32 students on a randomly chosen day recorded the time they spent on homework to the nearest minute. Following a table of the results, the following questions were asked:

a. Use interpolation to estimate the value of the median. (2)
   Given that
   $$\sum t = 1414 \text{ and } \sum t2 = 69{,}378,$$
b. Find the mean and the standard deviation of the times spent by the students on their homework. (3)
c. Comment on the skewness of the distribution of the times spent by the students on their homework. Give a reason for your answer. (2)

Sameera reported that focusing upon the verb group in the command structure of mathematics questions helped her students to answer all parts of a question. For example, in answer to c., the pupil wrote:
*so there's no skew because the answer is zero.*

A further question she gave the class was in relation to the time it took for a class of students to complete a Sudoku in a Sudoku competition, recorded to the nearest minute and summarised in a table.

The questions that followed were:

a. Write down the mid-point of the 9–12 interval. (1)
b. Use linear interpolation to estimate the median time
   taken by the students. (2)
c. Estimate the mean and standard deviation of the times
   taken by the students. (5)

The teacher suggested that a normal distribution could be used to model the time taken by the students to complete a different Sudoku.

d. Give a reason to support the use of a normal distribution in
   this case. (1)

*The coefficient skewness is very near zero so the distribution is symmetrical, hence a normal distribution.*

On another occasion, the teacher calculated the quartiles for the times taken by the students to complete a different Sudoku and found.

$$Q1 = 8.5, \quad Q2 = 13.0, \quad Q3 = 21$$

e. Describe, giving a reason, the skewness of the times on this occasion.

*The times are skewed because (Q2−Q1) is less than (Q3−Q2).*

The examples given above all demonstrate the regular features that occur in maths questions of this kind:

- A set of data relating to an activity is given.
- A set of questions are then asked for a statistical interpretation of the data.
- A final question asks for a prose interpretation of the statistical data.
- Often, between the first two parts given above, additional information is given that precipitates further mathematical interpretation and/or a further prose question, as in the examples above.

A further topic in A Level Maths is that of probability. Here, parts of a question also follow a regular pattern, where:

- information is given in relation to a set of events
- questions relate to finding probability
- further information is given that leads to further questions relating to probability
- a final prose question asking for an interpretation.

For example:
　Jake and Kamil are sometimes late for school.
　The events $J$ and $K$ are defined as follows

$$J = \text{the event that Jake is late for school}$$
$$K = \text{the event that Kamil is late for school}$$

P($J$) = 0.25; P($J \cap K$) = 0.15 and P ($J \cap' K'$) = 07.

　On a randomly selected day, find the probability that
a. at least one of Jake and Kamil is late for school
b. Kamil is late for school

Given that Jake is late for school,
c. Fine the probability that Kamil is late

The final two parts of the question then ask pupils to answer the question in d. as calculation and prose, and e. in prose as given below:

The teacher suspects that Jake being late for school and Kamil being late for school are linked in some way.
d. Determine whether or not $J$ and $K$ are statistically independent (calculation).

*The probability of K and the probability of J happening are not independent events.*

e. Comment on the teacher's suspicion in the light of your calculation in d.

*The teacher was correct in this suspicion which means that Jake and Kamil's lateness are linked.*

Language matters in maths then. Through paying explicit attention to the language used to ask questions and also to the language used in prose answers, Sameera helped her students to understand precisely what the questions required by way of answers and gave the confidence to answer questions that demanded prose answers.

## Conclusion

It is clear from the examples given in this chapter that discursive practices in both the sciences and mathematics are very different from those of English and the humanities. The chapter also illustrates how LBP can be incorporated into these two subjects to develop pupils' knowledge and understanding of knowledge codes. Writing answers to questions in science is much shorter than in the other subjects discussed in this book, concentrated upon vocabulary such nominalisations and expanded noun phrases that are semantically dense. As Osborne (2002) already quoted above pointed out, science is more than simply knowing the vocabulary, but also understanding how it is used. In science, links can be made between everyday concepts such as the example of the chair as a way of developing pupils' understanding of how to interpret examination questions so that they answer answers according to the right kind of information being asked for. Writing answers to questions in maths is shorter still due to the highly abstract nature of mathematical symbols. Nevertheless, the questions themselves are written in prose and thus require students to understand the nature of the verb group in relation to what it is they are being asked to do.

The main genres in which pupils write in science and maths are those of explanation and interpretation, with register features in science including:

- single clause sentences or clause complexes comprising mainly of two coordinating clauses;
- few adverbs and adjectivals;
- high concentration of nominalisations and nominal groups;

- subjects/participants of clauses are usually nominalisations and nominal groups referring to the physical phenomenon;
- high proportion of relational processes;
- no conclusion normally necessary.

In maths, register features include:

- use of mathematical symbols;
- writing is usually in the present tense;
- clauses in questions follow the command structure of English, with the verb/process at the beginning and are made up of one or two clauses, either coordinating or relative with the relative clause occurring at the start of the sentence;
- nominal groups refer to mathematical concepts;
- verbs/processes are relational and centre upon the verb *be*.

# References

Adams, E. A., & Pegg, J. (2012). Teachers' enactment of content literacy strategies in secondary science and mathematics classes. *Journal of Adolescent & Adult Literacy, 56*(2), 151–161.

Biber, D., & Gray B. (2016). *Grammatical complexity in academic English*. Cambridge: Cambridge University Press.

Devrim, D. Y. (2015). Grammatical metaphor: What do we mean? What exactly are we researching? *Functional Linguistics, 2,* 3.

Elliot, G., Green, S., Constantinou, F., Vitello, S.,Chambers, L., Rushton, N., et al. (2016). *Variations in aspects of writing in 16+ examinations between 1980 and 2014. Research matters: A Cambridge Assessment Publication, Special Issue 4.* http://cambridgeassessment.org.uk/Images/340982-research-matters-special-issue-4-aspects-of-writing-1980-2014.pdf.

Kazemain, B., Behnam, B., & Ghafoori, N. (2013). Ideational grammatical metaphor in scientific texts: A Hallidayan perspective. *International Journal of Linguistics, 5*(4): 146–168.

Kearton, V. (2011). Developing literacy skills in science lessons: What does the research say? The Association for Science Education, 1–2. www.ase.org.uk. Accessed 10 June 2017.

Lakoff, M., & Johnson, G. (1980). *Metaphors we live by*. Chicago: University of Chicago Press.

Martin, J. (1993). Literacy in science. In M. Halliday & J. Martin (Eds.), *Writing science: Literacy and discursive power* (pp. 187–225). London: Routledge.

Osborne, J. (2002). Science without literacy: A ship without a sail? *Cambridge Journal of Education, 32*(2): 203–218.

# 7

# Conclusion

As Chapter 1 has discussed, the growing acknowledgement of the importance of the part language plays in learning has developed in tandem alongside an empirically grounded and well-theorised LBP, including a well-theorised grammar that can draw upon for pedagogic purposes. Current debates are thus centred not so much upon whether or not grammar should be taught, but *how*, and what kinds of theories of instruction best underpin its teaching. In relation to secondary teachers of English in particular, part of the underlying tension with regards to teaching grammar has been that the creativity and subversion evident in English teaching pedagogy is assumed to sit at odds with negative experiences of grammar pedagogy. However, such tension is predicated upon the notion of grammar as 'error.' Once the lens through which grammar is viewed alters from a preoccupation with error to that of developing articulate expression of thought, then understanding grammar can be liberating and powerful.

There is also the view that teaching grammar is somehow detrimental to the development of adolescents' creative expression. However, I would argue that whether or not such teaching is detrimental depends upon how teachers construe grammar, in relation to both its purpose and its associated pedagogy. A legacy of the NLS that has survived their demise is the foregrounding of language and literacy development across the secondary school curriculum. Often, it is to the English department that head teachers turn in developing language LLAC initiatives, and teaching grammar itself is located within the curriculum for English. However, as later chapters of this book have shown, the grammatical patterns—register—of the writing through which the knowledge of each individual school subject is expressed are different in each one. It thus follows that for any LLAC initiative to have any real purchase, teachers from different subject areas need to work together.

A pedagogy that construes grammar as sets of rules designed to combat 'error' such as that associated with traditional teaching of grammar has no place in LBP. Rather, within LBP grammar is framed more in terms of linguistic patterns and their choice, across and within texts as well as clauses and in relation to the twin concepts of register and genre. It thus follows that such teaching is best situated in the context of and integrated with subject content, rather than as decontextualized sets of (usually) made up sentences. All of the research evidence as discussed in earlier chapters of this book has indicated that this latter pedagogic approach does not result in any noticeable improvement in adolescents' writing. However, the evidence base from around the world is steadily growing which shows that an integrated approach such as that of LBP can be introduced to and practiced by teachers across the secondary school curriculum in ways that transfer successfully into teachers' curriculum aims, goals and practices in ways that can enhance adolescents' learning experiences and the quality of their writing. As the later chapters of this book show, the assumption that teachers' metalinguistic knowledge awareness cannot be developed has proved to be unfounded, as has the assumption that explicitly teaching metalinguistic terminology is either beyond adolescents' capabilities or somehow damaging to their language development. Indeed, much of the evidence points to the opposite: that explicit instruction and direct teaching of language structure in the context of its use improve, rather than inhibit, education outcomes, particularly but not exclusively, for those pupils and for whom English is an L2 and those from disadvantaged backgrounds.

EAL adolescents are by their very nature, bilingual, and thus arguably more attuned to language than their monolingual counterparts.

Research by for example, Garraffa et al. (2017) and Murphy (2015) all point to the ways in which bilingualism can be beneficial for children and adolescents' development in terms not only in relation to language development but also of being more aware of different cultures, other people and other points of view. Monolingual learners can also benefit from more explicit attention being paid to grammar whatever their sociocultural background, as this book has also shown. An LBP approach draws upon SFL/G and recontextualises it into pedagogic contexts, linking with both government policy and teachers' evaluative practices rather than with a whole scale adoption of SFG in its entirety. The aspects of SFG that are the most beneficial in terms of informing a pedagogic grammar are (a) extending the unit of grammatical analysis beyond the sentence to the text, (b) teaching grammar in the context of adolescents' own reading and writing practices and (c) developing the twin notions of genre/text type and register in the context of school curriculum subjects and thus extending linguistic repertoires. Account also has to be taken of the fact that the time given to delivering curriculum objectives and preparing pupils and students for assessment, is finite. As too are school's financial resources. It thus follows, that incorporating LBP into initial teacher education programmes or professional development courses for in-service teachers has a greater chance of success if it is focused and targeted in the context of subject-specific literacy development. The pacing and sequencing of activities centred around the notion of apprenticeship and scaffolding that underpin the LTC also imply a change to teachers' existing pedagogic practices. For such change to warrant the time commitment needed to be effected, then it has to link into teachers' everyday affordances in ways that make sense to them.

LBP is an approach that is essentially dialogic in nature between teachers and their pupils and students. It does not seek to dictate or prescribe the pace or sequence of learning and teaching activities, nor propound a 'one size fits all' model. Rather, pacing and sequencing is left to teachers to determine, governed by the educational needs of the pupils and students they teach, the communities within which they are situated and the wider sociocultural landscape beyond. In this respect, an LBP approach is teacher, rather than method, driven. It is also appropriate a pedagogy for pupils and students for whom English is an L1 as it is for those for whom English is an additional one. This is because explicit attention is paid to the development of language alongside knowledge, in symbiotic relationship. Whilst this book has focussed upon LBP in England, the LBP principles and practices outlined in it are such that they can transfer into any education context anywhere in the world.

An LBP approach also integrates the writing required for assessment as part and parcel of the curriculum learning experience, rather than as something separate from it. It also draws upon SFG/L and recontextualises it into a pedagogic grammar of English that in turn, links into the framework of the curriculum not only for English but also that of other school subjects. Such recontextualisations cannot derive totally from a modern grammar, be it transformational generative, systemic functional, pattern, cognitive or any other. Grammar is not a religion, and the key here is the recontextualisation of as many key concepts drawn from SFG as are necessary for a pedagogic context. Such a recontextualisation selects and draws upon SFG in so far as it adds, extends and reconfigures existing traditions and practices, those of their pupils and students.

Research into the introduction of an LBP approach to language and literacy across the curriculum in England in a secondary context, particularly where EAL pupils and students are in the majority, demonstrates its potential as a potent resource for their language development in ways that integrate with both subject content and its assessmentAs the illustrative vignettes throughout Chapters 3–6 show and in line with research undertaken in Australia and the USA, an LBP approach works best when introduced in the context of teachers' day to day assessment and curriculum goals and practices and integrated into them. These, in turn, relate to the individual institutional context in which teachers work, the nature of the community the school serves and the wider national education context. Lack of any explicit knowledge on the teacher's part is not *of itself*, as the vignettes throughout this book have shown, a barrier to adopting an LBP approach.

# Developing Language and Literacy Across the Secondary School Curriculum: An Inclusive Approach

Throughout this book, I have demonstrated how LBP can inform an integrated approach to LLAC in ways that all benefit pupils and students, and not only those from predominantly EAL backgrounds. An LBP approach can be drawn upon to inform LLAC initiatives in any school, whatever the constituent linguistic and sociocultural make up of the community which it serves. LBP is an overarching 'grand theory' that theoretically embraces a range of concepts drawn from linguistics, sociology and socio-psychology in formulating its own, as outlined in Chapter 2. It can underpin any LLAC initiative in four distinctive ways. Firstly, it impacts upon the pacing and sequencing of how teachers organise classroom activity. Typically, teachers teach a subject topic that can be described metaphorically as adopting the shape of a semantic wave. Typically, teachers unpack concepts related to the topic being taught in terms of simplified contextual meanings as *riding down the wave*. They then *move back up the wave*, repacking concepts in condensed linguistic forms to allow relationships to be made with broader subject concepts. They then assess the degree of their pupils' or students' understanding through an individually written exercise of some kind, which is marked both formatively and summatively. Even where teachers make use of a writing frame or scaffold of some kind to support a summative assessment, results are often disappointing.

Adopting a pedagogy centred upon the LTC separates out formative from summative assessment through: the use of exemplar or mentor texts which are then deconstructed in terms of their academic language use; exploring the meanings of key concepts in more depth in the context in which they are used to supplement vocabulary lists; group writing activities, centring upon writing frames or scaffolds that help to organise a text's organisation and structure and more opportunities for drafting writing. Secondly, patterns of register relating to the textual organisation associated with different genres/text types that characterise the discursive practices of different school subjects are foregrounded and made explicit, rather than assumed. Vocabulary becomes ever increasingly specialised and semantically more dense as adolescents' move through the school system. Such vocabulary is characterised grammatically through grammatical metaphor, where typically a process or clause is turned into a noun or noun group, or a process into a thing, which includes the process of nominalisation (turning verbs into nouns) as discussed in Chapter 6. Finally, its starting point is the summative assessment that is to be undertaken at the end of any learning and teaching cycle.

Previous to taking part in the project, the pattern of delivery in all three schools and across all subjects taking part normally followed a similar cycle:

- teaching subject topic content in class,
- a piece of writing to be assessed then set, sometimes started in class and completed at home,
- the writing then peer and teacher assessed with a summative mark given and including formative comments on how the work could have been improved.

In all three schools discussed throughout this book, LBP impacted upon teachers' practices in terms of (a) making time in class to talk about the textual structure of the writing teachers asked their pupils and students to write through various activities such as modelling exemplar texts and group writing activities; (b) beginning to pay attention to patterns of register as outlined in Chapter 2 and making more explicit connections between the curriculum and its assessment.

As a result of taking part in the project, teachers changed the pacing and sequencing of their lessons so that it resembled the learning and teaching cycle as outlined in Chapter 2, particularly the introduction of phases two and three. A key concern with regard to implementing LBP is that it is perceived to 'take time away' from delivering curriculum content. However, taking the time in class to talk about the nature of the writing itself helped to apprentice adolescents into the discursive practices and subject positioning associated with individual school subjects which in turn, supported them in gaining more independent control over their written expression. It also helped teachers to pinpoint issues any individuals who required additional support in relation to understanding what was required of them. LBP then, has an inbuilt mechanism for differentiation. For example, in A Level History discussed in Chapter 5, discovering that some students had misunderstood how to use source extracts in their writing. Paying greater attention to the nature and purpose of source extracts in relation to answering a question increased the students' chances of improving their marks. In A Level Maths discussed in Chapter 6, understanding and responding to questions that required a prose answer also increased the number of marks students could be awarded in total for their work.

Focusing in on the LTC in respect of developing their pupils' and students' writing made sense to the teachers, particularly as the project coincided with changes to the curriculum at key stages 3, 4 and 5 and assessment by public examinations at GCSE and A Level. Such changes had increased curriculum content and the need to write at greater length than previously in some subjects such as science and geography coupled with a decrease in assessment by coursework in subjects such as history and English. In that context, paying greater attention to the textual organisation and structure of their pupils' and students' writing made sense to teachers. They thus drew upon aspects of the pedagogic grammar to which I introduced them in so far as it helped their pupils' and students' write more successfully and without necessarily engaging with theoretical underpinning. They also incorporated an LBP approach with existing LLAC cross-curricular initiatives and practices such as marking policies and local arrangements for CPD.

What became apparent then is that when it comes to recontextualising LBP into teachers' pedagogic practices, teachers by and large are less interested in its theoretical underpinning per se and much more in its practical applications. Whilst attempts to take SFG in its totality into the classroom may have a place, it quickly became clear in the CPD sessions I ran with the teachers (one teacher of English apart), that they were not interested in theory so much as its practical application. It was not so much the case then that teachers were taking SFG into the classroom, but that they were drawing upon SFG in so far as it served their specific curriculum and assessment goals. Grammatical concepts and related terminology were thus drawn upon firstly in the context of the textual organisation of the writing pupils and students were asked to write and secondly only in so far as it served the purposes of that writing.

As Chapter 1 has discussed, two dimensions to pedagogic grammar can be distinguished. The first, is the development of grammatical concepts and terminology of the kind discussed in Chapter 2 that have their place in subject English. This includes knowing the grammatical terms of the kind that make up the Key Stage 2 Grammar Glossary and the one at the end of this book. Secondly, there are the ways in which grammatical patterns are configured into specific patterns of register and corresponding genres/text types that characterise the discursive practices through which subject knowledge is expressed.

A major difference between developing LLAC in secondary schools as opposed to primary ones is that the curriculum divides into subjects as well as the three further key stages of 3, 4 and 5. The internal organisation of schools alters from being centred upon classes as they relate to a year group where one teacher predominantly teaches all curriculum subjects to class in any one year group to teachers in individual subject departments who teach all the respective classes for their subject. Cross-curricular activity is thus much easier to initiate in primary schools. It is also difficult in a secondary context to introduce and monitor a curriculum initiative such as LBP in relation to a single key stage, since teachers teach across more than one and in some cases across all three. In addition, teachers in secondary schools remain largely unaware of the discursive practices that characterise school subjects other than the one or at the most two that they teach. Through collecting samples of pupil and student writing related to the curriculum subjects of English, RE, history, geography, science and maths, it was possible to analyse them in relation to register patterns as discussed in Chapters 4–6. The key challenge then was how to raise the teachers' awareness of the different kinds of writing each curriculum subject. The next section discusses how this was achieved.

## Writing Across the Secondary School Curriculum

As detailed in previous chapters, teachers had responded to an LBP approach originally through engaging with the LTC by discussing mentor texts, ways in which the texts were put together, paying more attention to the drafting process and to grammatical aspects of textual organisation such as cohesion. In previous CPD sessions I had collated examples of writing across subject areas written for pupils at key stages 3 and 4 such as history, a science and English and organised activity around identifying verb processes and SPOCA patterns in each one, identifying how they were different. In a similar way, from the writing samples of pupil and student writing given to me by teachers, I compiled extracts from across year groups and subjects to exemplify differences in register, again by way of exemplifying the different register patterns and subject positions evident in each one:

*Yr 8 English: In the extract from Touching the Void, how does Joe Simpson make his description so intense and powerful?*

*Joe Simpson shortens adverbs to emphasise the word, to create a tense and powerful text. "Unexpected, it made my heart leap." He shortens the adverb "unexpectedly" to "Unexpected", which puts emphasis upon the word and makes the sentence pass quicker. This suggests that it was not expected at all, which makes the sentence very tense. He also uses imagery in the phrase "make my heart leap". This shows that he is fearing whatever is coming, which adds tension to the extract. The whole sentence shows that he is scared, and means that he has to consider if he is safe in the next few sentences. Joe Simpson uses shortened words and imagery to create a tense atmosphere to this extract.*

*Yr 9 Describe the trends/patterns in the graph below (4 marks).*

*The general **trend** of the graph is that the higher the GDP per capita, the longer the life expectancy. Some examples are the Central African Republic with a GDP of around $500 and a life expectancy of around 53 (units). Another example is Kuwait with a GDP of over $40,000 and a life expectancy of around 80 (units). However, there are some **anomalies** such as Swaziland with a GDP of around $9000 and life expectancy of around 49 (units).*

**Yr 10 Science: Explain how the distribution of organisms within the ecosystem can be affected by at least _three_ abiotic factors (6 marks).**

Abiotic factors affect the number and distribution of organisms within the ecosystem. The distribution of organisms is where they are found in an ecosystem. Abiotic factors are non-living factors such as temperature, light and water.

Light affects the distribution of plants because the more light there is the more plants that will be present. This is because plants need light energy from the sun to make their own food (photosynthesise). If there are more plants present then you will have more animals there as well because they will have more plants to eat.

The amount of water present also affects the number of organisms. The more water there is available in the environment the more organisms you would find however, if there is too much water for example during flooding the plants can die as well and this can affect the animals as well. If there is too little water the plants can also die as they need water for photosynthesis and hence to grow.

Temperature also affects where organisms live. Some organisms are adapted to live in cold climates however they cannot survive in warmer climates, for example polar bears. Some plants like cacti would not be found in cold climates as they are not adapted to survive there.

**Year 10 RE: Every person makes their own destiny. Evaluate this statement considering arguments for and against.**

I believe that everyone does have their own destiny because when you are doing things good or bad you do it purely because it is your own choice that is called free will. Allah has given us free will to do anything. When a person commits a deed they don't do it because Allah has told them to do it, that is incorrect. Allah has written down everything a person does their whole lifetime before they were even alive, this is written in a book called the loh-e-quran.

Many people think that because it is written down why should they be blamed for their actions. They think that if all of their actions are written and they are truly in control of what they do? This means can they really accomplish what they want to if it's all just written down for them.

In the Quran it states 'there is the one who gives, who is mindful of God, who testifies to goodness – we shall smooth his way towards ease.' This shows that the Quran reassures Muslims that they should continue to do good to work towards *their destiny because it will make their life easier. It helps guide Muslims and keeps them steadfast in their faith and belief in Allah.*

*However, others believe that because it is written down for them they cannot choose their path so it will not be their fault. They think that maybe if they don't have a choice on anything. The understanding of this comes from the people who think that they are on the wrong path or do bad deeds they justify it with that.*

**Yr 12 History: How far do sources 1-4 concur or differ in their interpretations of Mao's motives for introducing the Hundred Flowers campaign in 1957?**

*Source one is an extract written in 2005 which is long after the death of Mao. It is written by Jung Chang, who is Chinese. He explains the negative viewpoint of the Hundred Flowers Campaign. He describes how very few had guessed that Mao was setting a trap for the people, only so that he could later use this as an excuse to victimise them. This shows that Jung was aware of Mao's ill intentions which was not very common, despite the fact that it was in the year 2005. This is because even today, the majority of China's remains ignorant of Mao's destructive acts. They still see him as a godly figure.*

**Year 12 Maths: Satistics**

*The coefficient skewness is very near zero so the distribution is symmetrical, hence a normal distribution.*

For the teachers, this was the first time that they had considered their pupils' or students' writing in any subject other than their own, and expressed astonishment at the register differences between each one. Showing them this writing brought home to them how important it was for pupils and students to have control over the register of any one subject in terms of being able to order their thoughts coherently and logically in writing. I provided them with the list of register features as identified through their pupils' and students' writing, and asked them to identify them in the corresponding written text:

**English**:

Register features associated with this genre as evident in the texts pupils and students have written are:

- textual organisation centred upon an introduction, main body and conclusion;
- writing predominantly in the present tense;
- writing predominantly in the third person, particularly when referring to the author of a text but sometimes first or second person, and especially when expressing judgements and opinions;
- subjects of clauses and clause-complexes are normally concepts, characters and events in a text or the author being discussed;
- use of additive and causal conjunctions to signal explanations and to form two or three clause sentences;
- all verbal groups/processes drawn upon: behavioural, existential, material, mental, relational and verbal but in critical appreciation mainly relational, mental and verbal;
- use of pronouns as referents to link back to preceding sentences;
- use of modals and mental processes to signal interpretation;
- technical vocabulary to identify literary techniques in texts;
- describing/evaluating the effect of language features used in the text being written about through abstract verb groups and extended noun phrases;
- use of quotes to support developing argument;
- increased nominalisation;
- increased semantic density and gravity.

**RE and history:**

- textual organisation centred upon an introduction, main body and conclusion;
- clause complexes usually one or two co-ordinating linked by *and* and *because* that give reasons for opinions through conjunctions such as *because; despite, by, therefore, however*
- use of pronouns as referents to refer back to nouns in previous clauses
- verb processes mainly mental, verbal and relational
- participants/subjects are first person, people, ideas and texts
- complements/objects are ideas, groups of people, people, texts
- use of expanded noun groups and nominalisations

- use of adverbials and adjectives
- subject-specific vocabulary
- interweaving of abstract principles with textual references to religious texts (RE) and sources (history)
- extended writing through use of paragraphs
- increased semantic density and gravity.

**Geography:**

- textual organisation centred upon an introduction, main body and conclusion;
- clause complexes of usually co-ordinating clauses linked by conjunctions *and, because* that give reasons for opinions and others such *despite, by, therefore*; relative clauses
- verb groups/processes: mainly mental, material and relational
- participants/subjects are people, animals, physical phenomena
- complements/objects are ideas, groups of people, people
- use of expanded noun groups and nominalisations
- less use of adverbials and adjectives
- subject-specific vocabulary
- use of maps, graphs and diagrams
- short paragraph answers
- increased semantic density and gravity.

**Science:**

- textual organisation centred upon an introduction, main body and often no conclusion;
- clause complexes comprised of co-ordinating clauses;
- few adverbs and adjectivals;
- high concentration of nominalisations and nominal groups;
- subjects/participants of clauses are nominalisations and nominal groups referring to physical phenomenon;
- high proportion of relational processes;
- increased semantic density and gravity.

**Maths**:

- use of mathematical symbols;
- textual organisation of prose answers centred upon clauses, normally no more than two
- clause structure of questions follows the command structure of English, with the verb/process at the beginning and made up of one or two clauses, either co-ordinating or relative with the relative clause occurring at the start of the sentence;
- nominal groups refer to mathematical concepts;
- verbs/processes are relational and centre upon the verb *be*.

English RE and history share many patterns of register that have much in common with those of geography. The key difference lies in the ways in which interpersonal relationships are construed in terms of nature of the subjects/participants of clauses and the use or absence of any personal pronouns. There is less use of adverbials and adjectives in geography than English, RE and history which also includes maps, graphs, photographs and other visualisations in the texts that are studied; use less use if any of verbal groups/processes. Clause complexes tend towards two or three clause sentences at the most. Writing also tends to be shorter in geography characterised by a greater proportion of noun groups and nominalisation within clause structure. Geography thus shares many of the characteristics of writing in science, where again the key difference between geography and the sciences is in the nature of subjects/participants and the different ways in which reality is construed. In maths, questions are written as commands and any writing undertaken is normally in terms of explaining some feature(s) revealed by previously undertaken mathematical reasoning in one sentence.

Through their engagement in such activities, the teachers—regardless of their own teacher autobiographies and their own knowledge about language—developed literacy aspects of their differing subjects in the main through firstly, identifying the patterns associated with the textual organisation of the writing tasks they asked pupils and students to undertake. Only then did teachers feel able to focus in on the register patterns that characterised their pupils' and students' writing tasks, and particularly after seeing examples of the different kinds of writing drawn from different curriculum subjects.

## Concluding Thoughts

It is evident from the discussion throughout this book that introducing any initiative across the curriculum in secondary contexts that impacts upon teachers' pedagogic practices is not an easy endeavour to undertake, for the reasons already given. In relation to LLAC, this is particularly challenging given the internal organisation of schools into discrete subject areas/departments/faculties. Literacy initiatives in the three schools discussed throughout this book, in common with many others, had tended towards ones such as consistency of marking practices that included the application of a consistent set of codes in marking work initiatives such as peer assessment and paying explicit attention to learning outcomes in terms of assessment objectives. Many subject areas drew upon scaffolding frames such as IDEA, PEEL, PETER and TEA or any of the plethora of structure strips that can be found on twitter, but without explicitly teasing apart the register patterns of each of its sections. Where explicit attention was paid to grammar, it generally took the form of a decontextualised 'literacy ladder' or a piece of writing, usually from English, displayed with 'grammatical term' labelling surrounding it. Equally, teachers often provide vocabulary lists for key concepts and terms associated with any topic they are teaching, and/or lists of grammatical features such as conjunctions but without considering these items in the context of pupils' and students' constructing their own writing.

An LBP approach can build upon such initiatives, by teachers drawing upon it in terms of firstly, the textual organisation that characterises pupil and student writing in their subject areas and any corresponding scaffolding frames that seem appropriate to them. If pupils' and students' writing has no structure or internal logic, comprising ill-thought through sentences and paragraphs that are randomly selected and stray from the topic of the question being answered, then their chances of successful assessment lessen commensurately. Secondly, an LBP approach pays attention to the phrasing and wording of assessment questions and the register patterns within the textual organisation of the writing pupils and students write in response to them. The simile often used is that an LBP approach teaches pupils and students to think, speak and write 'like a historian', 'like a scientist', 'like a geographer' and so on. Such attention can also be paid to the texts pupils and students read. Pedagogic practice in turn is affected through teachers paying far more attention to the ways in which their pupils and students express their ideas and giving more time and space to activities centred around improving that expression in planned lesson time than they had hitherto. Thirdly, paying explicit attention to the specific register features that includes attention to vocabulary and grammar, including the use of grammatical metaphor through understanding the process of nominalisation, by way of initiating pupils and students into any individual subject's discursive practices.

To implement such an initiative requires a team of teachers drawn from different curriculum areas/subjects to work together, led by one of them acting as the co-ordinator. Many secondary schools in England have designated literacy co-ordinators and although this person is normally drawn from the English department, this not need necessarily be the case. In School A, Makepeace School for example, the literacy co-ordinator was the Head of the Modern Languages Department. Effective use of CPD or increasingly JPD, provide mechanisms through which an LBP informed LLAC initiative can be disseminated throughout a school or groups of schools. The discussion in the later chapters of this book also shows how two main barriers to an LBP approach, namely teacher's own lack of grammatical knowledge and finding the time to incorporate 'language work' into their lesson planning and delivery, can be overcome. This is particularly the case when developing teacher's grammatical knowledge and their confidence in applying it is undertaken in targeted, focused ways and in the context of their own pedagogic practices and goals.

## References

Murphy, V. (2015). *A systematic review of intervention research examining English language and literacy development in children with English as an Additional Language (EAL).* https://www.bell-foundation.org.uk/assets/Documents/EALachievementMurphy.pdf?1422548394. Accessed December 30, 2015.

Garraffa, M., Obregon, M., & Sorace, A. (2017). Linguistic and cognitive effects of bilingualism with regional minority languages: A study of Sardinian–Italian adult speakers. *Frontiers in Psychology, 8*, 1907.

# Glossary

**active voice:** a clause where the subject performs the action stated by the verb

**adjectivals:** any word or group of word that modifies a noun or noun group such as *adjectives; articles; determiners; posssessives*

**adjectival clause:** a clause that functions like an adjective to modify a noun, e.g. a relative clause

**adjective:** a class of words used to modify nouns, *e.g. large, square, beautiful*

**adjunct:** supplementary as opposed to essential information in a clause

**adverb/s:** a class of words used to specify the circumstances of an action or event, e.g. the manner (*slowly*), the time (*soon*), the place (*here*); it also includes conjunctive adverbs (*however*) and adverb particles (*up, out*)

**adverbial:** a type of element in sentence structure, referring to the circumstances of the sentence rather than to a place or person, often expressed by an **adverb, adverbial phrase, prepositional phrase** or **adverbial clause**. Often function as **adjunct** in a clause

**adverbial clause:** a clause, often introduced by a subordinating conjunction (*if, because, although*) that functions as an adverbial in sentence structure

**alliteration:** a sound pattern in which the first sound of two or more words is the same. e.g. *Peter Piper picked a pickled pepper*

**article:** a type of *determiner* that is followed by a noun: *a, an, the*. Expresses the definiteness and specificity of a noun

**assonance:** like alliteration, assonance refers to a particular sound patterning in words using repetition, only this time it is applied to the repetition of a vowel sound within a word. e.g. *Br<u>ea</u>k, Br<u>ea</u>k, Br<u>ea</u>k/ On thy c<u>o</u>ld, gr<u>ey</u>, st<u>o</u>nes. (Br<u>ea</u>k and gr<u>ey</u> c<u>o</u>ld and st<u>o</u>ne)*

**authorial voice:** Any written text has an author, known or unknown, although the extent to which she or he intrudes into text varies. In factual texts the author is usually at pains to keep him or herself at a distance from what they are writing, whereas in fiction the author can take a more active and positive role in telling the story. Telling a story from either narrative perspective involves further choices as to whether the narrator knows everything about the characters and events known as **authorial omniscience** or to restrict their narrative perspective, known as **authorial reportage.** Both of these perspectives can be referred to as **authorial voice**

**auxiliary verb:** a small set of verbs, including the modal verbs, *be, have* and *do*, which accompany lexical verbs and indicate modality, progressive and perfect aspects, and passive voice

**clause:** a syntactic unit having the essential structure of a **verb/verb group/process**, embedded in (functioning as part of) a clause. Can also be analysed in terms of **subject/predicate/object/complement/adjunct**

**clause- complex:** a head or main clause that combines with other clauses that modify it in some way, usually elaborating upon it or addidint verbal process. The main categories of such clauses are **coordinate, subordinate, relative** and **embedded. Parataxis** refers to co-ordinating clauses and **hypotaxis** to all others where the interdependence is of unequal status

**coherence:** the sense that a text is a meaningful whole; the psychological counterpart of cohesion

**cohesion:** the grammatical and lexical devices that serve to make a text hold together, *e.g. pronouns, conjunctive adverbs, lexical repetition*

**collocation:** a lexical feature relating to the mutual attraction of words; if two words are collocates; then there is a greater than chance likelihood of them both occurring. *e.g. dark* and *night, sour* and *milk*

**coordinate clauses:** the joining together of sentences, clauses, phrases or words by means of *and, but, or*

**complement:** an element of clause structure, typically realised as an adjective or nominal group, that has the potential to be a subject but is not, adding information about the subject and sometimes the object

**compound:** a word made up of the combination of two independent words, *e.g. rainfall, see-through*

**conjunction:** words used for joining ideas in clauses within a sentence; coordinating conjunctions *(and but, or)* provide coordination; subordinating conjunctions *(e.g. because, if, when, although)* join subordinate adverbial clauses to a sentence

**connective:** words used to join ideas in clauses of a preceeding sentence *e.g. also, furthermore, in addition, finally, meanwhile*

**consonant:** in writing, every other letter of the alphabet which is not a vowel

**deictics:** features of language which are not referred to directly, but are heavily dependant on context for their meaning *e.g. here v there; now v then etc*

**demonstrative:** a subclass of determiners and pronouns, comprising the words *this/these, that/those*

**determiner:** a class of words that accompany or qualify nouns in noun phrases, including **articles,** pronouns and quantifiers

**dialect:** the regional and social variations of a language, especially in respect of grammar and vocabulary

**embedded clause:** a clause which is inserted into a main clause, marked by commas: *the street, where he lived, was often busy*

**ellipsis:** leaving out part of a sentence which can be readily understood and to avoid unnecessary repetition, *e.g. Two pints (of beer) please*

**finite verbs:** verbs that have a past and present form: has an expressed or implied subject, can function as the root of a clause and thus standa alone as a single clause sentence

**genre:** sometimes called **text type**. texts classified according to purpose and structural features, *e.g. narrative, descriptive, expository* that share similar characteristics or patterns of **register**

**grammar:** the study of the spoken and written forms of language, particularly in relation to words, clauses and texts

**grammatical metaphor:** meaning realised in a different way from the literal in terms of a different grammatical construction. For example, when a *clause* is coded as a *phrase*. 'The brakes failed' becomes 'brake failure.'

**graphology:** the writing system of a language, handwritten or typed and related features such as punctuation, paragraphing, spacing, size of print etc

**hypotaxis:** the logical dependency between clauses of unequal status

**imagery:** a term commonly used in literary criticism to describe the way language creates visual images or pictures with words; e.g. the use of **metaphor** and **simile**

**intransitive:** a type of verb that is not followed by an object in sentence structure, also used of such a sentence; compare 'transitive.'

**lexical items:** items drawn from the stock of words belonging to the language as a whole

**lexico-grammar:** a system of grammar that takes account of lexis and semantics as well as syntax in devising its categories

**lexis:** the term used to describe the total stock of words of a language

**linguistic competence:** the grammar of a language is an idealization and that speakers know the rules of the 'correct' grammar of their language

**linguistic repertoire:** sets of linguistic practices associated with specific speech communities; ways in which linguistic choice is related or is tied to social categories and constraints

**metafunctions:** three general functions of language at a higher (meta) level than their instances of actual use mapped onto a clause and in relation to groups of semantic meanings: *ideational,* (*experiential* and *logical*) representing situations in the world and entities, actions and processes involved); *interpersonal,* expression of attitudes and evaluations; and *textual:* information structure and cohesion.

**metaphor:** a term from rhetoric, meaning the substitution of a word or phrase for a non-synonymous word or phrase, so that attributes of the new word are taken as referring to the original

**modality:** those features of a text (including modal verbs, evaluative adjectives and adverbs and so on) which seem to encode the author's attitude to the content

**morpheme:** a unit of word structure *e.g. prefix, suffix*

**morphology:** the study of the forms of words, including inflections, derivations and compounds

**morphosyntax:** the internal structure of words (morphology) and the ways in which they combine to form phrases, clauses and sentences (syntax)

**narrative:** a story, happening or events, real or imaginary, which a **narrator** considers interesting or important

**narrator:** A person who narrates, tells a story, either factual or fictional

**non-finite verb:** verbs in their infinitive, genrund and participle form

**noun:** the largest class of words, referring to 'things,' 'ideas' or 'people' of which the main subdivisions are: **abstract, collective, common, proper** and **pronouns.** Also **countable** and **uncountable**

**noun group:** a group of words consisting of a noun as head, with accompanying modifiers such as **determiners, adjectivals, prepositional phrases**

**object:** an element of clause structure, usually a noun group or nominal clause, occurring with a transitive verb and representing the thing affected by the action of a verb

**parataxis:** the logical dpendency between clauses of equal status

**participle:** one of two non-finite forms of a verb either present participle, with *-ing* suffix (*e.g. laughing*), or past participle, usually with *-ed* suffix (*e.g. laughed*)

**part of speech:** see word class

**passive voice:** the counterpart to active voice, where an active sentence is rearranged by making the verb passive (with *be* + past participle) bringing the object of the active sentence to subject position in the passive sentence, and optionally putting the subject of the active sentence into a *by*-phrase in the passive; e.g. active *The judge sentenced the prisoner to life imprisonment*—passive *The prisoner was sentenced to life imprisonment (by the judge)*

**phonology:** the study of speech sounds, their articulation, acoustics and auditory perception

**phrase:** a group of words that form a unit in the structure of sentences, clauses or other phrases, usually having a head word and accompanying modifying words e.g. noun phrase, verb phrase

**point of view:** the angle of vision or perception by which the events of a narrative are narrated and presented

**possessive:** relating to possession, including nouns and pronouns

**predicator:** a verb group which expresses the process involved; material action; mental; verbal and relational

**prefix:** a bound morpheme that is attached to the front of a root, used to derive new words *e.g. re-apply, anti-nuclear*

**preposition:** a small class of words, including *along, from, in, of, on* used for joining noun phrases to other elements of clause structure

**pronoun:** a class of words that function in place of nouns, including the personal pronouns *I, you, he, she etc*

**punctuation:** the system of marks in writing used to indicate the structure of sentences, including comma, semi-colon, full-stop, question mark

**received pronunciation:** the accent associated with spoken standard English

**reference:** the semantic relation between a word and the entity it relates to in the world of our experience; the raltionship between **nouns** or **pronouns** and the objects named by them. For example, the word *Harry* refers to the person named *Harry*

**referent:** a word or a phrase that stands in place of another, often a pronoun. *The sun shone brighter than **it** did yesterday; Lucy's dogs got wet. **They** shook water all over the place.*

**reflexive:** a type of pronoun, including *myself, yourself, themselves,* used for emphasis *(She did it herself)* or for self-reference *(She has cut herself)*

**register:** the different ways in which language is used in different situations of everyday life *e.g. a telephone conversation; a business letter; a sports commentary* determined by contextual variables of **field:** subject matter or topic of what is being talked, spoken or read about; **tenor: tenor:** social rules and relations that govern language use and **mode:** communication channel, degree of interacivity and spontaneity.

**register continuum:** is a continuum on which differing text types in speech and writing can be plotted, depending upon the levels of abstractness

**relative clause:** adapts, describes or modifies a noun group functioning as the subject of the main clause, introduced by a relative pronoun (*e.g. who, which, whose*) adding extra information about the subject. *Lucy liked her new haircut,* ***which was very flattering***

**rhyme:** where two phonemes in different words are matched for sound, e.g. end rhyme, where the last two words of two consecutive lines rhyme

**rhythm:** the pattern of stressed and unstressed syllables in a language. Regular patterns of stress produce different metrical patterns

**semantics:** the study of meaning in all its aspects, especially in relation to words and sentences

**semantic density:** the degree to which meaning is linguistically condensed, for example, through **nominalisation** and **grammatical metaphor**

**semantic gravity:** the degree to which the meaning of a word or phrase relates to subject content and context in ways that evoke a broader knowledge base. E.g. the word *cilia* in biology evokes different ways of classifying parts of a body; *tragedy* in English Literature evokes a certain kind of literary genre and its characteristics

**semantic waves:** the ways in which teachers and pupils engage with specific subject concepts. Typically, unpacking concepts in simplified contextual meanings occurs as riding down the wave and moving back up is repacking concepts in condensed linguistic forms to allow relationships to be made with broader subject concepts

**sentence:** a syntactic structure comprised of one clause or more, consisting minimally of a Subject and a Verb/Process, but also possibly containing a Complement, Objects and Adverbials

**simile:** comparing a word or phrase with a non-synonymous word or phrase, usually by using *like* or *as. e.g., as white as snow; my love is like a red, red rose*

**standard English:** the dialect of English that has been most codified and is promoted as a national variety of English in both spoken and written forms

**stress:** the relative prominence given to syllables in speech, e.g. in *certain* the first syllable is stressed and the second unstressed

**subject:** an element of clause structure. A noun group which is the topic of the clause. Normally precedes the verb in the neutral form of **declarative** sentences

**subordinate clause:** a clause that contains a subject and a verb/process attached to a main clause by a subordinating conjunction (*e.g. because, if, since, when*) and often preceded by a comma, but which does not make sense on its own e.g. *I first met her in Rome, **where I lived as a young girl***

**substitution:** the replacement of one expression for another *e.g. I bought a new shirt but I don't like it*

**suffix:** a bound morpheme that is added to the ends of roots, either to derive a new word (*e.g. pur-ify, fair-ness*) or as an inflection (*e.g. paper-s, wait-ing*)

**syllable:** a phonological structure consisting of a vowel (see below) as nucleus and consonants (see above) as peripheral sounds; words may consist of one or more syllables, *e.g. can/kan/, canteen /kan-t:n/*

**syntax:** (the study of) the structures of clauses and their combination into sentences

**systemic functional grammar:** a form of grammatical description derived from *systemic functional linguistics* where language is perceived as a network of systems or interrelated sest of options for the expression of meaning

**systemic functional linguistics:** a theory of language where the function of language is central (what language does, and how it does it), rather than a theory which is more structurally based, where elements of language and their combination are central. SFL starts at social context, and how language both acts upon, and is constrained by, this social context

**tense:** the grammatical category that relates to real-world time; in English only past and present tense are marked by inflections

**text:** a sequence of written clauses marked by punctuation into sentences and characterised by cohesion and coherence

**text type:** texts classified according to purpose and structural features, *e.g. narrative, descriptive, expository.* Often used synonymously as **genre**

**theme and rheme:** relates to the textual metafunction of language. The *theme* is the topic of what is being talked or written about, and the *rheme* is what is being said about the topic

**transitive:** a type of verb that takes an object in clause structure, also used of the clause structure itself; compare 'intransitive'

**transitivity:** relates to the ideational metafunction of language, in relation to particpants, processes and cirucmstances involved in any one clause. Viewed as a continuum rather than the traditional binary category of 'transitive' and 'intransitive'

**verb phrase:** a word or group of words that refer to actions, events (material action); states, feelings, perception (mental); expressive (verbal) and relational (be, have). Also subdivided into auxiliary verbs (see above) and lexical or main verbs

**verb phrase:** a group of words with a lexical verb as head and optionally preceded by auxiliary verbs and the negative *not*

**vowel:** a type of speech sound, articulated without any restriction to the airflow in the mouth and formed by modifications to the shape of the mouth, composing the nucleus of syllables; in writing associated with the letters *a,e,i,o,u.*; compare 'consonant'

**word:** a basic unit of syntax, entering into the structure of phrases and sentences, composed of morphemes

**word class:** a grouping of words according to shared features of reference, morphology and syntax, such as nouns, verbs, adjectives and prepositions. Divided into kinds, **open** and **closed**

# References

Achugar, M., & Carpenter, B. D. (2012). Developing disciplinary literacy in a multilingual history classroom. *Linguistics and Education 23*(3), 262–276.

Adams, E. A., & Pegg, J. (2012). Teachers' enactment of content literacy strategies in secondary science and mathematics classes. *Journal of Adolescent & Adult Literacy, 56*(2), 151–161.

Anderson, A., & Shattock, J. (2012). Design-based research: A decade of progress in education research? *Educational Researcher, 41*(1), 16–25.

Andrews, R. (2005). Knowledge about the teaching of [sentence] grammar: The state of play. *English Teaching: Practice and Critique, 4*(3), 69–76.

Andrews, R. (2010). *Re-framing literacy*. New York: Routledge.

Andrews R., Torgerson C., Beverton S., Locke T., Low G., Robinson A., & Zhu D. (2004a). *The effect of grammar teaching (syntax) in English on 5 to 16 year olds' accuracy and quality in written composition*. London: EPPI-Centre, Social Science Research Unit, Institute of Education. Retrieved December 12, 2005 from http://eppi.ioe.ac.uk/reel.

Andrews R., Torgerson C., Beverton S., Locke T., Low G., Robinson A., & Zhu D. (2004b). *The effect of grammar teaching (sentence-combining) in English on 5 to 16 year olds' accuracy and quality in written composition*. London: EPPI-Centre, Social Science Research Unit, Institute of Education. Retrieved December 12, 2005 from http://eppi.ioe.ac.uk/reel.

Andrews, R., Torgerson, C., Beverton, S., Freeman, A., Locke, T., Low, G., et al. (2006). The effect of grammar teaching on writing development. *British Educational Research Journal, 32*(1), 39–55.

Androutsopoulos, J., & Georgakopoulou, A. (2003). *Discourse constructions of youth identities*. Amsterdam: Benjamins.

Alexander, R. (2008) *Towards dialogic teaching: Rethinking classroom talk*. York: Dialogos.

Barnes, D. (1976/1992). *From communication to curriculum*. Portsmouth, NH: Boynton and Cook Heinemann.

Barnes, D., Britton, J., & Rosen, M. (1969 & 1971). *Language, the learner and the school*. London: Penguin Education.

Barton, D., & Hamilton, M. (2000). Literacy practices. In D. Barton, S. Hamilton, & R. Ivanic (Eds.), *Situated literacies* (pp. 7–15). London and New York: Routledge.

Barton, G. (2012). *Don't call it literacy!* London: Routledge.

Benesch, S. (2001). *Critical English for academic purposes*. Mahwah, NJ: Lawrence Erlbaum Associates.

Bernstein, B. (1975). *Class and pedagogies: Visible and invisible*. Paris: Centre for Educational Research and Innovation (CERI).

Bernstein, B. (1991). *The Structuring of pedagogic discourse Vol 4. Class, codes and control*. London and New York: Routledge.

Bernstein, B. (1996). *Pedagogy, symbolic control and identity*. London: Taylor and Francis.

Bernstein, B. (1999). Horizontal and vertical discourse: An essay. *British Journal of the Sociology of Education, 20*(2), 157–173.

Biber, D., & Conrad, S. (2009). *Register, genre and style*. Cambridge: Cambridge University Press.

Biber, D., Conrad, S., & Randi, R. (1998). *Corpus linguistics: Investigating language structure and use*. Cambridge: Cambridge University Press.

Biber, D., & Gray B. (2016). *Grammatical complexity in academic English*. Cambridge: Cambridge University Press.

Biber, D., Johansson, S., Leech, G., Conrad, S., & Finnegan, E. (1999). *The Longman Grammar of spoken and written English*. London: Longman.

Black, P., & William, D. (1998). Assessment and classroom learning. *Assessment in Education: Policy & Practice, 5*(1), 7–74.

Blackledge, A., & Creese, A. (Eds.). (2014). *Heteroglossia as practice and pedagogy*. Dordrecht, Heidlelberg, New York, and London: Springer.

Blommaert, J. (2010). *The sociolinguistics of globalisation*. Cambridge: Cambridge University Press.

Blommaert, J., & Backus, A. (2011). *Repertoires revisited: 'Knowing language' in superdiversity.* London: Kings College Working Papers in Language and Literacies.

Bourdieu, P. (1973). Cultural reproduction and social reproduction. In R. Brown (Ed.), *Knowledge, education and social change: Papers in the sociology of education.* Tavistock: Tavistock Publications.

Bourdieu, P., & Passeron, J. (1977). *Reproduction in education, society and culture.* London: Sage.

Bragg, S., Kehily, M. J., & Buckingham, D. (Eds.). (2014). *Youth cultures in the age of global media.* Basingstoke: Palgrave Macmillan.

Brisk, M. (2015). *Engaging students in academic literacies: Genre based pedagogy for K-5 classrooms.* London and New York: Routledge.

Britton, J. (1970). *Language and learning.* London: Penguin.

Bruner, J. S. (1966). *Towards a theory of instruction.* Cambridge, MA: Belkapp Press.

Bruner, J. S. (1983). *Child's talk: Learning to use language.* New York: W.W. Norton.

Bruner, J. S. (1996). *The culture of education.* Cambridge, MA: Harvard University Press.

Burns, A., & Joyce, H. (1991). The teaching-learning cycle. In J. Hamond, A. Burns, & H. Joyce (Eds.), *English for social purposes.* Sydney: National Centre for English Language Teaching and Research.

Busch, B. (2012). The linguistic repertoire revisited. *Applied Linguistics, 33*(5), 1–22.

Callaghan, M., & Rothery, J. (1988). *Teaching factual writing: A genre based approach.* Erskeneville, NSW: Metropolitan East Disadvantaged Schools' Program.

Carroll, J. E., (2016). Exploring historical 'frameworks' as a curriculum goal: A case study examining students' notions of historical significance when using millennia-wide time scales. *The Curriculum Journal, 27*(4), 454–478.

Carroll, J. E. (2017a). 'I feel if I say this my essay it's not going to be strong': Multi-voicedness, 'oral rehearsal' and Year 13 students' written arguments. *Teaching Hoistory: The Secondary Education Journal of the Historical Association, 167,* 8–16.

Carroll, J. E. (2017b). From divergent evolution to witting cross-fertilisation: The need for more awareness of potential inter-discursive communication regarding students' extended historical writing. *The Curriculum Journal, 28*(4), 504–523.

Carter, R. A. (2004). *Language and creativity: The art of common talk.* London: Routledge.

Carter, R. A., & McCarthy, M. J. (2004). Talking, creating: Interactional language, creativity and and context. *Applied Linguistics, 25*(1), 62–88.

Carter, R. A., & McCarthy, M. J. (2015). Spoken grammar: Where are we and where are we going? *Applied Linguistics, 38*(1), 1–20.

Carter, R. A., McCarthy, M. J., Mark, G., & O'Keefe, A. (2011). *English grammar today: An A-Z of spoken and written grammar*. Cambridge: Cambridge University Press.

Centre for Educational Research and Innovation (CERI). (2007). *Understanding the brain: The birth of a learning science*. http://www.oecd.org/edu/ceri/understandingthebrainthebirthofalearningscience.htm. Accessed December 30, 2015.

Charmaz, K. (2014). *Constructing grounded theory* (2nd ed.). London and New York: Sage.

Chomsky, N. (1957). *Syntactic structures*. The Hague and Paris: Mouton.

Chomsky, N. (1965). *Aspects of the theory of syntax*. Cambridge: MIT Press.

Christie, F. (2002). The development of abstraction in adolescence in subject English. In M. Schleppegrell & M. Colombi (Eds.), *Developing advanced literacy in first and second languages* (pp. 45–66). Mahwah, NJ and London: Erlbaum.

Christie, F. (2016). Secondary school English literary studies: An example of a knower code. In K. Maton, S. Hood, & S. Shay (Eds.), *Knowledge-building: Educational studies in Legitimation Code Theory* (pp. 156–158). London and New York: Routledge.

Clark, U. (1994). Bringing English to order. *English in Education, 28*(1), 33–38.

Clark, U. (2001). *War words: Language, history and the disciplining of English*. Oxford: Elsevier Science.

Clark, U. (2005). Bernstein's theory of pedagogic discourse: Linguistics, educational policy and practice in the UK English/literacy classroom. *English Teaching: Practice and Critique, 4*(3), 32–47.

Clark, U. (2010a). Grammar in the curriculum for English: What next? *Changing English: Studies in culture and education, 17*(2), 189–200.

Clark, U. (2010b). The problematics of prescribing grammatical knowledge: The case in England. In L. Terry (Ed.), *Beyond the grammar wars: A resource for teachers and students on developing language knowledge in the English/literacy classroom* (pp. 120–136). London: Routledge.

Clark, U. (2011). What is English for?: Language structure and the curriculum for English. *Changing English: Studies in Culture and Education, 18*(3), 287–296.

Clark, U. (2013). *Language and identity in Englishes*. London: Routledge.
Clay, M. (1991). *Becoming literate: The construction of inner control*. London: Hienemann.
Clay, M. (1993). *An observation survey of early literacy development*. London: Heinemann.
Christie, F. (2007). Ongoing dialogue: Functional language and Bernsteinian sociological perspectives in education. In F. Christie & J. Martin (Eds.), *Language, knowledge and pedagogy: Functional linguistic and sociological perspectives* (pp. 3–13). London and New York: Continuum.
Christie, F. (2012). *Language education throughout the cchool years: A functional perspective*. Chichester and Malden, MA: Wiley-Blackwell.
Christie, F., & Derewianka, B. (2008). *School discourse: Learning to write across the years of schooling*. London and New York: Continuum.
Christie, F., & Macken-Horarik, M. (2007). Building vertically in subject English. In F. Christie & J. R Martin (Eds.), *Language, knowledge and pedagogy: Functional linguistics and sociological perspectives* (pp. 14–36). London and New York: Continuum.
Christie, F., & Martin, J. R. (Eds.). (2007). *Language, knowledge and pedagogy: Functional linguistic and sociological perspectives*. London and New York: Continuum.
Christie, F., Gray, P., Gray, B., Macken, M., Martin, J. R., & Rothery, J. (1990a, 1990b, 1992). *Language a resource for meaning: Procedures,* Books 1–4 and Teachers Manual; Reports Books 104 and Teachers' Manual; Explanations Books 1–4 and Teachers' Manual. Sydney: Harcourt Brace Jovanovich.
Cloran, C., Butt, D., & Williams, G. (1996). *Ways of saying, ways of meaning: Selected papers of Ruqaiya Hasan*. London: Caswell.
Cobbett, W. (1818). *A grammar of the English language*. New York: Peter Eckler.
Coffin, C. (1996). *Exploring literacy in school history*. Sydney: Disadvantaged Schools Program.
Coffin, C. (2006). *Historical discourse: The language of time, cause and evaluation*. London: Continuum.
Coffin, C., & Donohue, J. (2014). *A language as a social-semiotic-based approach to teaching and learning in higher education*. Oxford: Wiley-Blackwell.
Collins, A. (1992). Toward a design science of education. In E. Scanlon & T. O'Shea (Eds.), *New directions in educational technology* (pp. 15–22). New York: Springer.

Cope, B., & Kalantzis, M. (2012). *Literacies*. Cambridge: Cambridge University Press.

Cox, B. (1991). *Cox on Cox: An English curriculum for the 1990s*. London: Hodder & Stoughton.

Coupland, N., & Bishop, H. (2007). The ideologised values for British accents. *Journal of Sociolinguistics, 11*(1), 74–93.

De Silva Joyce, H., & Feez, S. (2016). *Exploring literacies: Theory, research, practice*. Basingstoke: Palgrave Macmillan.

Denham, K., & Lobeck, A. (Eds.). (2010). *Linguistics at school: Language awareness in primary and secondary education*. Cambridge: Cambridge University Press.

Department of Education and Science (DES). (1975). *The Bullock Report. A language for life*. London: HMSO.

Department of Education and Science. (1988). *The Kingman Report. Report of the Committee of Inquiry into the Teaching of English Language*. London: HMSO.

Derewianka, B. (1998). *A grammar companion for primary teachers*. Sydney: Primary English Teaching Association.

Derewianka, B. (1990). *Exploring how texts work*. Rozelle, NSW: Primary English Association.

Devrim, D. Y. (2015). Grammatical metaphor: What do we mean? What exactly are we researching? *Functional Linguistics, 2*, 3.

Dixon, J. (1991). *A schooling in English*. Milton Keynes: Open University Press.

Doeke, B., & Breen, L. (2013). Beginning again: A response to Rosen and Christie. *Changing English; Studies in Culture and Education, 20*(3): 292–305.

Doughty, P., Pearce, J., & Thornton, G. (1971). *Language in use*. London: Schools Council.

Elliot, G., Green, S., Constantinou, F., Vitello, S., Chambers, L., Rushton, N., et al. (2016). *Variations in aspects of writing in 16+ examinations between 1980 and 2014. Research Matters: A Cambridge Assessment Publication, Special Issue 4*. http://cambridgeassessment.org.uk/Images/340982-research-matters-special-issue-4-aspects-of-writing-1980-2014.pdf.

Ellis, V., & Briggs, J. (2011). Teacher education and applied linguistics: What needs to be understood about what, how and where beginning teachers learn. In S. Ellis & E. McCartney (Eds.), *Applied linguistics and primary school teaching* (pp. 276–289). Cambridge: Cambridge University Press.

Fielding, M., Bragg, S., Craig, J., Cunningham, I., Eraut, M., Gillinson, S., Horne, M., Robinson, C., & Thorp, J. (2005). *Factors influencing the transfer of good practice.* http://webarchive.nationalarchives.gov.uk/20130402091155/https://www.education.gov.uk/publications/eOrderingDownload/RR615.pdf.pdf. *Accessed August 3, 2017.*

Fisher, D., & Frey, N. (2008). *Better learning through structured teaching: A framework for the gradual release of responsibility.* Alexandria, VA: Association for Supervision and Curriculum Development.

Fontaine, L. (2012). *Analysing English grammar.* Cambridge: Cambridge University Press.

Foucault, M. (1972). *The archeology of knowledge.* New York: Pantheon Books.

Freedman, A. (1994). 'Do as I say': The relationship between teaching and learning new genres. In A. Freedman & P. Medway (Eds.), *Genre and the new rhetoric* (pp. 191–210). London: Taylor & Francis.

French, R. (2012). Learning the grammatics of quoted speech: Benefits for punctuation and expressive reading. *Australian Journal of Language and Literacy, 35*(2), 206–222.

Garcia, O., & Wei, L. (2014). *Translanguaging: Language, bilingualism and education.* Basingstoke: Palgrave Macmillan.

Gardiner, J. (2006). *Assessment and learning.* London: Sage.

Garraffa, M., Obregon, M., & Sorace, A. (2017). Linguistic and cognitive effects of bilingualism with regional minority languages: A study of Sardinian–Italian adult speakers. *Frontiers in Psychology, 8,* 1907.

Gartland, L., & Smolkin, L. (2016). The histories and mysteries of grammar instruction. *The Reading Teacher, 69*(4), 391–399.

Gee, J. (1992). *The social mind: Language, ideology & social practice.* New York: Bergin & Garvey.

Gee, J. (2012). The old and the new in the new digital literacies. *Education Forum, 76*(4), 418–420.

Gee, J. (2014). Decontextualised language: A problem, not a solution. *International Multilingual Research, 8*(1), 9–23.

Georgakopoulou, A. (2014). 'Girlpower or girl (in)trouble?' Identities and discourses in the (new) media engagement of asolescents' school-based interaction. In J. Androutsopoulos (Ed.), *Mediatization and sociolinguistic change* (pp. 428–455). Berlin: Mouton de Gruyter.

Gibbons, P. (2002a). *Bridging discourses in the ESL classroom: Students, teachers and researchers.* London: Continuum.

Gibbons, P. (2002b). *Scaffolding language, scaffolding learning: Teaching second language learners in the mainstream classroom.* London: Heinemann.

Gibbons, P. (2006). *Bridging discourses in the ESL classroom: Students, teachers and researchers.* London: Continuum.

Giovanelli, M. (2014). *Teaching grammar, structure and meaning: Exploring theory and practice for post-16 English language teachers.* London: Routledge.

Giovanelli, M. (2015). Becoming an English language teacher: Linguistic knowledge, anxieties and the shifting sense of identity. *Language and Education, 29*: 416–429.

Giovanelli, M., & Clayton, D. (Eds.). (2016). *Knowing about language: Linguistics and the secondary English classroom.* London: Routledge.

Glazer, B., & Strauss, A. (1967). *The discovery of grounded theory—Strategies for qualitative research.* New Brunswick and London: AldineTransaction.

Goodwyn, A., & Fuller, C. (2011). *The great literacy debate.* London: Routledge.

Graham, S., & Perin, D. (2007). *Writing next: Effective strategies to improve writing of adolescents in middle and high schools—A report to Carnegie Corporation of New York.* Washington, DC: Alliance for Excellent Education.

Gray, B., Cowey, W., & Rose, D. (2000). *What do we mean by an educational culture of survival* (Report prepared for the Department of Education). Canberra: Training and Youth Affairs.

Green, B., & Lee, A. (1994). Writing geography: Literacy, identity and schooling. In A. Freedman & P. Medway (Eds.), *Learning and teaching genre* (pp. 207–224). Portsmouth, NH: Heinemann.

Gumperz, J. (1960). Formal and informal standards in the Hindi regional language area (with C. M. Naim). In C. Ferguson & J. Gumperz (Eds.), *Linguistic diversity in South Asia.* Bloomington: Indiana Univeristy Research Center.

Gumperz, J. (1964). On the ethnology of linguistic change. In *Proceedings of the UCLA Sociolinguistics Conference.* Los Angeles, CA: Mouton & Company.

Halliday, M. (1961). Categories of the theory of grammar. *Word, 17*(3), 242–292.

Halliday, M. (1973). *Explorations in the functions of language.* London: Hodder Stoughton.

Halliday, M. (1977). Text as semantic choice in social context. In T. van Dijk & J. Petofi (Eds.), *Grammars and descriptions* (pp. 176–225). Berlin: Mouton de Gruyter.

Halliday, M. (1983). *Spoken and written language.* Geelong, VIC: Deakin University Press (Republished by Oxford University Press, 1989).

Halliday, M. (1991). Linguistic perspectives on literacy: A systemic-functional approach. In F. Christie (Ed.), *Literacy in social processes: Papers from the Inaugural Australian Systemic Linguistics Conference.* Centre for Studies of Language in Education, Darwin.

Halliday, M. (1993). Towards a language-based theory of learning. *Linguistics and Education, 5*(2), 93–116.

Halliday, M., & Hasan, R. (1976). *Cohesion in English.* London: Longman.

Halliday, M., & Hasan, R. (1985). *Language, context and text: Aspects of language in a social semiotic perspective.* Oxford: Oxford University Press.

Halliday, M., & Martin, J. (1993). *Writing science: Literacy and discursive power.* London: Routledge.

Halliday, M. (1996). Literacy and linguistics: A functional perspective. In R. Hasan & G. Williams (Eds.), *Literacy in society* (pp. 339–376). London: Longman.

Halliday, M., & Matthiessen, C. (1999). *Construing experience through language: A language-based approach to cognition.* London: Cassell (Republished by Continuum, 2006).

Halliday, M., McIntosh, A., & Stevens, P. (2007/1964). The users and uses of language. In J. J. Webster (Ed.), *Language and society. Volume 10 in the Collected Works of M. A. K. Halliday* (pp. 5–37). London and New York: Continuum.

Hamond, J. (Ed.). (2001). *Scaffolding: Teaching and learning in language and literacy education.* Newtown: Primary English Teaching Association.

Hamond, J., & Gibbons, P. (2005). Putting scaffolding to work: The contribution of scaffolding in articulating ESL education. *Prospect, 20*(1): 6–30.

Hasan, R. (1973). Code, register and social dialect. In B. Bernstein (Ed.), *Class, codes and control, Vol 11: Applied studies towards a sociology of language* (pp. 253–292). London: Routledge and Kegan Paul.

Herrington, M., & Macken-Horarik, M. (2015). Linguistically informed teaching of spelling: Toward a relational approach. *Australian Journal of Language and Literacy, 38*(2), 61–71.

Hudson, R. (1992). *Teaching grammar: A guide for the national curriculum.* Oxford: Blackwell.

Hudson, S., & Francis, G. (2000). *Pattern grammar: A corpus-driven approach to the lexical grammar of English.* Amsterdam: John Benjamins.

Hudson, R., & Walmsley, J. (2005). The English patient: English grammar and teaching in the twentieth century. *Journal of Linguistics, 41*(3), 593–622.

Humphrey, S. (1996). *Exploring literacy in school geography*. Sydney: Metropolitan East Disadvantaged Schools Program.

Humphrey, S. (2015). A 4 x 4 literacy toolkit for employment: Englishlanguage learners for academic literacies. In M. B. Schaefer (Ed.), *Research on teaching and learning with the literacies of young adolescents* (pp. 49–72). Charlotte: Information Age Publishing.

Humphrey, S. (2016). *Academic literacies in the middle years: A framework for enhancing teacher knowledge and student achievement*. London and New York: Routledge.

Humphrey, S., & Macnaught, L. (2015). Functional language instruction and the writing growth of English language learners in the middle years. *TESOL Quarterly, 49*(4), 252–278.

Humphrey, S., Sharpe, T., & Cullen, T. (2015). Peeling the PEEL: Integrating language and literacy in the middle years. *Literacy Learning: The Middle Years, 23*(2), 53–62.

Jewitt, C., Bezemer, J., & O Hallora, K. (2016). *Introducing multimodality*. London: Routledge.

Kazemain, B., Behnam, B., & Ghafoori, N. (2013). Ideational grammatical metaphor in scientific texts: A Hallidayan perspective. *International Journal of Linguistics, 5*(4): 146–168.

Kearton, V. (2011). *Developing literacy skills in science lessons: What does the research say?* The Association for Science Education, 1–2. www.ase.org.uk. Accessed June 10, 2017.

Kendrick, M. (2016). *Literacy and multimodality across different global sites*. New York and London: Routledge.

Knapp, P., & Watkins, M. (1994). *Context-text-grammar: Teaching the genres and grammar of school writing in infant and primary schools*. Broadway, NSW: Text Productions.

Knobel, M., & Lankshear, C. (2007). *A New Literacies Sampler*. New York: Peter Lang.

Knobel, M., & Lankshear, C. (2014). Studying new literacies. *Journal of Adolescent & Adult Literacy, 58,* 97–101.

Kress, G. (2003). *Literacy in the new media age*. London: Routledge Falmer.

Lakoff, M., & Johnson, G. (1980). *Metaphors we live by*. Chicago: University of Chicago Press.

Lambert, D. (2011). Reviewing the geography curriculum two decades on. *Curriculum Journal, 22*(2), 243–264.

Langacker, R. W. (1983). *Foundations of cognitive grammar.* Indiana: Indiana University Press.

Langacre, R. (2013). *Essentials of cognitive grammar.* Oxford: Oxford University Press.

Lantolf, J., & Thorne, S. L. (2007). Sociocultural theory and Second language learning. In B. van Patten & J. Williams (Eds). *Theories in second language acquisition.* Mahwah, NJ: Lawrence Erlbaum Associates.

Lee, P. (2005). Walking backwards into tomorrow: Historical consciousness and understanding history. *International Journal of Historical Learning, Teaching and Research, 4*(1), 10–24.

Lillis, T. (2013). *The sociolinguistics of writing.* Edinburgh: Edinburgh University Press.

Locke, T. (Ed.). (2010). *Beyond the grammar wars: A resource book for developing teachers and students language knowledge in the English/literacy classroom.* London and New York: Routledge.

Macken-Horarik, M. (2008). Multiliteracies and 'basic skills' accountability. In L. Unsworth (Ed.), *New literacies and the English curriculum: Multimodal perspectives* (pp. 283–308). London: Continuum.

Macken-Horarik, M. (2011). Why schools English needs a 'good enough' grammatics (and not more grammar). *Changing English: Studies in Culture and Education, 19*(2), 46–53.

Macken-Horarik, M., Love, K., & Horarik S. (2018). Rethinking grammar in language arts: Insights from an Australian survey of teachers' subject knowledge. *Research in the Teaching of English, 52*(3).

Macken-Horarick, M., Sandiford, C., Love, K., & Unsworth, L. (2015). New ways of working 'with grammar in mind' in School English: Insights from systemic functional grammatics. *Linguistics and Education, 31,* 145–158.

Marsh, J., Merchant, G., Gillen, J., & Davies, J. (2012). *Virtual literacies: Interactive spaces for children and young people.* New York: Routledge.

Martin, J. (1993). Literacy in science. In M. Halliday & J. Martin (Eds.), *Writing science: Literacy and discursive power* (pp. 187–225). London: Routledge.

Martin, J. (2007). Construing knowledge: A functional perspective. In F. Christie & J. Martin (Eds.), *Language, knowledge and pedagogy: Functional linguistic and sociological perspectives.* London and New York: Continuum.

Martin, J. (2009). Genre and language learning: A social semiotic perspective. *Linguistics and Education, 20,* 10–21.
Martin, J. (2013). Embedded literacy: Knowledge as meaning. *Linguistics and Education, 24,* 23–37.
Martin, J. (2014). Evolving systemic functional linguistics: Beyond the clause. *Functional Linguistics, 1*(3), 1–24.
Martin, J., & Christie, F. (Eds.). (2007). *Language, knowledge and pedagogy: Functional linguistics and social perspectives.* London: Continuum.
Martin, J., & Rose, D. (2007). Working with discourse (2nd ed.). London: Continuum.
Martin, J., & Rose, D. (2008). *Genre relations: Mapping culture.* London: Equinox.
Martin, J., & Rose, D. (2012). *Learning to write: Reading to learn: Genre, knowledge and pedagogy in the Sydney school.* London: Equinox Publishing.
Martin, J., & Rothery, J. (1986). Writing project: Report. *Working Papers in Linguistics 4.* Sydney: Department of Linguistics, University of Sydney.
Maton, K. (2013). Making semantic waves: A key to cumulative knowledge-building. *Linguistics and Education, 24*(1), 8–22.
Maton, K. (2014). *Knowledge-building: Educational studies in Legitimation Code Theory.* London and New York: Routledge.
Maton, K., & Muller, J. (2007). A sociology for the transmission of knowledges. In F. Christie & J. Martin (Eds.), *Language, knowledge and pedagogy: Functional linguistic and sociological perspectives* (pp. 14–33). London: Continuum.
Maune, M., & Klassen, M. (2014). Filling in the gaps: Genre as a scaffold to the text types of the Common Core State Standards. In L. C. Oliveira & J. Iddings (Eds.), *Genre pedagogy across the curriculum: Theory and application in U.S. classrooms and contexts.* Sheffield and Bristol, CT: Equinox.
Maybin, J. (2014). Researching children's language and literacy practices in school. In C. McAlister & S. Ellis (Eds.), *Genre pedagogy and literacy across learning.* Paper presented at SERA Annual Conference 2014, Edinburgh, UK.
Mercer, N., & Edwards, D. (1987). *Common knowledge: The development of understanding in the classroom.* London: Methuen and Routledge.
Mercer, N. (2000). *Words and minds: How we learn to think together.* London: Routledge.
Moss, G. (2004). Changing practice: The National Literacy Strategy and the politics of literacy policy. *Literacy, 38*(3), 126–133.

Murphy, V. (2015). *A systematic review of intervention research examining English language and literacy development in children with English as an Additional Language (EAL)*. https://www.bell-foundation.org.uk/assets/Documents/EALachievementMurphy.pdf?1422548394. *Accessed December 30, 2015.*

Myhill, D. (2008). Writing; Crafting and creating. *English in Education, 35*(3), 13–20.

Myhill, D. (2018). Grammar as a meaning-making resource for improving writing. *L1. Educational Studies in Language and Literature, 18*, 1–21.

Myhill, D., & Watson, A. (2013a). Creating a language-rich classroom. In S. Capel, M. Leask, & T. Turner (Eds.), *Learning to teach in the secondary school: A companion to school experience* (pp. 403–413). London: Routledge.

Myhill, D., & Watson, A. (2013b). Grammar matters: How teachers' grammatical knowledge impacts on the teaching of writing. *Teaching and Teacher Education, 36*, 77–91.

Myhill, D., & Watson, A. (2014). The role of grammar in the writing curriculum: A review. *Journal of Child Language Teaching and Therapy, 30*(1), 41–62.

Myhill, D., Jones, S., Lines, H., & Watson, A. (2012). Re-thinking grammar: The impact of embedded grammar teaching on students' writing and students' metalinguistic understanding. *Research Papers Education, 27*(2), 139–166.

Nesi, H., & Gardener, S. (2012). *Genres across the disciplines: Students writing in higher education*. Cambridge: Cambridge University Press.

Ofsted. (2009). *English at the crossroads: An evaluation of English in primary and secondary schools 2005/8*. London: HMSO.

Ofsted. (2012). *Moving English forward*. London: HMSO.

Ofsted. (2014). *The national curriculum in England key Stages 3 and 4 framework document*.

O'Halloran, K. L. (2005). *Mathematical discourse: Language, symbolism and visual images*. London and New York: Continuum.

O'Hallaron, C. (2012). *Using SFL to support the development of elementary ELL's argumentative writing*. Presentation at *American Association of Applied Linguistics*. Boston, MA.

Oliveira, L. C., & Iddings, J. (2014). *Genre pedagogy across the curriculum: Theory and application in U.S. classrooms and contexts*. Sheffield and Bristol, CT: Equinox.

Olson, D. (1994). *The world on paper: The conceptual and cognitive implications of writing and reading*. Cambridge: Cambridge University Press.

Osborne, J. (2002). Science without literacy: A ship without a sail? *Cambridge Journal of Education, 32*(2): 203–218.

Painter, C. (2005). *Learning through language in early childhood.* London: Continuum.

Painter, C., Martin, J. R., & Unsworth, L. (2013). *Reading visual narratives: Image analysis of children's picture books.* London: Equinox.

Pahl, K., & Roswell, J. (2012). *Literacy and education: The new literacy studies in the classroom* (2nd ed.). London: Sage.

Parry, B., Burnett, C., & Marchant, G. (Eds.). (2016). *Literacy, media, technology: Past, present and future.* London: Bloomsbury Publishing.

Pearson, P., & Gallagher, M. (1993). The instruction of reading comprehension. *Contemporary Educational Psychology, 8,* 317–344.

Polias, J., & Dare, B. (2006). Towards a pedagogic grammar. In R. Whittaker, M. O'Donnell, & A. McCabe (Eds.), *Language and literacy: Functional approaches.* London and New York: Continuum.

Quinn, M. (2004). Talking with Jess: Looking at how metalanguage assisted explanation writing in the middle years. *Australian Journal of Language and Literacy, 27*(3), 245–261.

Raban, B., Clark, U., & McIntyre, J. (1994). *Evaluation of the implementation of English in the national curriculum at key Stages 1, 2 and 3 (1991–1993).* London: Schools Curriculum and Assessment Authority. http://www.educationengland.org.uk/documents/warwick/warwick1994.html.

Reeves, T., Herrington, J., & Oliver, R. (2005). Design research: A socially responsible approach to instructional technology researcher in higher education. *Journal of Computing in Higher Education, 16*(2), 96–115.

Richmond, J. (2015). *Grammar and knowledge about language.* UKLA and Owen Education.

Richmond, J., Burn, A., Dougill, P., Goddard, A., Raleigh, M., & Traves, P. (2017). *Curriculum and assessment in English 11 to 19: A better plan.* London: Routledge.

Rose, D., Gray, B., & Cowey W. (1999). Scaffolding reading and writing for indigenous children in school. In P. Wignell (Ed.), *Double power: English literacy in indigenous schooling* (pp. 23–60). Melbourne: NLLIA.

Rosen, M. (2013). How genre theory saved the world. *Changing English: Studies in Culture and Education, 20*(1), 3–10.

Rothery, J. (1989). Learning about language. In R. Hasan & J. Martin (Eds.), *Language development: Learning language, learning culture* (pp. 152–198). Norwood, NJ: Ablex Publishing.

Rothery, J. (1994). *Exploring literacy in school English (write it right resources for literacy and learning)*. Sydney: Metropolitan East Disadvantaged Schools Program.
Rothery, J. (1996). Making changes: Developing an educational linguistics. In R. Hasan & G. Williams (Eds.), *Literacy in society* (pp. 86–123). London: Longman.
Rothery, J., & Stenglin, M. (Eds.). (1997). Exploring experience through story. In F. Christie & J. Martin (Eds.), *Genres and institutions: Social processes in the workplace and school* (pp. 231–263). London: Pinter.
Rothery, J., & Stenglin, M. (2000). Interpreting literature: The role of APPRAISAL. In L. Unsworth (Ed.), *Researching language in schools and functional linguistic perspectives*. London: Cassell.
Sandoval, W. A., & Bell, P. (2004). Design-based research methods for studying learning in context: Introduction. *Educational Psychologist, 39*(4), 199–201.
Schemilt, D. (2000). The Caliph's colin: The currency of narrative Frameworks in History Teaching. In P. Stearns et al. (Eds.), *Knowing, teaching and learning history: National and international perspectives*. New York: New York University Press.
Schemilt, D. (2009). Drinking an ocean and pissing a cupful. In L. Symcox & A. Wilschut (Eds.). *National history standards. The problem of Canon and the future of teaching history.* Charlotte, NC: Information Age Publishing.
Schleppegrell, M. (2013). The role of metalanguage in supporting academic language development. *Language Learning, 63,* 153–170.
Schleppegrell, M. (2015). *Learning to situate SFL-inspired pedagogies in new contexts*. Paper presented at the Education Semiotics conference, Aachen, Germany.
Schleppegrell, M., Greer, S., & Taylor, S. (2008). Developing a metalanguage for historical inquiry. *Australian Journal of Language and Literacy, 27*(3), 174–187.
Schleppegrell, M., Greer, S., & Taylor, S. (2012). Literacy in history: Language and meaning. *Australian Journal of Language and Literacy, 31*(2), 174–187.
Sebba, M. (2012). Orthography as social action: Scripts, spelling, power and identity. In A. Jaffe, J. Androutsopoulos, M. Sebba, & S. Johnson (Eds.), *Orthography as social action: Scripts, spelling, power and identity* (pp. 1–20) Berlin: Mouton de Gruyter.
Snell, J. (2013). Dialect, interaction and class positioning at school: From deficit to difference to repertoirw. *Language and Education, 27*(2), 110–128.

Stiggins, R. (2007). Assessment through the student's eye. *Educational Leadership, 64*(8), 22–26.

Strand, S. (2015). *English as an Additional Language (EAL) and educational achievement in England: An analysis of the National Pupil Database.* https://www.bellfoundation.org.uk/assets/Documents/EALachievementStrand.pdf?1422548358. Accessed December 30, 2015.

Street, B. V. (1995). *Social literacies: Critical approaches to literacy in development, ethnography and education.* London: Longman.

Tienson, J. (1983). *Linguistic competence Transactions of the Nebraska Academy of Sciences and Affiliated Societies.* Paper 259. http://digitalcommons.unl.edu/tnas/259.

Unsworth, L., & Macken-Horarik, M. (2015). Interpretive responses to images in picture books by primary and secondary school students: Exploring curriculum expectations of a 'visual grammatics'. *English in Education, 49*(1), 56–79.

Unsworth, L., & Thomas, A. (Eds.). (2014). *English teaching and new literacies pedagogy: Interpreting and authoring digital multimedia narratives.* New York: Peter Lang.

Upward, C., & Davidson, G. (2011). *The history of English spelling.* Oxford: Wiley-Blackwell.

Velghe, F., & Blommaert, J. (2014). Emergent new literacies and the mobile phone: Informal languages learning, voice and identity in a South African Township. In B. Geraghty & J. Conacher (Eds.), *Intercultural contact, language learning and migration* (pp. 89–111). London: Bloomsbury.

Vertovec, S. (2007). Super-diversity and its implications. *Ethnic and Racial Studies, 30*(6), 1024–1054.

Vygotsky, L. (1962). *Thought and language.* Cambridge, MA: MIT.

Watson, A. (2015). The problem of grammar teaching: A case study of the relationship between a teacher's beliefs and pedagogic al practice. *Language and Education, 29*(4), 332–346.

Wells, G. (1999). *Dialogic inquiry: Towards a sociocultural practice and theory of education.* Cambridge: Cambridge University Press.

Wignall, P., Martin, J. R., & Eggins, S. (1993). The discourse of geography: Ordering and explaining the referential world. In M. Halliday & J. Martin (Eds.), *Writing science: Literacy and discursive power* (pp. 151–183). London: Taylor & Francis.

Williams, G. (1998). Children entering literate worlds: Perspectives from the study of textual practice. In F. Christie & R. Misson (Eds.), *Literacy and schooling* (pp. 18–46). London and New York: Routledge.

Williams, G. (2000). Children's literature, children and uses of language description. In L. Unsworth (Ed.), *Researching language in schools and communities: A functional perspective* (pp. 111–129). London and New York: Continuum.

Williams, G. (2004). Ontogenesis and grammatics: Functions of metalanguage in pedagogic discourse. In G. Williams & A. Lukin (Eds.), *The development of language* (pp. 241–267). London and New York: Continuum.

Wolleb, A., Sorace, A., & Westergaard, M. (2017). Linguistic and cognitive effects of bilingualism with regional minority languages: A study of Sardinian–Italian bilingual children. *Bilingualism: Language and Cognition*, 1–30.

Wood, C., Kemp, N., & Plester, B. (2014). *Text messaging and its impact on literacy skills: The evidence.* London: Routledge.

Wyse, D. (2017). *How writing works: From the invention of the alphabet to the rise of social media.* Cambridge: Cambridge University Press.

Wyse, D., Jones, R., Bradford, H., & Wolpert, M. A. (2013). *Teaching English, language and literacy* (3rd ed.). London and New York: Routledge.

# Index

**A**

Academic literacy 8–9, 11, 19, 42, 67
Assessment 6, 7, 11, 14, 17, 18, 29, 80–82, 90, 96, 99–106, 115, 116, 119, 123, 124, 129, 135–137, 143, 147–150, 152, 153, 161, 162, 168, 170, 181, 193, 201, 202, 221, 224, 225

**C**

Christie, F. 13, 43, 52, 54, 56, 72, 73, 113, 114
Clause structure 29, 53, 66, 91, 148, 153, 167, 200, 201, 208, 232, 238, 240, 241, 243
Cobbett, William 3–5, 134, 186

**D**

Derewianka, B. 13, 43, 56, 59, 61
Dialect 38–41, 50, 73, 239
Dialogic teaching 75–76
Differentiation 209, 225

**E**

English as an additional language (EAL) 6, 16, 37, 78, 89, 90, 93–95, 100, 112, 114, 123, 173, 221–223

**G**

Genre/text type 97, 127, 134, 182, 185, 221
Grammatical metaphor 114, 199–200, 224, 234, 242

## H

Hasan, R. 28, 39, 52, 54
Humphrey, S. 10, 13, 17, 42, 73, 89, 93, 101, 122

## J

Joint practice development (JPD) 98–99, 234

## K

Knowledge about language (KAL) 10, 12, 14, 24, 25, 89, 91, 124, 131, 132, 232
Knowledge structures 72, 154–155, 156, 159

## L

Language based pedagogy (LBP) 1, 6, 9–14, 16–21, 25, 27–30, 37, 42, 45, 49, 51, 52, 56, 67, 76, 77, 80–82, 89, 91, 92, 93, 95–100, 104, 106, 107, 112, 113, 116, 118, 119, 122–124, 127, 131, 133, 139, 142, 143, 148, 152–154, 156, 159–161, 169, 172, 185, 191, 192, 195, 196, 201, 202–205, 209, 210, 219–227, 233, 234
Language development 5, 9, 13, 19, 29, 30, 43, 45, 52, 56, 77, 78, 90, 93, 123, 124, 152, 220–222
Levels of language 57

## M

Martin, J. 16, 17, 21, 52, 73–75, 77, 80, 111, 184, 197–200
Maton, K. 52, 72, 74, 75
Mentor texts, use of 97, 117

## N

National Curriculum 2, 7–9, 23–25, 38, 55, 59, 69, 90, 92, 127–129, 154, 168, 182, 183, 198, 200, 209
Nominalisation 101, 104–107, 149, 155, 188, 189, 191, 193, 194, 199–201, 208, 215, 224, 230–232, 234

## P

Pedagogic discourse 6, 67, 68, 70–72, 80
  horizontal discourse 71, 73
  vertical discourse 70, 71, 73
Pedagogic grammar 2, 3, 6, 53, 81, 82, 129, 154, 159, 192, 195, 201, 221, 222, 225, 226

## R

Register 8, 21, 24, 29, 37, 40–42, 45, 50, 51, 54–56, 58, 66, 73, 80, 81, 97, 101, 105, 108, 115, 116, 118, 129–133, 139, 142–144, 153–156, 159, 160, 163, 172, 182, 185, 186, 191, 193–195, 197, 198, 200, 201,

215, 220, 221, 223, 224, 226, 227, 229, 233, 234

## S

Schleppergrell 89
Semantic density 75, 120, 155, 193, 194, 198, 230, 231
Semantic gravity 75, 242
Speech and writing 24, 44, 45–51, 53, 54, 242
Subject specific academic register features
    English 66, 69
    Geography 58
    History 66
    Maths 58
    RE 66
    Science (biology) 58
Systemic functional linguistics/grammar 52–67

## T

Teaching and Learning Cycle 74, 78–81, 96, 97, 108, 114, 116, 119, 122, 129, 134, 149, 152–154, 192, 196, 221, 223–225, 227
Textual organisation 3, 4, 29, 95, 97, 123, 134, 142, 154, 155, 160, 172, 185, 191, 192, 202, 208, 223, 225, 227, 230–233
Theme 99, 110, 111, 115, 117, 121, 143, 149, 156, 168

## V

Verbs and processes 8, 62, 96, 110, 145, 147, 203, 204, 216, 232
Vygotsky, L. 16, 52, 76, 77